REAL LIFE
paleo

175 GLUTEN-FREE RECIPES, MEAL IDEAS, *and an* EASY 3-PHASED APPROACH *to* LOSE WEIGHT & GAIN HEALTH

written by

STACY TOTH & MATTHEW MCCARRY

Victory Belt Publishing Inc.
Las Vegas

To all our fans, followers, and friends who continue to inspire us every day to learn something new, to share something interesting, and to be the best we can be. Your support made this possible. Thank you!

First Published in 2014 by Victory Belt Publishing Inc.

ISBN 13: 978-1-628600-45-2

The authors are not licensed practitioners, physicians, or medical professionals and offer no medical treatments, diagnoses, suggestions or counseling. The information presented herein has not been evaluated by the U.S. Food and Drug Administration, and it is not intended to diagnose, treat, cure, or prevent any disease. Full medical clearance from a licensed physician should be obtained before beginning or modifying any diet, exercise, or lifestyle program, and physicians should be informed of all nutritional changes.

The authors/owners claim no responsibility to any person or entity for any liability, loss, or damage caused or alleged to be caused directly or indirectly as a result of the use, application, or interpretation of the information presented herein.

Printed in the U.S.A.

RRD 0114

All photos by Aimee Buxton, except page 24 taken by Bill Staley of PrimalPalate.com, page 10 by April N. Thompson, and the front cover shot collaboratively by Aimee, Russ Crandall of TheDomesticMan.com, and Brent Schrader and Heather Gerum of VaHunterGatherers.com

Book design by: Yordan and Boryana Terziev

CONTENTS

RECIPE INDEX

CONDIMENTS, SAUCES, AND DIPS

110
Apple and Pumpkin Butters

112
Apple Butter BBQ Sauce

114
Coconut Butter

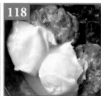
116
Sautéed Mushrooms and Onions

118
Hollandaise Sauce

120
Ketchup

122
Mayonnaise and Mayo-Based Dips

124
Salad Dressings

126
Cashew Cheese Sauce

128
Pickled Onions

130
Roasted Garlic

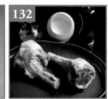
132
Stock (aka "Bone Broth")

BREAKFAST

136
Easy Peasy Pancakes

138
Strawberry Streusel Muffins

140
Blueberry Breakfast Cookies

142
CC's Perfect Hash Browns

144
Eggs in a Nest

146
Quick Banana-Chocolate Soufflé Cake

148
Green Salad with Poached Egg

150
Apple Cinnamon Crumb Cake

152
Eggs Stacy

154
Pumpkin Pudding

156
Cinnamon Bread

158
Sweet Potato Apple Hash

160
Breakfast Burritos

162
Egg Pizza (Frittata)

164
Breakfast Sausage

166
Waffles

SNACKS AND ON-THE-GO

Snack Balls
170

Cranberry-Orange No-Bake Coconut Bars
172

Kale Chips— Two Ways
174

Sweet Potato Chips
176

Roasted Pumpkin Seeds
178

Jerky
180

Almond Meal Crackers
182

Slightly Sweet & Salty Snack Mix
174

Nut Butter
186

Energy Bars
188

Smoothies
190

CHILDHOOD FAVORITES

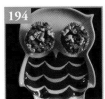
Chunky Monkey Muffins
194

Honey Nut Cereal
196

Pumpkin Cider Latte
198

Not Beanie Weenies
200

Chicken Fingers with Honey Mustard
202

Mini Corn Dog Muffins
204

Zucchini Cauliflower Tots
206

Meatza
208

Monkey Bread
210

Gummy Snacks
212

APPETIZERS

Braunschweiger Burger Sliders
216

Chinese Lettuce Cups
218

Chicken Liver Mousse
220

Prosciutto-Wrapped Pears
222

Pork Belly Bites with Arugula
224

Spinach and Artichoke Dip
226

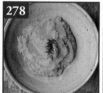

DRINKS

Coconut Milk and
Almond Milk

Chai Thai Iced Tea

Eggnog

Salted Caramel
Frappé

Iced Mocha

Peppermint
Hot Chocolate

Flavored Water

MAINS

Sage and Citrus
Roast Chicken

Juicy Pot Roast

Nona's Paprikosh
(Chicken and
Dumplings)

Stacy's Soup

Leftover Casserole

Macadamia-Crusted
Tilapia

Crab Balls

Mongolian Beef

Kung Pao Chicken

Drunken
Carrot Noodles

Turkey Thai Basil

Panang Beef Curry

Cider-Braised Brats

Slow-Roasted
Pork Shoulder

Lamb Stew

Apple Short Ribs

Epic Bacon Meatloaf

Linguine with
Baby Clams

342
Peruvian Chicken

344
Turkey Breasts Stuffed with "Cheese" and Cranberries

346
Restaurant Steaks

348
Brisket with Onion Jam

350
Beef Tongue Carnitas

352
Eastern Market Shrimp Salad

354
Garden Tuna Salad

356
Chicken Waldorf Salad

358
Grilled Kabobs with Pineapple

360
Grilled Spareribs

362
Butternut Squash Lasagna

SWEETS AND TREATS

366
Chocolate Layer Cake with Fresh Fruit

368
Frosting

370
Snickerdoodle Whoopie Pies

372
Marshmallows

374
Rocky Road Blondies

376
Samoa Brownies

378
Chocolate Chip and Walnut Cookies

380
Creamy Dreamy Frozen Custard

382
Peach Cobbler

384
Healthiest Ice Cream Ever

386
Jack-O'-Lantern Cookies

388
Pecan Pralines

390
Pumpkin Parfait

392
Key Lime Pie

394
Lemon Drop Thumbprint Cookies

396
Lemon Blueberry Bundt Cake

398
Chia Seed Pudding

400
Monster Cookie Dough Dip

402
Creamy Coconut Chocolate Chip Macaroons

404
Salted Dark Chocolate Truffle Cookies

406
Chocolate Custard

FOREWORD

By Sarah Ballantyne, PhD (aka The Paleo Mom)
New York Times bestselling author of *The Paleo Approach*
and *The Paleo Approach Cookbook*

The Paleo diet is a powerful nutritional approach to health. Clinical trials show that it improves cardiovascular disease risk factors, reduces inflammation, improves glucose tolerance, helps with weight loss, and can even improve autoimmune disease. Health improvements can be attributed to the fact that the Paleo diet provides balanced and complete nutrition with its focus on eating a variety of quality meats, seafood, vegetables, fruits, eggs, nuts, and seeds. The Paleo diet also eliminates foods that contribute to inflammation and hormone imbalances, including grains, legumes, refined sugars, refined oils, low-quality dairy, preservatives, food dyes, and processed foods.

As monumental as the health benefits can be, "going Paleo" isn't necessarily easy! Seeing a list of foods to avoid, many of which may be staples of your diet, can be overwhelming. Well, *Real Life Paleo* is here to come to the rescue!

Real Life Paleo guides you through the transition to a Paleo diet in three realistic, manageable phases: *Swap, Remove,* and *Heal.* With a detailed list of priorities for each phase as well as a huge collection of resources, such as a Food Swaps guide, meal ideas, and weekly meal plans, this book takes the guesswork out of going Paleo and sets you up for success. Best of all, with a collection of over 175 mouthwatering Paleo recipes, *Real Life Paleo* shows you just how delicious following a Paleo diet can be!

Real Life Paleo also does something completely unique: It teaches you how to put together an entire Paleo meal. Rather than simply giving you a collection of main and side dish recipes and leaving you to figure out how to combine them, *Real Life Paleo* teaches you how to use those recipes to create nutritionally balanced and complete meals, including ideas for flavorful breakfasts, lunches, and dinners. One-week meal plans for each phase further expand on your repertoire of meal templates to take the stress out of choosing what to eat.

A variety of other tools and information in this book will be invaluable during your transition to Paleo and will help you prioritize and get organized. And thanks to the tear-away guides, including such gems as a Going Out Guide, Grocery List Guide, Pantry Staples list, and Family Fun Guide, you'll be able to take these resources with you wherever you go.

Real Life Paleo also helps you fit Paleo into your real life. The recipes are clearly labeled when they are nut-free, egg-free, nightshade-free, under-30-minute meals, one-pot meals, under-5-ingredient meals, recipes for great on-the-go foods, and recipes that are perfect for holidays. This easy navigation means that figuring out what to cook on a busy weeknight is a snap!

While supporting people who aren't ready to jump all in, *Real Life Paleo* ultimately focuses on nutrient density. The third and final phase, Heal, centers on delicious ways to add more nutrient-dense, healing foods to your diet. As a critical component of my own healing journey, I'm excited to see just how accessible *Real Life Paleo* has made these superfoods for you!

Real Life Paleo is the ultimate guide for those looking to adopt a Paleo diet. But don't think this book isn't for you if you've been following a Paleo template for a while! The recipes in this book are innovative, with extraordinary flavors. It is quite simply a spectacular collection of some of the best Paleo recipes out there. And they will keep you coming back to this book again and again and again!

So grab a fork, and maybe even a plate, and dive in!

INTRODUCTION

The story of our family's Paleo journey begins in the spring of 2010, when Stacy left the hospital with our third baby boy, three Cesarean scars, and no gallbladder. Weighing 336 pounds, she felt miserable, exhausted, and defeated. She had been morbidly obese for most of her life and had no lasting success with any weight loss plan she'd tried. She was not, however, new to the idea of foods affecting her health. With her first baby, she noticed early on that he always got colic when she consumed dairy products. And it was while searching for dairy-free recipes that she first encountered the term *Paleo*. After falling down the Google research rabbit hole, Stacy was convinced to give Paleo a try. Finally, she'd found a dietary approach that made sense, based on evolution, biology, and the foods our bodies really need.

The weight immediately started melting off; Stacy's friends, family, and doctor couldn't believe it. Best of all, she was much healthier. She had more energy, a desire to get up and accomplish things, and no postpartum depression. The intestinal problems that had begun after her gallbladder was removed disappeared, along with heartburn and difficulty sleeping. After a year on the Paleo diet, her cholesterol, blood pressure, and blood sugar, which had consistently been dangerously elevated, were back within a normal range. Even a seriously high white cell count that made her bloodwork look like that of someone with a severe infectious disease miraculously resolved itself. (She later discovered that it was related to undiagnosed celiac disease, which improved dramatically on the Paleo diet.) By the time the next spring rolled around, she had lost more than 120 pounds.

Meanwhile, Matthew was so impressed with Stacy's success that he lugged his own 233-pound, Internet-jockey body to the starting line as well. He, too, experienced immediate changes. He lost over 60 pounds of fat and went from a sack of lard to a lean athlete. His severe anxiety and depression improved, and his near-debilitating seasonal and pet allergies disappeared entirely.

Now the two of us were on the same journey and regaining our health. So it seemed like a natural progression when we looked at our three kids munching on their pizza slices and thought, "Well, if Paleo is good for us . . . ."

Cole, our oldest, had always had behavioral and self-control issues, which led to his nearly being expelled from preschool for repeated incidents of accidentally hurting other children. He was a wonderfully nice boy and never had any malicious intent, but his brain and body just weren't connecting to enable him to find self-control—hugs became tackles and playful games of superheroes led to choke holds. The change to a Paleo diet immediately put him in control of his body. Almost overnight, he became a new person, the one we knew was there all along. By the end of kindergarten, he was praised as not only the best behaved child in class but also the healthiest eater. As a cherry on the Paleo sundae, the daily need for his asthma inhaler was gone for good and his weight gain had tapered off, allowing his next entry on the height-weight chart to fall squarely in the normal range.

Finian, our middle child, had a variety of skin and allergy sensitivities, ranging from eczema and a bumpy rash to severe pet allergies that induced high fevers. He also showed early signs of ADD, and his doctor and preschool worried that he might need to be medicated in order to succeed in school. Since he started eating a Paleo diet, the rash that doctors wanted to treat with steroid cream is no longer an issue; the eczema has cleared up; and he is able to visit family and friends who have pets without getting a fever, runny nose, or watery eyes. He is now able to focus and pay attention in school and has integrated into elementary school and summer camp with no problems at all. He, too, stopped growing wide and has shot upward like a weed.

So it seemed like a natural progression when we looked at our three kids munching on their pizza slices and thought, *"Well, if Paleo is good for us...."*

This brings us to Wesley, our Paleo baby. Wes proves how much we can all benefit from Paleo foods—he is the happiest child you'd ever hope to see, with an ear-to-ear grin at all times. The lucky kid never had to struggle with colic, gas, or even a rough night's sleep. (He has slept through the night almost since birth; we credit his mom's nutrient-dense breast milk.) Additionally, while the other boys had frequent fevers as babies, Wes, now 4 years old, has only rarely been sick and has never needed antibiotics.

Shortly after beginning our transition to Paleo, we started a small Tumblr blog to track our progress and share our more unusual recipes. We quickly discovered that the Paleo community lacked voices like ours. Among all the fitness advocates and single twenty-somethings, there weren't a whole lot of families talking about how they were incorporating Paleo into their regular, suburban lives. So we decided to create the website PaleoParents.com to show that Paleo can be great for everyone, even children!

Our family has experienced health changes we never thought were possible. Combined, we've lost over 200 pounds since switching to Paleo. Stacy is even a competitive athlete now! Dietary changes saved our family, and now we want to help you save you and yours.

WHAT IS PALEO?

The word *Paleo* refers to *Paleolithic* (the same nutritional approach is also referred to as primal or caveman). Originally, Paleo advocates tried to find the types of foods that Paleolithic people used to eat in order to design a diet around those foods. This evolutionary approach is what initially appealed to us, but we don't blindly go back 50,000 years for our menus these days. The Paleo diet is really a philosophy of eating the foods that the human body evolved to thrive on: unprocessed, whole, real foods dense in nutrients and low in antinutrients and other inflammation-causing components. This means no grains, no legumes, no refined sugar, no processed oils, and no artificially added chemicals. It often, though not always, means no dairy and a shift away from starches as the base of the diet.

Exactly which foods are eaten on a Paleo diet may be different for different people. We don't eat dairy, but you may do just fine with it. We're more liberal with sweeteners than others may be—we like to have Paleo(ish) treats made with whole ingredients on occasion. We focus on living a socially "normal" life while also optimizing our health. By following the steps outlined in this book, you will be able to figure out your family's food priorities and how best to meet them.

Our definition of **PALEO** *is simple:*

It's a way of eating that focuses on unprocessed, whole foods that make our bodies feel good.

WHY TRY PALEO?

Paleo is about thinking "outside the box" about the food that inhabits your kitchen. You can get your body into a great state of health—quickly and without much effort—by throwing out the dated food pyramid and looking into filling your plate with real, natural, whole, nutrient-dense foods. With the right fuel, your body can naturally find health—and for most people that means losing weight and feeling more energized. And you get to keep eggs and bacon on your plate!

HOW CAN *REAL LIFE PALEO* HELP?

We have developed this book to aid your family's transition to Paleo. In it, we provide shopping advice, recipes, and a few ideas on how to fully embrace the Paleo lifestyle as a family. We will help you figure out what to buy, how to cook it, and how to get active with your family.

We are here to help you with the "how" of transitioning to Paleo. If you would like more information on the "why"—the nitty-gritty scientific details of how different foods affect our bodies and our health—we highly recommend looking at the Resources section (page 413), which lists the tools and resources we used to educate ourselves about Paleo.

GETTING STARTED

It starts with you deciding to make a change.

Begin with a healthy plate at every meal. Don't allow yourself to become overwhelmed; **JUST STAY POSITIVE** *and* **MAKE IT FUN!**

Going Paleo isn't always easy, especially when it comes to integrating it into your lifestyle. Not only do you need to learn a new way of eating and preparing foods, but you're also living in a world filled with temptations. With holidays, birthdays, dinner parties, and other social events filling our busy lives, sticking to a Paleo diet can be difficult. That's why we wrote this book! Having transitioned our family of five to a Paleo lifestyle several years ago, we know all too well how hard it can be, but we've also learned how to succeed.

Thirty-day programs are popular in the Paleo world, but that wasn't an option for our family; our transition was much slower. We didn't fully realize how slow until years later, when we were able to look back and see just how far we'd come and how much the health of our whole family had improved. But after years of successfully living a Paleo lifestyle and helping thousands of families do the same through our blog, we developed a three-phase approach to transitioning to Paleo.

The most important step in the transition is simply making the decision to change and then starting. Don't let anxiety about making changes cause you to give up before you've begun; we're here to guide you, step by step, and we can help you stay consistent.

SET YOURSELF UP *for* SUCCESS: GET THE FAMILY ON BOARD

Sometimes people ask us how to get children on board with the dietary changes they're making. It is certainly not uncommon to have children who are picky eaters or who are opposed to change. Here are a few tips for encouraging your children to join you in improving your health through dietary change. Please note that we are talking about children of typical development. Children with special needs, of course, have needs that should be handled with the advice of a professional.

First, be consistent and firm in your belief that you are in charge of their food. As you begin each phase, let your kids know that they will be committed to making the change as well. As the parent, you are buying all the food and preparing all the meals. Don't let your kids' complaints, refusals, and declarations of breath-holding dissuade you from the path that you know is best for their health and well-being. In our house, we do not prepare special children's meals that are separate from what the adults are eating. Separate meals not only encourage children to hold out for the chicken nuggets they prefer, but also create a divide between parents and children that discourages bonding at the dinner table.

That said, we do encourage you to make some concessions to help your child feel empowered in this big change. For example, our kids really don't like eggplant, so we don't prepare it for them. Having that kind of input makes children feel less like they're being dictated to and more like they're participating, so they're less likely to be resistant.

We often remind our kids that their taste buds are changing constantly— "shedding like a snake sheds its skin" is how we phrase it—and that something they didn't like in the winter may become a favorite by fall. Encourage your children to try the foods that they find intimidating, but don't attempt to force it. Sometimes a reward can work in these situations: "You can have more applesauce if you try a bite or two of your kale."

Involving kids in food selection and preparation will also go a long way toward getting them invested in the meal. We take our kids grocery shopping with us, and they get to select foods that we will make that week. Let them pick out recipes with you, and then shop together for ingredients. Children who go to school can also be encouraged to pack their own lunch boxes (with supervision, so as to prevent the inclusion of only an apple, an orange, and a banana).

Cooking is, to us, one of the best ways to bond with your children. Nothing will make them feel more grown up than preparing food just like you do. It will be helpful to you as well once they've had significant practice. Let them stir and mix when they're young, and then let them graduate, as you feel comfortable, to using knives and the stove. This will pay off in many ways as they start to be able to prepare food for themselves and grow into self-sufficient young adults.

But most important, remember that the more fun it seems to your kids, the more of an adventure it is for them and the more willing they are to participate. The more positively you frame things, the better for everyone!

Eating Paleo has brought our family closer together, and we wish you the same bonding experience as you embark on your journey!

ABOUT THE PHASES

The original concept for a phased approach to going Paleo came from years of answering questions on our blog and podcast from frustrated individuals and families. Over time we realized that our answers were generally pretty simple: We recommended that people first swap out the most offending foods for healthier packaged options, then remove the remaining non-Paleo items, and finally heal through a focus on nutrient-dense ingredients and lifestyle factors.

Through this coaching and mentorship, we've helped thousands of individuals succeed. You may move through the phases in mere weeks, or, if you have a stubborn family, it could take years. No matter what, we like to focus on patience and consistency while moving forward, not looking back with guilt. This is a lifestyle, and no one, not even the godfathers of Paleo themselves, approaches it looking for perfection. The key is finding what works for you and your family and then focusing on accomplishing it, consistently, for life!

Clean out the pantry and the fridge and use the Grocery List Guide and Food Swaps list to make the best choices at the store. Eliminate gluten, refined sugar, and processed, chemical-laden foods.

As your family becomes accustomed to living gluten-free (and free of refined sugar), *gradually eliminate* all grains, dairy, legumes, and processed oils.

Take healing a step further by introducing nutrient-dense foods as well as *healthy lifestyle choices.*

Phase 1: Swap (pages 20–27)

To start, you first have to stop. Stop buying foods that contain the worst offenders—gluten, refined sugars, and chemicals—and switch to healthier, gluten-free alternatives (which will make it easier to eliminate grains completely in Phase 2). Stop buying prepackaged meals and snacks that are filled with chemicals and refined sugars. Our handy Grocery List Guide (page 25), Food Swaps list (page 26), and Going Out Guide (page 27) will help you make smart choices for your family's favorites.

Phase 2: Remove (pages 28–39)

Once you've cut out gluten, refined sugar, and artificially added chemicals, eliminate the remaining non-Paleo foods: all grains, dairy, legumes, and processed fats and oils. These foods can promote systemic inflammation and prevent your body from achieving optimal health. We'll make it easy to figure out what to eliminate with our guide to Simple Safe Foods (page 37). You'll also learn more about our favorite ingredients for success in the kitchen in the Stocking Your Paleo Home section (page 32). Of course, if your family isn't on board, successfully transitioning to Paleo becomes difficult, if not impossible. Try making the transition a fun adventure for everyone. Perhaps our Family Fun Guide (page 39) will help you and your family with the big change.

Phase 3: Heal (pages 40–47)

You're on your way to the healthiest you ever. Now that you feel more comfortable avoiding foods that aren't Paleo-friendly, you'll learn how to add health-promoting foods and activities. Our True Superfoods guide (page 46) covers adding nutrient-dense foods such as vegetables, seafood, organ meats, gelatin, stocks, and fermented foods. Then the Making Healthy Lifestyle Choices guide (page 47) focuses on lifestyle factors such as sleep, stress management, play, sunlight, and movement.

Making a major dietary change can be overwhelming. That's why we suggest doing it in phases, tackling one step at a time. Although we've found that these phases work well for many people, it is not our intention for them to be the "be-all, end-all" of your Paleo journey. They are guides, or templates, to help you figure out how best to make your own transition. We highly encourage you to evaluate your and your family's life and health when starting each phase. Some people move through each phase in a week, while others take years. Be patient and understanding, and refer to the ideas, recipes, meal ideas, and guides in this book; they will help you achieve long-term success with a Paleo lifestyle, for a lifetime of good health.

① PHASE I: SWAP

Trade
Gluten, Refined Sugar, and Chemical-Laden Processed Foods
for **HEALTHIER ALTERNATIVES**

In this first phase, we remove the biggest offenders, which are doing the most damage to your body: gluten, refined sugar, and chemical-laden processed foods. These foods actually act like toxins and can cause chronic illness, such as obesity, autoimmune conditions, cancer, and type 2 diabetes. We recommend swapping out these foods for healthier versions to make the transition easier for you and your family.

SWITCH *to* GLUTEN-FREE

It can be overwhelming to think about giving up your favorite breads, pasta, and sweets. The good news is, there are quite a few gluten-free options available in grocery stores that taste as good as—if not better than—traditional breads, pasta, and treats. Eventually, you'll want to cut out all grains, which we'll walk you through in Phase 2 (see page 28). At this point, though, just switching to gluten-free cereal and breads is progress. Swapping some of your most beloved foods with gluten-free alternatives and working on eating them less frequently allows the change to set in slowly over time and helps you to gradually create new habits.

The recipes in this book all follow strict Paleo standards and are grain-free, so try to incorporate as many of them as you can into your meals. And, just as our taste buds are constantly overstimulated by hyperpalatable food, so are our other senses overstimulated by bright packaging and brilliant colors. So if suddenly changing everything to homemade seems too jarring, trying out packaged organic and gluten-free options first might ease the transition. Make sure to read labels and use your best judgment—too many packaged foods (even the "healthy" variety) can do a number on your waistline, not to mention your wallet.

We've found that our family feels best when our gluten-free products are made with almond, coconut, white rice, potato, buckwheat (which doesn't actually contain wheat at all), arrowroot, or tapioca flour. Just be sure to read the ingredients label, because gluten-free products often contain refined sugar and chemicals. You may need to check a few labels before you find the right gluten-free products for you.

✕ GLUTEN

Gluten is a lectin (a class of protein) found in wheat and other grains. Lectins are a plant's natural defense against predators and pests, and in some people, they can cause the tightly joined cells that line the intestines to break apart, creating holes in the intestinal lining. This allows bacteria to leak into the bloodstream, causing systemic inflammation. Gluten can hide in many foods. Check labels for wheat, hydrolyzed wheat protein, barley, rye, malt, and glucose. The *Be a Gluten Detective* guide in Diane Sanfilippo's book *Practical Paleo* is an excellent resource for learning about all the places gluten can hide.

✕ REFINED SUGARS

We'll talk later about natural sugars and how we use them, but this phase is about avoiding refined sugar. Essentially, refined sugar is sugar that has been completely removed from its natural source. Without other nutrients, refined sugar hits your bloodstream harder. All sugar is highly addictive, though, and while we need a certain amount of glucose to live, the modern American diet has way too much. Too much sugar can deplete your body of nutrients and cause myriad health problems, such as insulin resistance (which leads to type 2 diabetes), hormonal dysregulation, and weight gain. It also stimulates the release of the stress hormone cortisol and decreases the production of leptin, a hormone that regulates appetite and causes the stomach to feel full. Make sure that any sweeteners you consume are unrefined (raw or natural), such as raw cane sugar or syrup, honey, maple syrup, and palm or coconut sugar. Avoid foods with labels that list corn syrup, high-fructose corn syrup (HFCS), or cane sugar.

✕ PROCESSED FOODS

Both gluten and refined sugar are found in nearly all processed foods, which also have added chemicals to keep the products shelf-stable. These added chemicals have been linked to many illnesses, from migraines to cancer. The worst offenders are monosodium glutamate (MSG), food dyes (such as Red 40), artificial sweeteners (such as aspartame), sodium benzoate, potassium benzoate (a known carcinogen), butylated hydroxyanisole (BHA), and butylated hydroxytoluene (BHT). Just be sure to read labels! Packaging that boasts "all natural" or "organic ingredients" doesn't mean much in the food industry; the only way to know for sure if a food contains unhealthy ingredients is to read the label.

Processed foods are designed to appeal to our most basic instincts. Our cravings for fat and sugar come from a time in human history when these things were scarce, and it made sense to eat as much of them as we could when they were available. But today, those cravings are exploited by the manufacturers of processed foods. By using fat and refined sugar to make their products hyperpalatable, they are not only causing addiction, but also making the healthier alternatives seem less appealing. After all, what's sweeter: a strawberry or strawberry ice cream?

We know that it can seem impossible to eliminate foods that you and your family like. That's why we created the Food Swaps list (page 26): to provide some ideas for similar but better, healthier foods. That list is just a starting point, however. Feel free to make your own substitutions that work for your family's unique tastes. There is also no need to make all these changes at once, either. We found that letting the children choose a new snack to try each week at the store worked well. It took months to swap out all the snacks they were used to having, but now they love to snack on veggies!

The important thing to remember is that you are establishing a lifestyle that will be sustainable over the long term. Children often don't understand making a complete overhaul in one day, or even thirty days. Follow the steps we have laid out and set a pace that works for your family. If you try to do too much too quickly, the likelihood of long-term success diminishes. It's better to take your time getting to that end target.

REMOVE UNHEALTHY FOODS *from* YOUR HOME

One necessary evil of Phase 1 is taking a look at what you already have in your home. It's time to clean out the pantry and fridge so you're not tempted to eat unhealthy foods; that is a lot easier to do if you simply don't have them around. We recommend that you finish what you have remaining of these foods, unless there's something super offensive that you want to get rid of right away, and then buy healthier replacements. As the cereal boxes empty and pasta disappears from the pantry, it's a good opportunity to talk with your family about how once it's gone you'll be trying something new (which they'll be more likely to try if they get to help pick it out at the store).

Then, as you stop buying foods that contain gluten, refined sugars, and chemicals, fill that space with healthy staples like canned coconut milk, natural nut butters, and olives. You can even feel good about buying gluten-free pasta, bread, and wraps and simply using them less frequently over time. Our Grocery List Guide (page 25) and Food Swaps list (page 26) will help get you started. Of course, it would be unreasonable to think that you'll be eating only at home, where we hope you're stocking safe foods, so refer to our Going Out Guide (page 27) for tips on how to survive in the wild!

As you use up the dairy products in your home, try to replace them with less-processed versions. That means full-fat, organic, and/or grass-fed (raw if your state allows). It's nearly impossible to find low-fat dairy products without added sugar (remember to check the labels to make sure that there's no refined sugar or chemicals). In Phase 2, you will eliminate dairy completely, so making this transition to less-processed dairy is not only a huge improvement in itself, but will also help to prepare you for that elimination.

EAT MORE VEGGIES

Once you've eliminated gluten, refined sugars, and chemical-laden foods from your family's diet, the next step in Phase 1 is to start eating more veggies.

Vegetables not only often contain carbohydrate, but also provide fiber, vitamins, and minerals that our bodies need. If vegetables replace grain-based carbohydrates on your table, you'll get more nutrients as well as lower your blood sugar. It's a win-win!

Adding vegetables doesn't have to be expensive, either. Starchy tubers—such as sweet potatoes, yuca, carrots, beets, turnips, parsnips, and rutabaga—can fill that desire for carbohydrate without breaking the bank. And fiber-rich greens such as kale, spinach, and cabbage can be incredibly filling. Then there are the multifunctional vegetables like zucchini and cauliflower, which are so versatile that Paleo people love to sneak them into meals in an incredible number of ways.

Though you're likely to agree that vegetables are healthy and often affordable, the hard part is getting them onto the table. Try to find new and fun ways to incorporate more vegetables into your meals. Start with small amounts in omelets and lunch boxes. If you have picky eaters, ensure that they will eat something by letting them choose their favorite veggies to add to the family dinner table. Use the recipes in this book to try out new flavors, or choose new and exciting ingredients at the grocery store and make cooking with them an adventure. Eating more vegetables is a great way to start reducing the pasta, rice, breads, and other less-healthy foods on the table.

For little ones (or big ones who act like little ones), the keys are to not make a big deal of eating veggies and to make it fun. Add veggies to your own plate and talk about how the different nutrients in them help our bodies grow healthy and strong, which everyone wants to be! If all else fails, we love to joke that pirates got scurvy and rickets from not eating enough veggies, and that we hope it doesn't happen to our boys. Said with the right pirate accent, this often works to both incite giggles and get them to at least try what's on their plate.

If you've tried a particular veggie before and didn't like the flavor, remember that taste buds change! They go through a life cycle from basal cells to taste cells and then die and are sloughed away, much like a snake sheds its skin. Our taste buds' normal life cycle is anywhere from ten days to two weeks, so if it's been more than two weeks, it's time to try at least a bite again.

Finally, our recipes will help you make great meals for your family. All of the recipes in this book are Paleo, although the ones marked "Phase 1" may be the most palatable for your family right now. For this first step of the transition, we think you'll love:

Blueberry Breakfast Cookies (page 140)

Honey Nut Cereal (page 196)

Iced Mocha (page 298)

Salted Caramel Frappé (page 296)

Mini Corn Dog Muffins (page 204)

Cinnamon Bread (page 156)

Samoa Brownies (page 376)

Chocolate Chip and Walnut Cookies (page 378)

We've outlined a meal plan for a week of Phase 1 foods on pages 102–103.

SWAP

GROCERY SHOPPING BASICS

Shopping around town takes a lot of work. As you start to cook most of your food at home, you may feel frustrated and overwhelmed. You may feel like you're spending all your time shopping and cooking. But think about how important fueling your body is.

Consider it a reprioritization—you're putting in the effort at the beginning, and you'll reap the benefits to your health and wellness down the road. Our kids are rarely sick, and our health has never been better. I'd much rather spend time cooking and shopping with the kids than spend time in the hospital, at the doctor's office, or in the dentist's chair.

Here are our strategic recommendations to make shopping easier and faster. We've done the prep work for you; the best places to buy your Paleo ingredients, based on convenience and cost, are listed below. The brands mentioned are our own personal favorites, but there could be better options out there. And while we recommend pastured, organic, and grass-fed where possible, if that's not an option for you, just make the best choice you can.

You'll find our favorite ingredients to buy online and at farmers markets in the lists below. While we talk specifically about Amazon Subscribe & Save, a service that automatically delivers items to you at appointed intervals for a significant discount, this service is obviously not your only online option. On the following page, you'll find a Grocery List Guide that you can take with you to your local stores (a tear-out version is included at the end of the book). And finally, our handy Food Swaps list (page 26) will give you ideas on how to transition to Paleo-friendly versions of your family's favorites.

Buy Online and at Farmers Markets

Amazon Subscribe & Save or other online options

Banana chips in coconut oil

Bare Fruit apple chips

Brothers-All-Natural dried fruit

Equal Exchange dark chocolate chips

GoGo Squeeze apple squeezers

Natural Value full-fat coconut milk

Navitas cacao nibs

Navitas chia seeds

Navitas cocoa powder

Navitas organic palm sugar

SeaSnax (roasted seaweed)

Sweet Leaf liquid stevia

Farmers Markets

Eggs

Local honey

Humanely raised, pastured meat (if you're not participating in meat shares or getting it direct from farms)

Produce (anything you can find from local farms is best!)

24 | Phase 1: SWAP

GROCERY LIST *Guide*

SUPERMARKETS

Organic veggies*

Grass-fed, pastured, organic meat

Pastured poultry

Rotisserie chicken

Lunch meat

Free-range, pastured, organic eggs

Kerrygold butter

High-quality cheeses

Grass-fed, organic heavy cream

Yogurt

Coconut aminos or wheat-free tamari

Palm shortening

Fermented foods (e.g., Bubbies pickles, sauerkraut)

Kombucha

LaraBars

*Buying produce that is already cleaned, chopped, or prepped will save you time in the kitchen.

TRADER JOE'S or NATURAL GROCERS

Applegate Farms deli meat

Canned salmon

Canned tuna

Frozen fish

Salami (we like the stick kind)

Smoked salmon

Boxed almond and coconut milk for drinking

Cold-brew coffee

Coconut milk yogurt

Ketchup

Mustard

Olive oil

Canned black olives

Pre-bagged trail mix, nuts, and dried fruit

Applesauce and squeezers (no sugar added)

Organic bananas

Canned fruit in 100% juice

Frozen fruit

Fruit juice (100% juice)

Low-sugar juice boxes

Butternut squash

Beets

Mirepoix

Sliced and cleaned mushrooms

Seasonal produce*

Bagged salad

COSTCO or other BULK STORES

Coconut oil

Fresh dates

Honeyville almond flour

MaraNatha almond butter

Raw bagged nuts (almonds, pecans, walnuts)

Bulk nuts

Organic frozen wild berries

Organic canned diced tomatoes

Produce (organic salad mix, baby spinach, carrots, asparagus, Brussels sprouts, romaine lettuce, and more)

Lunch meat

Frozen natural sausage patties

Frozen seafood

Canned and deboned wild salmon and tuna

Smoked salmon

FOOD SWAPS

NOW	BETTER	BEST
Fruit cup in syrup	Organic fruit cup in juice	Organic fruit
Pancake syrup	100% maple syrup	Apple and Pumpkin Butters *(page 110)*
Deli meat	Minimally processed deli meat (MSG- and gluten-free)	Beef Tongue Carnitas *(page 350)*, Chicken Waldorf Salad *(page 356)*, or Garden Tuna Salad *(page 354)*
Breakfast cereal	Gluten-free rice or corn cereal	Honey Nut Cereal *(page 196)*
Jelly	Organic jams	Homemade compotes and fruit preserves, Apple and Pumpkin Butters *(page 110)*
Fruit snacks	Organic fruit snacks	Dried fruit
Slim Jim/jerky	Gluten-free, nitrate-free jerky	Jerky *(page 180)*
Standard salad dressing	Organic dressings and dips	Ranch Dressing, Caesar Dressing, or Berry Balsamic Dressing *(page 124)*
Tortillas and wraps	Gluten-free tortillas	Lettuce or collard green wraps *(page 356)* or Tostadas *(page 262)*
Bread	Tapioca- or rice-based gluten-free bread	More vegetables, Cinnamon Bread *(page 156)*, or Biscuits *(page 250)*
Skim milk	Organic and/or raw whole milk	Coconut or Almond Milk *(page 290)*
Ice cream	Store-bought grass-fed or coconut milk ice cream	Healthiest Ice Cream Ever *(page 384)* or Creamy Dreamy Frozen Custard *(page 380)*
Chips	Store-bought sweet potato chips or avocado oil potato chips	Kale Chips *(page 174)* or Sweet Potato Chips *(page 176)*
Vegetable oil	Olive oil, avocado oil, or butter	Lard, duck fat, or coconut oil
Pasta	Rice-based, gluten-free pasta	Spaghetti squash or zucchini noodles
Conventional eggs	Organic, cage-free eggs	Pastured eggs
Conventional meat	Organic or pasture-raised meat from the grocery store	Local pasture-raised meat direct from a farm
Conventional produce	Use the Dirty Dozen and Clean 15 lists to strategically buy organic produce	All organic and/or local and seasonal produce

TRUSTED SOURCES

TROPICAL TRADITIONS:	U.S. WELLNESS MEATS:	TESSEMAE'S:	STEVE'S PALEO GOODS:	CAPPELLO'S:
Coconut oil, palm shortening, maple syrup, raw honey	Pasture-raised meats and lard	Salad dressings, marinades, and sauces	Jerky, dried fruit, grain-free granola	Almond flour–based pasta

GOING OUT *Guide*

EVERYONE NEEDS A BREAK *from* COOKING SOMETIMES, EVEN THE MOST SEASONED PALEO PRACTITIONER. WITH THAT IN MIND, HERE ARE SOME SUGGESTIONS *for* PLACES TO GO *and* WHAT TO LOOK FOR WHEN YOU'RE EATING OUTSIDE YOUR HOME.

GENERAL TIPS

▶ When you arrive, ask if the restaurant has a gluten-free menu. Many restaurants have one available; if not, your server may be able to tell you which menu items are gluten-free.

▶ While you are being seated, be sure to ask for no bread basket or they'll bring one for you automatically.

▶ Ask questions about ingredients! "What is in this side dish?" "Is it coated in flour, or is flour used as a thickener?" "Can I replace the rice with vegetables?" "Do you have an alternative to the bread?" Everyone who works at the restaurant has a vested interest in satisfying you. We always joke, "We're high maintenance, but we tip well!"

▶ When in doubt, a steak, broiled fish, or bunless burger is usually available and generally within the Paleo bounds.

TAKE-OUT OPTIONS

▶ You may be able to find gluten-free pizza made with a non-gluten-grain crust, but be careful! Chains often take zero precautions against cross-contamination and may actually dust their gluten-free crusts with wheat flour on purpose. A truly gluten-free pizza will be cooked in a separate pan and prepared on a separate surface.

▶ Chinese food may be off-limits unless the restaurant in question offers gluten-free options, which is rare. Also ask about MSG.

▶ Thai food, if prepared in the traditional way, is often naturally gluten-free. Just confirm that items are made with rice and without soy sauce.

▶ Our favorite take-out is Peruvian chicken, which we replicate on page 342. If you do not have this option where you live, most supermarkets offer rotisserie chicken.

FAST-CASUAL AND FAST-FOOD OPTIONS

▶ Avoid McDonald's and Burger King, whose patties contain a lot of soy, and Burger King coats its fries in flour. Wendy's has soy-free patties and flour-free fries.

▶ Burger joints are almost always safe, offering lettuce wraps or gluten-free bread.

▶ More upscale, build-your-own fast-casual restaurants, such as Chipotle, are much more likely to cater to your needs than other fast-food restaurants. They will likely be able to tell you the ingredients of any of their components and steer you toward building a safe meal.

▶ Casual American restaurants such as Jason's Deli and Ruby Tuesday often offer gluten-free bread and an excellent salad bar.

▶ If coffee is what you're after, you may be able to find independent coffee shops that offer almond milk. The major chains do not offer it, so you may be stuck with black coffee. Starbucks will blend their Kerrygold butter into your coffee if you are brave enough to ask!

RESTAURANTS *for* FINER DINING

▶ Sushi restaurants are safe if you avoid dishes that contain soy sauce and imitation crab. Be sure to inquire about the crab, as many menus will say "crab" even when it's imitation. Bring your own coconut aminos or tamari for dipping sashimi. Salad rounds out the meal nicely.

▶ Brazilian steakhouses are an all-you-can-eat meat experience and offer many safe options.

▶ Often, the fancier the restaurant, the less likely it uses unhealthy ingredients and the more likely it can accommodate your needs. Ask questions and make requests!

② PHASE 2: REMOVE

ELIMINATE GRAINS, DAIRY, LEGUMES, *and* PROCESSED OILS

As you move through Phase 2, you will be transitioning to a true Paleo diet. We don't think of it as what we would normally call a diet, a plan for losing weight, but rather as a lifestyle choice. We eat this way for our health; weight loss is only a part of our success. When you're eating optimal foods in the right portions, weight normalization (or weight loss, for most people) happens naturally. But the health benefits of Paleo, unlike those of other diet plans, do not come simply from reduced calories or carbohydrates or fat. Paleo also helps you to maintain your health by eliminating foods that can cause significant problems in many people.

The traditional Paleo diet removes foods that cause inflammation and gut irritation in most people—grains, dairy, legumes, and processed oils—and calls for a higher quality of the foods you do consume. You can see how these foods affect you with what is known as an elimination diet: Remove them from your diet entirely, allowing your body to heal in their absence, and then gradually reintroduce them one at a time. As you reintroduce each food, you will be able to see how it truly makes your body feel. In Phase 3 (see page 40), we'll go into detail on the Paleo superfoods we recommend to promote healing, but as you eliminate highly inflammatory foods in Phase 2, the healing process begins immediately.

Within the Paleo community, many people find that their own Paleo diet varies from the original template. However, we still absolutely believe that it's best to start with the traditional approach and remove the following foods.

GRAINS

We know that this may be contrary to the traditional ideas you have grown up believing, but after we read the science and saw our own results, the truth spoke for itself!

Grains are refined carbohydrates, which act like sugar in the body. They also contain inflammatory lectins, including gluten, and omega-6 fatty acids. Gluten is especially problematic—our family is strictly, absolutely gluten-free. But all grains, whether glutinous or not, contain antinutrients, which prevent other nutrients from being absorbed properly and directly cause gut irritation. Continuous gut irritation that's caused by the consumption of irritants leads to increased intestinal permeability, also known as leaky gut syndrome, which allows bacteria to leak into the bloodstream. Leaky gut syndrome has been shown to cause a variety of autoimmune diseases. It makes sense: If waste products are leaking from your bowels, your immune system is bound to respond. Reports are now surfacing that because it eliminates gut-irritating and inflammatory foods, a Paleo diet can help to control autoimmune and other diseases.

DAIRY

Research indicates that dairy consumption interferes with insulin regulation and that, like breast milk, cow's (or any mammal's) milk has insulin-like growth factor (IGF-I), which speeds up cell production and growth. For infants, this is great! But for an overweight individual or a cancer patient, the results can be catastrophic. Some people also find that they do not tolerate lactose, a dairy sugar, or casein, a protein found in dairy. Lactose-intolerant people, who don't have the enzyme to break down lactose, often have severe bloating, cramping, and gas after dairy consumption, and casein intolerance can cause constipation, brain fog, and joint pain. However, unprocessed dairy products from healthy animals (like grass-fed, organic, low-heat heavy cream) are incredibly rich in micronutrients, so if you are not affected by dairy consumption, then dairy can be a part of your personalized approach to Paleo. But we recommend that you remove all dairy from your diet for at least thirty days and then reintroduce dairy to see how you respond. Many people don't realize that acne, allergies, and even behavioral problems in children (like bedwetting, tics, or backtalk) can be linked to casein intolerance.

> **EVEN IF YOU THINK YOU DO NOT HAVE AN INTOLERANCE,** *just try a* **THIRTY-DAY ELIMINATION AND THEN YOU WILL KNOW.**

LEGUMES

Legumes are heavy in lectins and carbohydrates, just like grains. If you are looking for the fiber and protein found in legumes, we recommend consuming more greens and protein-rich foods that aren't bound up in carbohydrates, such as meat, seafood, and eggs. The vitamins and minerals in these foods are easier for your body to absorb, and the proteins and fat are easier to digest. If you are a vegetarian, legumes can be one of the safer forms of non-meat-based protein, but we recommend the traditional preparation of soaking and sprouting the beans so that they are optimal for better digestion.

PROCESSED OILS

Avoid oils that come from things that are not naturally high in fat, such as canola oil, corn oil, soybean oil, and vegetable oil. These manufactured food products are often oxidized and high in omega-6 fatty acids, which increase inflammation in the body. Instead, use a stable, solid fat like coconut oil, lard, butter, or ghee. If you need a liquid fat, then one from a fatty whole food, like avocado oil, macadamia nut oil, or olive oil, is your best bet—just make sure that it's 100 percent oil from the source, is identified as either "low-heat" or "expeller-pressed," and comes in a dark bottle to prevent oxidation.

For more specific information on the whys and hows of the Paleo diet, check out our recommendations in the Resources section (pages 413–414). Dr. Sarah Ballantyne's The Paleo Approach *offers the most scientific information.*

As we're sure you've noticed, unlike a weight-loss diet, Paleo doesn't specify a certain number of calories or macronutrients (carbohydrates, protein, and fat). It's more about getting back to basics and focusing on quality ingredients that are high in micronutrients like vitamin B, iron, beta-carotene, and many, many more. That way, each calorie you consume provides the most nutrients possible. By consuming a vibrant, colorful, and varied whole-foods diet, most of us are able to eliminate the need for vitamin supplements. Not only do we get more vitamins and minerals from our food, but we're also able to absorb them better, because the micronutrients in whole-food sources are synergistic. Synergistic micronutrients work together in the body and are usually found in appropriate ratios in whole foods. For example, both calcium and phosphorus are needed for healthy bone growth, and they are usually found together in the same foods.

If you're worried about not getting enough calcium, fiber, and vitamins when you eliminate grains and dairy, keep in mind that grains and cow's milk are fortified—vitamins and minerals are added back to the final product, so they aren't as absorbable as they would be in a whole-food source. On a Paleo diet, we eat nutrient-dense foods, like pastured eggs and meat, seafood, bone broth, and leafy greens and other vegetables, so we end up with more nutrients than we were getting from eating fortified processed foods.

Although the Paleo diet is often defined by what is eliminated, we like to focus on what is included: vegetables, fruit, meat, nuts and seeds, and healthy fats. Obviously, stating that is much easier than actually figuring out what to eat. That's why we've put together guides and tools to help you transition at your own pace.

Healthy Alternatives

DAIRY: While raw and organic full-fat dairy were fine in Phase 1, in Phase 2 we remove them in order to check for intolerances. When you cook, start replacing butter with lard or coconut oil and milk with almond or coconut milk, or simply go without. For beverages, water is a great choice—after all, we like to get our nutrients from foods, since chewing is the trigger for the body to start the digestive process.

LEGUMES: Most of us associate legumes with beans, but peanuts also fall into this category. The hardest legumes to remove will likely be soy and peanuts, which are often found in prepackaged foods. Prepare as many homemade foods as possible to avoid soy. Instead of peanut butter, use almond, sunflower seed, or other nut butters.

PROCESSED OILS: Saying goodbye to vegetable and canola oil is tough, we know. Processed oils were one of the last things to leave our home because we struggled to find replacements. The great news is that now you can find healthy oils and fats at Costco and regular grocery stores, so they're more affordable. Our favorites are avocado oil, coconut oil, and lard.

GRAINS: In Phase 1, you successfully transitioned to gluten-free grain products. But chances are that there are still a lot of processed grain products in your diet. It's time to cut them out completely. (Your body and your wallet will thank you.)

NUTRITION in STANDARD FOODS

FOOD	CARBS	PROTEIN	FAT	FIBER	CALCIUM	VITAMIN A	VITAMIN C
2% milk, 1 cup	12 g	8 g	5 g	0 g	286 mg	461 IU	0.5 mg
Chicken, 1 boneless skinless breast	0 g	43 g	5 g	0 g	21 mg	29.4 IU	0 mg
Whole grain bread, 2 slices	36 g	10 g	2 g	6 g	84 mg	0IU	0 mg
Whole wheat spaghetti, 1 cup	37 g	7 g	1 g	6 g	21 mg	4 IU	0 mg
Bagel	56 g	11 g	2 g	2 g	19 mg	0 IU	0 mg
Corn tortillas, 1 cup	11 g	1 g	1 g	2 g	19 mg	0.5 IU	0 mg
Cornflakes, 1 cup	24 g	2 g	0 g	1 g	1 mg	751 IU	0 mg
Oatmeal, 1 cup	32 g	6 g	4 g	4 g	21 mg	0 IU	0 mg
Raisin Bran cereal, 1 cup	46 g	5 g	1 g	7 g	28 mg	868 IU	0 mg
Black beans, 1 cup	41 g	15 g	1 g	15 g	46 mg	10 IU	0 mg
Kidney beans, 1 cup	40 g	15 g	1 g	11 g	62 mg	0 IU	2 mg
White potato, 1 large	64 g	6 g	0 g	6 g	30 mg	30 IU	38 mg
Iceberg lettuce, 1 cup	2 g	1 g	0 g	1 g	10 mg	361 IU	1.5 mg

NUTRITION in COMMON PALEO FOODS

FOOD	CARBS	PROTEIN	FAT	FIBER	CALCIUM	VITAMIN A	VITAMIN C
Almonds, 1 cup	29 g	32 g	73 g	15 g	313 mg	10 IU	0 mg
Tuna, 1 can	0 g	41 g	5 g	0 g	24 mg	34 IU	0 mg
Salmon, ¼ pound	0 g	25 g	8 g	0 g	15 mg	44 IU	0 mg
Grass-fed ground beef, ¼ pound	0 g	19 g	13 g	0 g	12 mg	0 IU	0 mg
Eggs, 2 large	0 g	12 g	10 g	0 g	26.5 mg	244 IU	0 mg
Liver, ¼ pound	5 g	27 g	5 g	0 g	6 mg	26091 IU	1 mg
Coconut milk, 1 cup	6 g	5 g	48 g	0 g	41 mg	0 IU	2 mg
Cauliflower, 1 cup	5 g	2 g	0 g	3 g	22 mg	13 IU	46 mg
Zucchini, ½ cup	4 g	2 g	0 g	1 g	19 mg	248 IU	21 mg
Broccoli, 1 cup	10 g	6 g	0 g	6 g	61 mg	1860 IU	74 mg
Kale, 1 cup	7 g	2 g	0 g	1 g	91 mg	10302 IU	80 mg
Sweet potato, 1 large	37 g	4 g	0 g	6 g	68 mg	34590 IU	35 mg
Spinach, 1 cup	1 g	1 g	0 g	1 g	30 mg	2813 IU	8 mg

After eliminating foods that fall outside the Paleo template and allowing their bodies to heal, some people find that returning to the foods they eliminated causes a reaction, such as digestive upset. This doesn't mean that the Paleo diet is giving you an allergy or intolerance. For most people, it means that on the Paleo diet your body was able to heal from a low level of systemic inflammation, resolving chronic diseases or health conditions, such as allergies, headaches, high cholesterol, or high blood pressure. When the problematic foods are reintroduced, they can cause bouts of inflammation or gut irritation that you never noticed before because your body was so inflamed to begin with. The good news is, as you work on healing your body, your body will react less over time, which is why we focus on healing in Phase 3.

STOCKING YOUR PALEO HOME

Fats and Oils

One of the hardest adaptations for us was replacing cooking and baking oils. "Normal" cooking oils, such as vegetable oil, canola oil, and soybean oil, are highly processed, chemical-laden, bleached, and oxidized "foods" that come from grains or legumes, so we had to switch. Finding a replacement that was flavorless and easy to work with was difficult, but we figured it out.

Today, we almost always use liquefied coconut oil, but we also occasionally use olive oil, avocado oil, and macadamia nut oil. Instead of oils, we often use fats now: ethically sourced palm shortening, which works well to replace butter or vegetable shortening; coconut oil (it's solid at room temperature); or lard or bacon fat, which offer incredible flavor.

If you want to use a different fat than a recipe calls for, just make sure that you use a solid if the recipe calls for a solid or a liquid if the recipe calls for a liquid.

Yes, most of these fats are high in saturated fat. However, studies are now showing that saturated fat was never the problem we were told it was, and that the true cause of heart disease, high cholesterol, and other modern diseases is the inflammation caused by omega-6 fatty acids—especially when hydrogenated, as they are in vegetable, canola, and soybean oils. In fact, of all the studies done over the past fifty years, none has shown a definitive link between saturated fat consumption and heart disease.

If you're still not gung-ho about unprocessed fats, there are lots of resources available online to help you understand how our bodies need dietary cholesterol for brain growth, hormone regulation, and proper absorption of vitamin D. After we removed most foods that are dense in omega-6 fats and added omega-3-rich foods and healthy fats to our diet, our blood tests amazed our physicians.

Coconut oil (which has a smoke point of 350°F/177°C) has all the wonderful gut-healing and healthy-fat properties of coconut milk in a very flavorful oil for baking or sautéing. It is a solid at room temperature, so keep in mind that it will return to that state if you leave it sitting out. Coconut oil should be available at most stores these days; look for one that has been pressed instead of solvent-extracted, to minimize the chemical processing.

Do not be afraid of lard or tallow (smoke point of 390°F/192°C). We make our own lard (we included the recipe in our previous book, *Beyond Bacon*), but you can get lard by the tubful from your local farmers market or from U.S. Wellness Meats. Since we are dairy-free, we love to use it for everything from pan-frying chicken to making mashed vegetables (it gives them a creamy, buttery taste). Real fresh lard is much more delicious than seed oil alternatives. Best of all, it's usually not much more expensive than a similar volume of canola oil, and it keeps for a very long time in the refrigerator.

If you're looking for a plant-based replacement for lard, palm oil (smoke point of 455°F/235°C) works well. We like Tropical Traditions brand, which is ethically sourced.

Flours

We often hear from people who say that missing baked goods, or the fear of losing them entirely, is their biggest struggle with going Paleo. Some people find that using Paleo ingredients to bake healthier versions of cookies, breads, and more helps them to transition successfully. In fact, our family incorporated a lot of what we call "Paleo-ish" baked goods when we were transitioning to Paleo, especially for our boys, who love bread, muffins, cookies, and pancakes. None of that would have been possible without a replacement for the standard all-purpose flour, which is made from wheat. We've tried quite a few flours, including ones made from nuts, root veggies, and seeds. For the most part, we prefer almond and coconut flours, which are high in protein, fiber, healthy fats, and vitamins and minerals. But when these heavy flours are too thick to allow something to rise or we need a binder, we also add starchy, light, and powdery flours, like tapioca or arrowroot flour.

Just as you might expect, these flours are simply ground almonds, coconut, and cassava (yuca) root and arrowroot, respectively. Not only do almond and coconut flours have protein and healthy fats, but they are also more nutrient-rich and much more flavorful than wheat flour. Unfortunately, they can be hard to find and expensive compared to wheat flour (which is subsidized enormously to keep it cheap). Also, watch out for blends that contain rice, potato, or other starches, which will affect the end result of your baking.

If you can't afford these flours or you have trouble finding them locally, you can find them at lower prices online. Or try making your own almond or coconut meal with either a food processor or a powerful blender. It will be a bit more coarse than store-bought, but it will still do the trick. We have extensively tested sunflower seed flour (made of finely ground, raw, shelled sunflowers) as a replacement for almond flour and can definitively say that it can be substituted for blanched almond flour at a one-to-one ratio. Read more about how to make nut-free and much more affordable flour in the Replace Common Allergens section (page 52).

Remember, though, that all baked goods are treats, and we encourage you to eat less of them over time. Our recipes for them are incredibly calorie-dense and do contain sweeteners and omega-6 fatty acids (although not nearly as many as grain-based baked goods). They are intended to be sometimes foods, not everyday foods.

When a recipe includes both baking soda and sunflower seed butter or flour, a chemical reaction with the chlorophyll in the sunflower seeds turns your baked goods bright green! This can be a fun and exciting science experiment if you give your kids a heads-up (if you wait for them to see it themselves, though, they may find it off-putting). It's great for making gnarly snacks on Halloween and St. Patrick's Day!

Nut and Seed Butters

Nut and seed butters, such as almond butter and sunflower seed butter, are made simply by grinding up the nuts or seeds and adding more fat or flavors. We've included several of our own nut and seed butter recipes in this book (such as Vanilla Cashew Butter and Salted Caramel Almond Butter, both on page 186), but we've also found that many store-bought brands work well, such as MaraNatha and Trader Joe's brands. We use almond butter in quite a few

Our recipes for homemade Nut Butters are on page 186.

recipes because it is easy to cook with and is a simple way to add almond flour and oil at once, as almond butter is already a combination of the two.

Roasted or raw, crunchy or creamy—it's all your preference. We recommend not purchasing any brand that advertises "no stir" because it likely has filler ingredients and will not work the same way in baked goods. We suggest raw, creamy butters for baking and roasted, crunchy butters for eating. Just as sunflower seed flour is a great substitute for almond flour, sunflower seed butter is a great one-to-one replacement for almond butter to make a recipe nut-free.

Chocolate

Chocolate is made from cocoa butter (the fat) and cocoa powder, both products of the cacao tree. You might be thinking, "But cocoa is a bean—that's a legume!" Actually, no. Cocoa is the seed from the pod, which makes it more like a nut or seed. In fact, good-quality dark chocolate has been shown to offer excellent health benefits because it's high in antioxidants—yippee!

We recommend finding the darkest chocolate you can (over 70 percent cacao is best) in a brand that's soy- and dairy-free. Read the labels; soy lecithin and other odd ingredients often find their way into chocolate. We also try to find sustainably sourced chocolate. Look for "fair trade" on the label to ensure that your chocolate was ethically sourced.

For more information on the health benefits of chocolate and the importance of finding ethically sourced brands, check out The Paleo Chocolate Lovers' Cookbook *by Kelly Brozyna.*

Sweeteners

Sugar isn't Paleo. But neither are printed books, electronics, and the rest of our modern-day advantages. What's important to understand is that sugar can be toxic to the body and seriously deter progress toward health and wellness. It causes hormonal changes and triggers the release of insulin, which is what caused our health problems to begin with. However, we firmly believe that we live in the real world. I don't know about you, but our kids like to have cupcakes when they go to birthday parties. And they like to make cookies for their teachers at the holidays. So we use sweeteners in the treats we make to help our family feel more normal.

Fortunately, nature provides many whole-food sources of sweeteners that our bodies are better equipped to handle, and those are the ones we choose to use. As often as we can, we sweeten our recipes with whole fruit, which includes fiber and nutrients that help our bodies to process the blood sugar spike. However, sometimes (because baking is a science) we have to use other sweeteners in our recipes, so we'll walk you through each one.

Honey is known to have immunological benefits, especially when it comes from local honeybees. However, heat destroys many of the nutritional benefits of raw honey, so it would be a waste of money to purchase local raw honey for baking. We like to use local raw honey in tea and for other non-baking purposes, but for baking, we purchase raw or creamed honey online because it is often more

WHEN IT COMES TO SWEETENERS, USE YOUR OWN *best judgment* FOR YOUR HEALTH AND WHAT WORKS FOR YOU AND YOUR FAMILY.

affordable. If you can't find or afford raw honey, just make sure not to purchase an overly fragrant variety (like clover), which can overpower the taste of your baked goods.

Maple syrup is boiled sap from maple trees. You might be surprised to know that syrups labeled "pancake syrup" often have no natural ingredients and are only flavorings and refined sugar, like high-fructose corn syrup. Make sure to check the labels and purchase only real maple syrup. The grade of a syrup refers to its translucency and the time at which it is made. Grade B maple syrup is made at the end of the season and is dark, with an intense, nutty flavor that is excellent for cooking. It also has been shown to have a higher mineral content.

Blackstrap molasses is a flavorful by-product of cane sugar that is a dark unrefined syrup. It contains all the mineral content of its original source and is used for its distinct flavor more than its ability to sweeten foods.

Palm sugar is an unrefined sweetener with a low glycemic index. It's made from the nectar of the coconut palm, so it even has vitamins and minerals. We use it because it is granulated but not highly processed, and it's much more familiar and easier to adapt to traditional baked good recipes than other natural sweeteners. Try putting it in a coffee grinder to make a superfine sugar for frostings and meringues. We've noticed that our kids' behavior is better when treats are sweetened with palm sugar instead of sucanat, so it's what we prefer.

Sucanat is raw cane sugar that hasn't gone through the refining process that strips it of some of its natural properties. It's similar to turbinado (the kind of sugar in the brand Sugar in the Raw), although turbinado is slightly more processed.

Umami Flavorings

Defined as a "pleasant savory taste," umami usually means "flavor punch" in the American vernacular. And we love to cook flavorful food! Usually we eat at least one Asian-inspired dish a week. Because the first ingredient in traditional soy sauce is wheat, creating a similar umami flavor requires some alternative ingredients.

Tamari is made from fermented soy, just like traditional soy sauce, so it has the same traditional flavor without the wheat. It is affordable and easy to find at most grocery stores and Asian markets. However, it is made with soy, and we make every effort to keep all legumes out of our diet. So we use **coconut aminos** instead, which is made from fermented coconut and has a similar but slightly sweeter flavor. It's a bit pricier and more difficult to find, but we highly recommend it; it should be available at your local health food store or Whole Foods.

Fish sauce is made from fermented fish and salt, but mostly—although it can smell bad initially and may seem gross to newbies—it is made of awesome. It's the thing that restaurants add to Asian dishes that makes you wonder how they

We prefer to use natural, unprocessed sweeteners such as maple syrup, honey, ripe bananas, applesauce, and dates, which offer a depth of flavor not found in standard American sweeteners. Each has not just a unique flavor profile but also a different ratio of sucrose to fructose and different vitamins and minerals—so you'll find that most of our recipes include a variety of sweeteners.

You can use granulated date sugar or granulated maple sugar as an alternative to granulated palm or cane sugar. Although they are more difficult to find and pricier, they have a better nutritional profile and add a deliciously rich flavor.

make it so delicious. When you add it to the dishes where we call for it, it'll give that "pop" you've been missing. Stacy likes to joke that it's the Paleo version of MSG. It's *that* good. The only things you need to worry about with fish sauce are the additives and scary ingredients in low-quality brands, like hydrolyzed wheat protein. Use a brand such as Red Boat, whose only ingredients are fish and salt.

Coconut Milk and Coconut Cream Concentrate

Coconut is one of our favorite foods. It's incredibly nutritious and has properties to help heal the gut. While coconut does have a distinct flavor, it's not overpowering when used in our recipes. With time, coconut can become a base flavor that you hardly notice.

Coconut milk is made from coconut meat that is grated and squeezed to produce a thick, milky substance. It has become such a staple in our home that we buy it by the case. It's a perfect replacement for milk and cream in general, and in specialty items like curries and ice cream. We have even made a faux béchamel sauce with coconut milk.

Our recipe for homemade Coconut Milk is on page 290.

Our recipe for homemade Coconut Butter is on page 114.

When a recipe calls for coconut milk, for best results use full-fat coconut milk that is free of additives, like guar gum. It should contain only coconut and water.

Coconut cream concentrate, also known as coconut butter or creamed coconut, is made from dried and ground coconut meat and coconut oil. Reconstituting this thick paste with water gives you an easy-to-make coconut milk, or you can use it directly in savory and sweet dishes for added creaminess and flavor.

These may seem like a lot of restrictions at first, but allow yourself to make these changes slowly, one at a time. Gradual changes, however long they take, are still steps in the right direction. With all of the recipes in this book, you'll be living the Paleo lifestyle in no time! For Phase 2, we think you'll love:

If you're ready to put more vegetables on your table and move away from the less nutrient-dense and bread-like Paleo foods, we recommend checking out all of the side dishes marked Phase 3–compliant.

SIMPLE SAFE FOODS

STARCHES

Acorn squash
Beets
Butternut squash
Parsnips
Plantains
Pumpkin
Rutabagas
Spaghetti squash
Sweet potatoes
Yams
Yuca

SWEETENERS

Date sugar
Honey
Maple syrup
Molasses
Palm sugar

NUTS and SEEDS

Almonds
Brazil nuts
Cacao nibs
Cashews
Chia seeds
Macadamia nuts
Pecans
Pine nuts
Pumpkin seeds
Sunflower seeds
Walnuts

VEGETABLES

Asparagus
Artichokes
Arugula
Avocados
Bell peppers
Broccoli
Brussels sprouts
Cabbage
Carrots
Cauliflower
Celery
Chile peppers
Collard greens
Cucumbers
Garlic
Kale
Leeks
Lettuce
Mushrooms
Onions
Radishes
Rhubarb
Romaine lettuce
Seaweed
Spinach
Tomatillos
Tomatoes
Turnips
Zucchini

FRUITS

Apples
Apricots
Bananas
Blackberries
Blueberries
Cantaloupes
Cherries
Coconut
Cranberries
Dates
Figs
Grapefruit
Grapes
Lemons
Limes
Mangos
Oranges
Papaya
Passion fruit
Peaches
Pears
Pineapples
Plums
Pomegranates
Prunes
Tangerines
Raspberries
Strawberries
Watermelons

MEAT/PROTEIN

Anchovies
Bacon
Chicken
Crab
Duck
Eggs
Elk
Gelatin
Lamb
Lobster
Pork
Prosciutto
Salmon
Sardines
Shellfish
Shrimp
Tuna
Turkey
Salami
Steak
Veal

OTHER

Cocoa powder
Coconut aminos
Coconut oil
Coffee
Ghee (clarified butter)
Tea

 **PALEO STAPLES**

For THE PANTRY

Fats and Oils

Coconut oil *(we recommend Nutiva and Tropical Traditions brands)*

Avocado oil *(we recommend Chosen Foods brand)*

Macadamia nut oil

Olive oil

Chocolate

Dark chocolate chips *(we recommend Equal Exchange and Enjoy Life brands)*

Unsweetened chocolate squares

Cocoa powder *(we recommend Navitas, Rapunzel, and Equal Exchange brands)*

Coconut Products

Full-fat canned coconut milk *(we recommend Natural Value brand)*

Coconut cream concentrate/ coconut butter *(we recommend Tropical Traditions and Nikki's Coconut Butter brands)*

Flours

Blanched almond flour *(we recommend Honeyville brand)*

Arrowroot flour *(we recommend Bob's Red Mill brand)*

Coconut flour *(we recommend Tropical Traditions brand)*

Tapioca flour *(we recommend Bob's Red Mill brand)*

Sweeteners

Unrefined granulated palm sugar *(we recommend Sweet Tree and Navitas brands)*

Unrefined granulated date sugar

Unrefined granulated maple sugar

Grade B maple syrup

Raw honey

Additional Items

Canned anchovies

Canned salmon

Canned sardines

Canned tuna

Canned black olives

Canned tomatoes

Apple cider vinegar

Balsamic vinegar

Dried fruit and nuts

Honey Nut Cereal *(page 196)*

Gelatin

Nut Butters

Almond butter *(page 186, or we recommend MaraNatha and Traders Joe's brands)*

Sunflower seed butter *(we recommend SunButter, MaraNatha, and Trader Joe's brands)*

Umami Flavors

Coconut aminos *(we recommend Coconut Secrets and Naked Coconuts brands)*

Wheat-free tamari

Fish sauce *(we recommend Red Boat brand)*

For THE FRIDGE

Ketchup *(page 120)*

Mayonnaise *(page 122)*

Mustard

Pickles

Sauerkraut

Salad Dressing *(page 124)*

Almond Milk *(page 290)*

Coconut Milk *(page 290)*

Organic deli meats

Premade salads *(page 50)*

Stock *(page 132)*

Fresh produce

Organic deli meats

Thawed meat

Kombucha

For YOUR PURSE or GLOVE BOX

Jerky *(page 180; we also recommend Steve's PaleoGoods brand)*

Dried fruit

Snack Balls *(page 170)*

FAMILY FUN *Guide*

PURSUING A HEALTHIER LIFESTYLE *as a* FAMILY ISN'T JUST ABOUT CHANGING WHAT YOU EAT, IT'S ALSO ABOUT MAKING A CHANGE TOGETHER. FAMILY ACTIVITIES ARE A GREAT WAY *to* ENCOURAGE EVERYONE TO GROW HEALTHIER TOGETHER. HERE ARE SOME *of* OUR FAVORITE WAYS TO PURSUE BETTER HEALTH *with* OUR FAMILY.

VISIT LOCAL FARMS Many farms, orchards, and other agricultural centers encourage visitors, and these trips are a great way to learn more about where your food comes from. The more natural and sustainable the farm's practices, the more likely they'll let you wander the fields and explore. For kids, this might mean getting to see and touch farm animals! EatWild.com is an excellent resource for finding sustainable farms in your area.

PICK YOUR OWN PRODUCE In many areas, farms let you onto their fields to pick in-season produce. Check out PickYourOwn.org to find one near you. Each farm tells you by phone or on its website what is available to pick, but you can expect to find a variety through the seasons, depending on your location.

HIKE, BIKE, *and* CAMP When we made our switch to Paleo, we suddenly had a huge jump in energy and wanted to go exploring. Going to local parks and wilderness areas is a great way to experience the natural world and get in touch with nature. We highly recommend geocaching as a reason to go exploring!

EXERCISE Whatever your preferred method—from swimming to CrossFit, from soccer to flashlight tag—playing and exercising together can be great fun. Getting active as a family sets a good example for the kids and creates healthy habits for years to come. Plus, it's fun! Our family has had dedicated months where we all practice something together, like handstands.

PLANT A GARDEN, RAISE CHICKENS Nothing is more organic than the vegetables you grow yourself! If you have the space, plant your own food and learn how much work it takes to put food on a plate. If your local laws allow it, you may even be able to raise chickens for eggs. We find inspiration in the truly adventurous homesteaders Liz Wolfe at RealFoodLiz.com and Diana Rodgers at SustainableDish.com.

COOK *and* EAT TOGETHER We know, it probably seems boring, but you would be surprised how often families don't participate in the most obvious communal activity in the home: eating together. If you are able, make cooking and eating a family affair. This goes for not just kids but adults as well. Many couples have found that working together in the kitchen translates into a more lasting bond. Just look at the websites PrimalPalate.com and VaHunterGatherers.com for inspiration. For date night, we love to grocery shop and then cook an extravagant meal that costs a fraction of what a restaurant would charge but is twice as healthy.

PHASE 3: HEAL

INTRODUCE HEALING FOODS and LIFESTYLE FACTORS

For those people who have been Paleo but want to improve their health further, Phase 3 will help! In this chapter on the final phase of transitioning to the Paleo lifestyle, we'll discuss in detail how to heal your body from the years of damage it may have incurred from unhealthy and processed foods. From eating Paleo superfoods to changing our lifestyle, these are the things we can do to focus on improving our health long-term.

Although descriptions of the Paleo diet often focus on what is removed, this phase is about what we add to create health and healing.

INTRODUCE HEALING FOODS

Now that you've made the transition away from the foods that were damaging your body and your health, it's time to start eating the foods that will help you recover. For some people, this might be the hardest step of all, but the repair will certainly be worth it!

The first step is to focus on nutrient density. Foods like salads, vegetables, egg yolks, and pastured meats should increase while Paleo baked goods and treats decrease. Then, when you're ready to branch out and really heal, we recommend making sure that your dietary routine includes these essential foods:

ORGAN MEATS, STOCKS, GELATIN, PASTURED PROTEIN, VEGETABLES, FERMENTED FOODS, and SEAFOOD

Don't freak out! We know it can seem overwhelming, or gross, or perhaps impossible. We have taken all the worry and fear out of figuring out how to add these foods by including over fifty delicious Phase 3 recipes. Many of them are kid-friendly, so even picky eaters can get their nutrients.

We've created a sample meal plan for integrating Phase 3 foods on pages 106–107.

Bonus! Once the body starts to heal, many people find that they are able to successfully reintroduce some foods that they previously had to eliminate.

Organ Meat

For many of us, organ meat (offal) initially seems distasteful. Foods like liver, kidneys, and heart have long been maligned, but they don't have to be like the disgusting image you have in your head.

Organs contain the densest possible concentration of nutrients. Heart is extremely rich in iron, and liver is the best whole-food source of vitamin A you can eat. While liver and onions and kidney pie are certainly classics, we encourage you to try a different approach if the idea of organ meat is unappealing. Our family was once grossed out by the idea, too, and now we've found flavorful and delicious ways to eat these healing, nutrient-dense foods!

If you want the nutrient benefit of organs but can't get past the flavor or texture, try grinding up liver and kidneys and adding it to your ground meat for burgers or meatballs. Heart has a similar texture to steak but can be tough, so acidic marinades work really well to soften the meat. We turn our beef hearts into jerky after marinating them overnight, and no one can tell the difference!

	BRAIN	SWEETBREADS	HEART	LIVER	KIDNEYS	TONGUE
VITAMIN A				+ + +		
VITAMIN C	+			+ +	+	
VITAMIN B12	+ +	+ + +	+ + +	+ + +	+ + +	+ + +
RIBOFLAVIN	+	+		+ + +	+ + +	+ +
NIACIN	+		+ +	+ + +	+ +	+ +
THIAMIN	+		+ +	+	+	
FOLATE				+ +		
CALCIUM						+ +
PHOSPHORUS	+ +	+	+	+	+	+ +
SELENIUM	+ +	+ + +	+	+ + +	+ + +	+ +
IRON		+	+ +	+ + +	+	+
COPPER			+	+ +	+	+

+ good   + + great   + + + excellent

Stock and Gelatin

Our household's favorite nutrient-dense food is stock made from animal bones. Homemade stock is rich in many micronutrients, including calcium, magnesium, and phosphorus. It's also a great source of gelatin, an easily digested protein that is essential for both gut health and the production of collagen, which helps to keep skin tight and joints working. Homemade stock also has digestible amino acids that help to heal the gut, which means that more of the other nutrients you consume will be absorbed.

Our favorite offal recipes are:

Braunschweiger Burger Sliders (page 216)

Beef Tongue Carnitas (page 350)

Chicken Liver Mousse (page 220)

Superfood Jerky (page 180)

Sweet Heart Jerky (page 180)

Our favorite recipes that incorporate stock and gelatin are:

Gummy Snacks (page 212)

Stacy's Soup (page 312)

Baked Potato Soup (page 252)

Butternut Bisque (page 264)

Brisket with Onion Jam (page 348)

Our favorite seafood recipes are:

Our favorite recipes using pastured protein are:

Seafood

Seafood of all types would ideally be eaten at least a couple times per week. Many of you may have been turned off by the taste of overcooked seafood when you were young, but now is the time to get over it! There are few foods on this planet as healthy as seafood. Fish and shellfish have an extremely high level of anti-inflammatory and heart healthy omega-3 fats and are very rich in nutrients.

Omega-3 fatty acids are essential to our health and healing; they help to counteract inflammation caused by an overabundance of omega-6 fatty acids in our diet. Instead of taking fish oil supplements for omega-3, though, we consume fish oil in its original, whole-food state.

Seafood is also a major source of iodine, a mineral that's essential for a healthy thyroid. Unfortunately, it's not uncommon for Paleo diet followers to develop an iodine deficiency. This mineral is generally missing from the American diet already, which is why table salt has been fortified with iodine. But when we remove processed foods that have been preserved with iodized salt, we lose the benefit of that added iodine, which is why we need to add it back into our diets with real food.

Fish and shellfish are also excellent sources of vitamins A and D. Eating a fish or two a week will certainly kick your health recovery into overdrive.

We know a lot of people don't like to prepare seafood at home, but it can be one of the quickest and easiest meals to throw together. Additionally, almost all grocery stores have wild-caught seafood in the frozen section, making it a perfect back-up dinner when you're running short on time.

We also highly recommend adding sea vegetables to your diet. We love to snack on roasted seaweed and use sea vegetable sea salt (found at health food stores or online) or furikake (a condiment made from seaweed, sesame seeds, dried fish, and salt that can be found at Asian markets) as a finishing salt on our foods. Just make sure to check the ingredients; some brands add MSG or processed oils.

Pastured Protein

Given the pro-vegetarian bent of our culture, it might surprise you to know that animal protein is one of the most nutrient-dense foods. Rich in amino acids, B vitamins, iron, and a multitude of other vitamins and minerals, protein is an incredible energy source that can also help heal your body. Some kinds of protein also contain conjugated linoleic acid (CLA) and omega-3 fatty acids, both of which help to reverse the damage and inflammation that omega-6 fatty acids can cause in the body.

The most nutrient-dense animal proteins are offal, seafood, pastured egg yolks, and meat from grass-fed ruminants such as beef, sheep, goats, and deer. When consuming these proteins for their nutrient density, it's important to make sure that the animals are fed their intended diet and allowed to roam free in fresh air and sunlight. All of these factors contribute to the animals' ability to convert their food into the nutrients you will consume later.

Many food producers, realizing that the market is driving purchases toward grass-fed or pastured protein, are tricking consumers with updated labels that don't really describe the product. If you read the label carefully, it may say that "cage-free" eggs are from hens given only vegetarian feed (which means that they can't hunt and peck for bugs, a natural part of a chicken's diet) or that beef is grass-*fed,* not grass-*finished* (which means that the animal was given grain in the last weeks or months of its life). That means the animals aren't able to provide you with the ideal nutritional profile, while you as a consumer are getting charged for a product that doesn't offer the benefits suggested by the label. We find that buying direct from a farmer, farmers market, or high-quality butcher shop is the best way to guarantee quality (as well as support local small businesses and the environment), but our Grocery Shopping Basics (page 24) will help you make better choices within grocery stores.

Vegetables

The Paleo diet is often perceived as an all-meat caveman diet, but many people find that it doubles their vegetable intake. Stacy herself was a vegetarian for seven years and often says that she eats more vegetables now than she ever did as a vegetarian. As you can see in our Meal Ideas (beginning on page 60), as you transition into Phase 3 and a healing and nutrient-rich version of Paleo, vegetables replace the pasta, breads, and fillers previously on the table.

Vegetables have a lot to offer us. Rich in antioxidants, vitamins, and minerals, they are essential to our long-term health. If you or someone in your family is a picky eater, we recommend finding a few staple vegetables that work well in your household and ensuring that one of them is always on the table. That way, if someone doesn't like the other foods, there's a vegetable they can count on for nutrients. For our boys, that's cabbage, carrots, cauliflower, and sweet potatoes.

Our family almost always has salad at mealtime. Salads don't have to be boring! We let each of our children pick a topping, which ensures that the salad is almost never the same. See our suggestions for building a salad on pages 50–51.

Fermented Foods

Finally, the cornerstone of gut health is the recolonization of healthy gut bacteria through the consumption of fermented foods. For years we've seen commercials about the benefits of active cultures in yogurt, and it sounded like yogurt was the healthy food we needed. Turns out, the overly processed, sugar-filled, and chemically laden yogurt was keeping the beneficial active cultures from getting the job done and healing our guts. Fermented foods are simply that active culture in real, whole-food sources that aren't filled with junk. The good bacteria from fermented foods help to clear out the bad bacteria that feed on sugar and often overrun intestines after years on the Standard American Diet.

Healthy gut bacteria also help to counter the negative effects of gluten and help you break down and properly digest food, ensuring that your body is able

If you're looking for new, unique ways to eat the rainbow of vegetables, we recommend:

Healthiest Ice Cream Ever (page 384)

Creamed Kale (page 254)

Cauli-Gnocchi with Brussels Sprouts and Lemon Zest (page 260)

Citrus Broccoli (page 276)

Thai Fried Cauli-Rice (page 247)

Green Onion and Bacon Mac 'n' Cheese (page 238)

Roasted Rainbow Carrots (page 266)

Pickled Onion and Arugula Salad (page 286)

Pizza Kale Chips (page 174)

Stacy's Soup (page 312)

Veggies can give you a big bang for your buck! Cabbage, carrots, cauliflower, onions, and sweet potatoes are all incredibly affordable and keep well in the fridge, so we always keep them on hand.

to properly absorb the nutrients you're putting into it. Additionally, a healthy balance of gut flora is associated with good mental health—though scientists don't yet know why, beneficial microorganisms in the gut seem to help reduce anxiety and improve mood. Don't you owe it to yourself to give your body a healthy population of beneficial organisms?

Give yourself a head start on your new healthy gut by eating fermented foods. Yogurt, pickles, sauerkraut, kimchi, and kombucha all have the starter cultures you'll need. You can also check out *Fermented* by Jill Ciciarelli to learn how to ferment foods in your own kitchen.

Supplements

If you're dealing with specific health problems, such as digestive issues, hair loss, or thyroid issues, and you're not yet seeing the results you had hoped for after focusing on nutrient-dense foods, it's best to consult with a medical professional and consider supplementation. We supplement with fermented cod liver oil, which provides a great boost of omega-3 fatty acids and a synergistic blend of easily absorbable vitamins and minerals. Additional supplementation may include probiotics or support for digestion, the thyroid, or the adrenal glands. We don't recommend blindly taking vitamin D, fish oil, magnesium, or other specific supplements unless you're working with a professional who has tested your blood levels and can monitor the effects of the supplements over time.

PURSUE *a* HEALTHY LIFESTYLE

Get Proper Sleep

Getting proper sleep is essential to our family's life, as it significantly contributes to the regulation of hormones and cellular regeneration. We see it easily in our boys, who are night and day behaviorally depending on their sleep! Sleeping in a dark room for eight to nine hours a day and following your body's circadian rhythms—going to bed when tired and waking up well rested, without frequent waking in the night—are the keys to overall health and wellness, not just "nice to have." Most people find that when they are getting enough sleep, they crave less sugar, experience less stress, and are generally able to think more clearly and handle stress better. It's hard to make it a habit, but sleep must be prioritized with the same vigor as food!

Reduce Stress

Once you have prioritized sleep, look for ways to reduce stress in your life, as excess stress hormones can be detrimental to brain and organ function. Stress plays a huge role in chronic illness, from autoimmune disease flares to heart attacks. Finding ways to relax and be happy are essential to long-term health.

Get Active

Finally, your body wants to move and absorb sunlight. Get outside and play! Hiking, walking around your neighborhood, and gardening are excellent ways to move and spend time outdoors. The natural vitamin D that your body gets from sunlight aids in the regulation of hormones and is a significant contributor to overall health. Vitamin D deficiency has been linked to many health conditions and unfortunately is rampant in the United States, where we spend too much time indoors. While you're outside moving around, you'll improve your metabolism and produce mood-boosting hormones.

Any kind of physical activity is a great addition to your lifestyle. Our family likes to explore nature in the warmer months, and we also participate in group CrossFit and weight-lifting classes year-round. We love the health benefits we get from strength training. It helps to regulate metabolism, improves blood sugar, and balances hormones. And it's especially great for women because it improves bone density, which helps to prevent osteoporosis.

REINTRODUCE FOODS

Now the fun part! You've fully transitioned to Paleo and are working on incorporating healing foods and following a healthy lifestyle. You feel great and are really seeing the health benefits. You want to indulge occasionally or try adding back some of the foods eliminated in Phases 1 and 2, but you aren't sure where to start or which foods really need to be avoided.

We recommend reintroducing only one eliminated food at a time for a week or more so that any reaction to it can be discovered.

We found that as our bodies healed, adding back some nutritionally beneficial foods, such as grass-fed butter and heavy cream, didn't upset our health (digestive or otherwise). We also found that eating white rice a couple of times a week, especially on active days, didn't bother us. (The brown husk of whole-grain rice is the most difficult to digest, so white rice tends to be easier on the digestive system.) Many people within the Paleo community consider white rice, high-quality dairy, and white potatoes part of their own Paleo template.

We recommend reintroducing only one eliminated food at a time for a week or more so that any reaction to it can be discovered. If you can't tolerate a certain food, you may experience acne, allergies, congestion, heartburn, upset stomach, constipation, headache, joint pain, and ear infection—and since everyone's body is different, keep an eye out for anything else out of the ordinary. Our family has found it best to adhere strictly to the Phase 3 guidelines, but on special occasions we'll sometimes eat a few of the foods removed in Phase 2, like gluten-free pancakes.

THE TRUE SUPERFOODS

AFTER YOU'VE ELIMINATED THE BAD STUFF, IT'S TIME TO REPLACE IT *with* HEALTHY *and* HEALING FOODS. HERE'S WHAT YOU SHOULD BE THINKING ABOUT *in* PHASE 3.

ORGAN MEATS Consuming organ meats, also known as offal, can be a big hurdle because of their unusual appearance, taste, and texture. But they're certainly the healthiest of all meats, rich in vitamins and minerals found in few other sources. To make them more palatable, we recommend grinding them up and adding them to ground meat dishes, such as Epic Bacon Meatloaf (page 338), or making them into a mousse or pâté, such as Chicken Liver Mousse (page 220).

STOCK *and* GELATIN The unique amino acid profile of stock and gelatin is ideal for supporting joint and bone health as well as building collagen and keratin. Ever admire a Paleo adherent's great skin, hair, and nails? This might be the secret!

PASTURED PROTEIN Studies have shown that one of the keys to good health, especially heart health, is eating more omega-3 fats and fewer omega-6 fats. One of the quickest ways to tilt the balance toward omega-3 is to switch from grain-finished meats to pastured or grass-fed, grass-finished meats. All pastured proteins have a better ratio of omega-3 to omega-6 than their grain-fed counterparts, as well as more nutrients.

VEGETABLES This may seem obvious, but it's worth emphasizing: Paleo is not a meat-only diet. Vegetables are very important sources of antioxidants, vitamins, and minerals and should make up a significant portion of your meals.

FERMENTED FOODS Healthy gut bacteria is very important to overall health. Sauerkraut, pickles, kefir, and kombucha all support healthy bacteria in your gut.

SEAFOOD Not only are fish and shellfish rich in vitamins and minerals, they're also the best source of omega-3 fats. Replacing chicken with salmon once a week is an excellent way to tilt your ratio of omega-3 to omega-6 in the right direction.

SUPPLEMENTS We use fermented cod liver oil for its boost of omega-3, vitamin A, and vitamin K, but you may want to consult with a health professional to see what you're deficient in and take steps to make up the difference.

MAKING HEALTHY LIFESTYLE CHOICES

FOOD ALONE CAN'T FIX EVERYTHING THAT AILS YOU. TO OPTIMIZE YOUR HEALTH, YOU ALSO NEED *to* CHANGE OTHER PARTS *of* YOUR LIFE.

GET PROPER SLEEP With a full night's sleep, you not only feel rested and have improved brain function, but also reduce your stress hormones, have a stronger immune system, and improve thyroid and insulin function—key factors for losing fat.

REDUCE STRESS Our stress hormones aren't activated only when death or injury is imminent. They also surge when we're stuck in traffic, working hard to meet a deadline, or facing a long to-do list. Learning to manage stress is beneficial to your heart health and any autoimmune conditions you may have, and it allows your hormones to regulate properly.

EXERCISE Exercise, particularly resistance and strength training, has been shown to increase overall health, including bone strength and cardiovascular health. It also increases your feel-good hormones. Incorporating some movement into your life, however small the commitment, will definitely pay off.

ABSORB SUNLIGHT It's easy to stay inside, where the temperature is regulated and comfortable and we don't have to expend much energy moving around. The human body, though, needs to be outside in the sun every day. Not only does sunlight activate mood-enhancing hormones, but your body also needs it to make vitamin D, a nutrient in which most people are now deficient.

HOW TO...

If you have no idea how to go from a person with a kitchen to a person who makes food, this chapter is for you.

We'll help you by providing the basic how-tos for our style of Paleo cooking.

CREATE SPICE BLENDS *and* FLAVOR COMBINATIONS

When you start cooking for yourself, one of the more intimidating tasks is figuring out how to flavor things with herbs and spices so that they taste good. There's a whole world of flavors out there, from the common, like basil and paprika, to the unusual, like allspice and saffron, to the downright bizarre, like grains of paradise and anardana. How are we supposed to manage all of that at home?

First off, don't worry! So much experimentation went on before you were even born that, we can assure you, the hard work of discovering flavor combinations has mostly been done for you. Pick up a book about spices and you'll find all kinds of ideas for spice mixes and suggestions for pairing spices with different meats or vegetables. You'll find that certain dishes have their own "best practice" flavor profiles. For example, roasted lamb and mint work very well together, as do rosemary and braised beef, and tarragon and chicken soup. In fact, tarragon is referred to in our house as the "chicken noodle soup flavor."

Certain spices are often used together as well, such as rosemary and thyme or paprika and cumin. They're very well suited to each other and make flavoring much simpler.

Finally, don't make it too complicated! Simple flavors with only a few components are usually better than ten different components, which can lead to a muddled mess. That's why Rick Bayless's twenty-ingredient mole is so celebrated; he used twenty ingredients and somehow it still tastes good!

Below you'll find our standard spice blends for various proteins. Use these as a guide to help you sort through your spice cabinet, or experiment and find what works best for you.

Chicken

½ tablespoon salt

1 teaspoon dried rosemary

1 teaspoon dried tarragon

1 teaspoon thyme

⅛ teaspoon ground black pepper

Pork

½ tablespoon salt

1 teaspoon paprika

1 teaspoon ground cumin

½ teaspoon garlic powder

⅛ teaspoon ground black pepper

Beef

½ tablespoon salt

½ teaspoon dried oregano

½ teaspoon dried basil

½ teaspoon dried parsley

⅛ teaspoon ground black pepper

Lamb

½ tablespoon salt

1 teaspoon cinnamon

1 teaspoon ground cumin

½ teaspoon ground cloves

½ teaspoon garlic powder

¼ teaspoon ground nutmeg

½ teaspoon chili powder

⅛ teaspoon ground black pepper

Fish

½ tablespoon salt

1 teaspoon dried dill

1 teaspoon garlic powder

1 teaspoon dried parsley

⅛ teaspoon ground black pepper

MAKE PALEO MASHES *and* RICES

Everyone is familiar with those starch-rich staples, potatoes and rice. Many people probably can't imagine a meal without one or the other, and they're a huge part of the diets of many cultures all over the world.

So for those who want to eliminate these foods or replace them with something more nutritious, getting started is often difficult. But what if we told you that it's easy to make foods with the textures of rice and mashed potatoes from other vegetables? And that, in fact, they're even tastier?

To make a mash, simply steam a dense, starchy vegetable until it is very soft and then mash or purée it. We routinely do this with a variety of vegetables, the most versatile of which is cauliflower. Cauliflower makes a nice puree, very much like a smooth mashed potato, but it's not good for a lumpy mashed potato. For that, we mash steamed turnips and cauliflower together with a potato masher. Other vegetables we love for a mash are sweet potatoes, carrots, parsnips, rutabagas, acorn squash, butternut squash, and pumpkin. To get an even smoother, creamier mash, pour in ¼ cup of coconut milk or cream and a couple tablespoons of lard or butter. Add salt and black pepper and any spices you desire.

Making rice from vegetables is similar, and we often use the same vegetables. For cauliflower rice, we pulse the florets in a food processor to get the desired rice-sized pieces and then steam them. For other vegetables, we recommend dicing them very finely with a knife before steaming. The result will be exactly the same kind of starchy side dish you're used to.

Our recipe for Cauli-Rice is on page 246.

BUILD YOUR OWN SALAD

When you ask people what their favorite food is, very few answer with a declaration of their love for salad. Many people only experience salad as iceberg lettuce, grated carrots, and a processed salad dressing. Frankly, that's unfortunate, because the world of salad is wide open, and salads are so easy to assemble that there's no excuse not to try to build a salad you will love.

The first step in building a good salad is to find the right greens. Avoid iceberg lettuce and go for a mixture of greens with varied textures and flavors. Lettuces come in a large variety, from the crunchy, mild romaine to the slightly bitter radicchio, and from the soft, sweet Boston to the peppery arugula. These days, it's easy to find common lettuce mixes such as mesclun. Or try baby cooking greens, like spinach or kale. Experiment with lots of different greens to find the ones you like. Also, adding herbs like dill or sorrel (our favorite) to a salad can be delicious.

Next, figure out what add-ins you prefer in your salad. Traditional options include vegetables like celery, bell peppers, tomatoes, and carrots; nuts and seeds like sunflower seeds, pepitas, walnuts, and sliced almonds; and fruit like berries, apples, and orange slices. Don't forget that you can easily change the texture of your salad by changing the size and shape of your add-ins. Think about the difference between shredded carrots, carrot rounds, carrot ribbons, and carrot ripple chips.

If your salad will be a full meal, make sure to add protein. This can be leftover meat from any meal, like a pork roast, chicken, or beef, or something you make when you build your salad, like bacon, shrimp, or chicken tenderloins. Perhaps you'd like a prepared salad, like our Chicken Waldorf Salad (page 356) or Garden Tuna Salad (page 354). Any of these proteins will turn a side salad into a main dish.

Finally, you will need salad dressing. There are several Paleo options in this book, including Caesar Dressing, Ranch Dressing, and Berry Balsamic Dressing (page 124).

Experiment with combining and recombining all your options, and make salad fun!

Our favorite salads are:

Winter Salad (page 272)

Green Salad with Poached Egg (page 148)

Caesar Salad (page 280)

Pickled Onion and Arugula Salad (page 286)

MAKE DRINKING WATER *more* INTERESTING

You've probably heard all the stories about how important water is: that the human body is 60 percent water, that water helps with weight loss and athletic performance, that "you're not hungry, you're just thirsty," and everything else. But when you're sitting opposite a glass of water and staring it down, you may still think it's boring and would much prefer to grab a can of soda or some juice. Instead, why don't you make water more interesting?

First of all, you can always carbonate your water. Obviously, sparkling water and mineral water are available at most grocery stores, but in recent years, there has been an explosion of carbonation machines. With these machines, such as the SodaStream, you simply attach a bottle, charge it with carbon dioxide, and you have your very own carbonated water.

Instead of bottled flavorings full of sugar and chemicals, add flavor extracts, such as vanilla or almond extract. Fruit juice will also improve your water. Lime and lemon juice are obvious options, but just a touch of apple juice, pomegranate juice, pineapple juice, or grape juice will help, too. If you want flavoring from fruits that are harder to juice, like berries or mangos, simply add the whole fruit pieces to the water. You can also use herbs; we enjoy mixing basil and mint with our water. Just make sure that the herbs are fresh!

REPLACE COMMON ALLERGENS

Here are some ways you can replace those tricky foods.

Some of the most common ingredients in our recipes also happen to be allergens for some people—almond flour, eggs, and coconut oil or palm shortening, for instance. And sometimes people have unique aversions to certain foods. For example, our photographer, Aimee, will not eat bananas.

Almond Flour or Almond Butter

Almond flour is all over the baked goods that we make at home. Unlike other Paleo-friendly flours, almond flour doesn't dry out confections or overpower them with its own flavor. But since tree nut allergies are so common and so severe, a number of people have asked us for an alternative. And there is one!

Take raw, shelled sunflower seeds and grind them into a fine powder in a food processor or blender. Do not overgrind, however, or you'll be left with sunflower seed butter instead of flour. We find that our Blendtec blender works best for this task.

The result can replace almond flour at a one-to-one ratio. If you need to replace almond butter, it can be replaced by sunflower seed butter—go ahead and overgrind this time. Plus, it's much more affordable!

Coconut Oil or Palm Shortening

The recipes in this book sometimes call for coconut-based fat, but some people cannot stand the taste of or are allergic to coconut. For those people, replacing these ingredients should be easy.

The most effective replacement for coconut oil in baked goods is lard. Ideally, you'd make your own from pork fat (if you're interested, there are detailed instructions in our previous book, *Beyond Bacon*), but butchers often sell fresh, unhydrogenated lard. For palm shortening, turn back the clock and return to butter—which palm shortening was invented to replace. Or use lard, which will work almost as well.

Eggs

Eggs are kind of magical in baked goods, and trying to figure out a way to replace them often leaves people stymied. There is no perfect solution. For example, there is really no way to make a soufflé or meringue without eggs. But in recipes that call for eggs as a binder, you can make do with a couple techniques.

Try using one tablespoon of ground chia seeds in two tablespoons of water per egg. Mix it first, and then add it to your batter in the place of the eggs. The gel that forms will act as a binder.

Another method, which we use to good effect in a couple recipes in this book, is to add ¼ cup of mashed banana or applesauce in place of each egg. The stickiness of the fruit will replicate the binding properties of the egg.

Bananas

If, like Aimee, you don't like bananas, just use applesauce, date puree, or pumpkin instead.

REPLACE AMERICAN STANDARDS

Some foods—particularly rice, pasta, bread, potatoes, dairy, flour, cornstarch, and fats—are so fundamental to the way most Americans eat that eliminating them becomes a real sticking point for making a diet change. Luckily, we have some solutions.

Rice

Rice is an important base for dishes from many cultures, from fried rice to paella to risotto. While we haven't found a good replacement for the slightly sticky texture of glutinous rice, steamed cauliflower rice works well otherwise. (Find more on making cauli-rice on page 246.) Another option is to use sautéed diced starchy vegetables, or try using sautéed greens as your base. In our Chia Seed Pudding (page 398), we replace rice in a sweet treat, too.

Pasta

Clearly, if you're not eating wheat, you'll be hard-pressed to find good pasta. If you're in Phase 1, you can certainly try rice pasta, quinoa pasta, or even corn pasta. After Phase 1, the best option is to cut vegetables into noodles, either by hand or using a tool called a Spiralizer. Zucchini works best for noodles, but we have used carrots and sweet potatoes as well. Simply blanch the noodles for 90 seconds before adding them to your dish. Also, check out our recipe for Cauli-Gnocchi with Brussels Sprouts and Lemon Zest (page 260), which cooks up just like wheat gnocchi!

Bread

Bread is such a basic part of the Standard American Diet that it can be hard to imagine life without sandwiches, toast, biscuits, or baguettes. But living without them isn't actually that hard. If you truly miss bread, you can, in Phase 1, buy gluten-free bread. Breads made from tapioca flour and rice flour are the most common; be careful of corn and potato breads, because they are almost always made with wheat. A better choice might be coconut wraps that contain only coconut meat and water, although these can be difficult to find.

When you're ready to give up sandwich bread entirely, wrap your sandwich meat in large greens or lettuce leaves, like our collard green wraps (page 356). Or make deli meat roll-ups without any outside wrapping and veggies inside. For dinner rolls, try our Biscuits (page 250). They're delicious and can certainly be eaten sliced open and buttered.

Potatoes

Although potatoes are a part of our Paleo template, there are more nutrient-rich options. If you're interested in mashed potatoes, we recommend steaming and puréeing cauliflower for a smooth mash, or turnips and parsnips for a chunky mash. (Find more on making vegetable mashes page 244.) If you're interested in French fries, fry yourself some Yuca Fries (page 284) or Sweet Potato Chips (page 176). For tater tots, try making our Zucchini Cauliflower Tots (page 206); for hash browns, try Sweet Potato Apple Hash (page 158) or CC's Perfect Hash Browns (page 142). There's a healthier version of pretty much anything made with potatoes that you can think of.

Flour and Cornstarch

We go into some detail about the various replacement baking flours on page 33. Whether you use coconut, almond, or sunflower seed flour, you'll find that they all have their strengths and weaknesses, but none can easily replace wheat flour alone.

Sometimes an old recipe will call for flour or cornstarch as a thickener. For this purpose, your best replacement is tapioca flour or arrowroot flour. Both of these are available in the natural foods aisle of your local grocery store or online. We prefer tapioca flour because it has less of a tendency to clump.

Dairy

Once, an English friend complained to us about American recipes, "You aren't content to have cheese on your burgers and pizza; you have to inflict yellow cheese on shepherd's pie and steaks, too!" Yes, we Americans do love our cheese! We created our Cashew Cheese Sauce (page 126) to act as a replacement for the cheesy flavor found in so many American foods. We use it in our Meatza (page 208) and Leftover Casserole (page 314).

To replace milk, we recommend homemade Almond Milk or Coconut Milk (page 290), although you can find good store-bought versions, too. Coconut milk yogurt is a great replacement for regular yogurt and sour cream; it's usually available at grocery stores. And the cream you can skim from canned coconut milk is a great replacement for regular cream. Be mindful that store-bought non-dairy products often contain stabilizers, and we try to limit our use.

Fats

In our cooking, we use three kinds of fat: butter or ghee; animal fats, such as lard, duck fat, or bacon fat; and coconut, such as coconut oil and palm shortening. We definitely recommend having all three on hand, but they can be used interchangeably in many circumstances. Animal fats work very well in place of butter for sautéing, and palm shortening is great for baking when butter isn't an option.

There are, however, a couple situations where one kind of fat is definitely the best choice. You will find yourself unable to make Hollandaise Sauce (page 118) without real butter or ghee, for example. Whenever the kind of fat you use does not make a difference in our recipes, we list our preferred fat and then add "or fat of choice." If you don't see that note in a recipe, stick to the fat listed.

MAKE COOKING QUICK *and* EASY

It's true, moving away from processed and prepackaged foods does mean spending more time in the kitchen preparing meals from scratch. If you find yourself lamenting the loss of time, here are some tricks to make cooking from scratch quicker and easier.

Make Dishes Ahead of Time

Before we went Paleo, we used a service where you would enter a storefront, toss the components of a whole meal in a bag, and freeze everything at once. The meals were designed to be simple, with no precooking and only oven baking. This system simplified our lives because all we needed to do was place the ingredients in the oven and bake our dinner. There is absolutely no reason why you can't do the same thing yourself at home. Assemble six of our recipes in freezer-safe containers on Sunday, freeze, and cook one a day for the rest of the week.

Keep Prepped Ingredients on Hand

From diced vegetables to precooked meats, you can always prepare some of your ingredients ahead of time to maximize your efficiency when it comes time to cook.

Make a Meal Plan

Both of the previous time-saving steps will be wasted if you don't know what you're making for the week and what ingredients you need to have on hand for those meals. If you don't take the time to plan ahead, you'll be standing in front of your fridge wondering what to make instead of having a list of things you need to do.

Don't Be Afraid of Frozen Vegetables

These days, grocery stores sell an abundance of flash-frozen vegetables, including organic varieties. Flash-frozen vegetables are usually better quality than canned and nearly as good as fresh, retaining almost all of their nutrients in the freezing process. Additionally, frozen vegetables are already chopped and ready to go, and sometimes skipping that extra step will save you a lot of time.

Utilize Your Microwave

Don't let your concerns about radiation stop you: There's nothing wrong with using a microwave. Many studies on microwave use and cancer have been done, and there's no link between the two. Your food does not become radioactive when it's microwaved. In fact, the microwaves that your appliance produces are too wide to penetrate the door of your oven, let alone your body. The only difference between steaming in a microwave and steaming on a stovetop is a tiny loss of nutrient content in the microwave. So if time is what you're after, we recommend that you cook a spaghetti squash for ten minutes in the microwave rather than for forty minutes in the oven.

Never Throw Away Leftovers

Okay, if you make something terrible, then by all means don't force yourself to eat it again. (We hope that something terrible wasn't one of our recipes!) But leftovers can simply and easily be transformed into tomorrow's lunch or dinner. In fact, we are always converting leftovers into soups, casseroles, or stir-fries. And we designate one night a week as a "leftovers for dinner" night, so the fridge is always cleared out.

Grab Helpers

Cooking is a team endeavor in a restaurant, so why is it a solo effort at home? Grab all the extra hands you can! Whether they're a four-year-old's hands, good only for supervised stirring, or a grown-up spouse's hands, usually trustworthy enough for using a knife, you'll be relieved that someone is assisting. And what a great bonding time it is to cook together.

KEEP PALEO EATING AFFORDABLE

Here are a few tips to keep that bill a bit lower.

When you take away the cheapest, most heavily subsidized foods—wheat, beans, corn, rice—you may find your grocery bill creeping up. It goes up even more if you opt to start buying organic produce and pastured meats.

Don't Make Nut-, Maple-, or Honey-Based Treats a Daily Indulgence

You'll quickly find that the replacements for wheat flour are not subsidized down to fifty cents a pound and that maple syrup and honey are extremely expensive as well. Honey prices are likely to continue to skyrocket as the bee population is experiencing a plague worse than any human population has ever seen.

If your habit is to bake several times per week, we recommend that you cut back. Is your sweet tooth a weakness? Perhaps this will be good motivation to wean yourself off sugar. If you make dozens upon dozens of cookies at a time, you may want to cut back your quantities. Check out our less sweet treats, like Snack Balls (page 170).

Buy More Affordable Cuts of Meat

Thanks to the fat and cholesterol scare that began some fifty years ago, fattier cuts of meat have long been cheaper than their lean counterparts. But research has proven that fat and cholesterol in the diet does not correlate to clogged arteries and heart disease, so take advantage of this price break.

The cheapest meats are the less-lean pork and beef roasts, and chicken thighs and legs. Pounce on these, especially when they're on sale, and avoid making steaks, chops, and breasts the main component of your purchases.

Take Advantage of Coupons and Sales

Coupons, Groupons, sales, and discount codes come up all the time. Check newspapers and flyers, scan social media (like the Paleo Parents Facebook page!), and see if you can save yourself some money.

Join a Meat Share

A whole animal purchased directly from a farm costs hundreds of dollars, but the per-pound price is half (or less) of what it costs to buy the meat piecemeal. If you want the benefits of pastured meat, find a local meat share. A meat share will divide up the cost of a whole animal among multiple parties so that no one person has to spend hundreds of dollars on several freezers full of meat. We talk in more detail about how to do this in *Beyond Bacon*.

Join a CSA

Community-supported agriculture, or CSA, is a system in which a local farm distributes a box of fresh produce directly to subscribers each week. It helps to spread the cost of local, seasonal, and often pesticide-free or organic produce among many participants, and it's better for the farmers, too. The selection varies from week to week depending on what's in season, but it's always fresh from the farm and usually much cheaper than produce found in grocery stores.

Go to the Farmers Market

Farmers markets cut out the middleman, so you can often get fresh produce cheaper than at a grocery store. Just be careful not to buy from a reseller. Ask questions; a real farmer will know where things came from and how they were grown. Look up where markets are held in your area and go visit.

Join a Co-Op

Some things are sold at a discount in bulk. How do you access this discount? Call up your friends and organize a co-op! This just means that you order together and share the savings you get once you qualify for wholesale pricing.

COOK *for* SPECIAL OCCASIONS

Since prehistoric times, humans have celebrated special occasions with food, drinks, and family gatherings, and over time, certain foods have become associated with certain holidays and events.

Even though going Paleo means giving up some of the ingredients that make up those traditional dishes, we still want to celebrate in a traditional way. Keep in mind that we're approaching this from a typical middle-American perspective, which is dominated by Christian religious traditions. If you happen to have a different cultural or religious background, there's probably someone else writing about that perspective. For example, Elana Amsterdam writes extensively on her blog, *Elana's Pantry,* about making gluten-free foods for Jewish holidays, and Michelle Tam from *Nom Nom Paleo* frequently writes about Chinese traditions.

Birthdays

What would a birthday be without cake? Certainly not a party! It was very important to us to include a Paleo-friendly recipe for a layer cake, the traditional birthday dessert, to make for that special day. Our Chocolate Layer Cake with Fresh Fruit (page 366) is perfect with Vanilla Bean or Strawberry Frosting (page 368).

Thanksgiving

The classic Thanksgiving meal is still possible, even if you're living a grain-free lifestyle. Roasting an unstuffed turkey falls naturally in line with Paleo; just season it with salt, black pepper, and herbs. But if the stuffing is what you're really after, try our Turkey Breasts Stuffed with "Cheese" and Cranberries (page 344). For sides, we recommend our Green Bean Casserole (page 248), Biscuits (page 250), and Cranberry-Orange No Bake Coconut Bars (page 172). For other typical Thanksgiving dishes, just a little change is enough. Simmering cranberries by themselves makes cranberry jelly, and sweet potatoes with marshmallows can be made with our Marshmallow recipe (page 372). Finish the night with Pumpkin Pudding (page 154) or Pumpkin Parfait (page 390).

Christmas

In our family, we love to have Monkey Bread (page 210) on Christmas morning. This recipe is usually made with canned biscuit dough, but our version uses homemade dough without any grains at all. And what wintertime event would be complete without Eggnog (page 294) and Peppermint Hot Chocolate (page 300)? We have many happy memories of enjoying these dishes as we unwrap our presents.

New Year's

On New Year's Day, the Western tradition is to eat foods that symbolize a successful coming year. We like to eat greens, like Creamed Kale (page 254), which represent money for obvious reasons, and pork, like our Slow-Roasted Pork Shoulder (page 332), because pigs represent progress.

Easter

Many of the celebrations around Easter are about birth, rebirth, and fertility, which makes sense considering both the religious celebration and the arrival of spring. The Easter egg hunt, which has become about finding plastic eggs filled with candy, can return to its roots with colored or painted hard-boiled eggs. Our boys were thrilled when their eggs were suddenly filled with coins instead of candy. Lamb and ham are typical main dishes and are easy to adapt to a Paleo diet. You could try our Lamb Stew (page 334), roast a rack or leg of lamb, or find a ham without a glaze.

Halloween

This is perhaps the most difficult of all celebrations for those avoiding processed foods and excess sugar. We now have an annual candy-free Halloween party at which the children exchange small trinkets and do a grain-free cake walk. We do go trick-or-treating, but we set a low limit on the amount of candy our children can keep, and then only with our approval. But the really fun parts of Halloween are the costumes and walking the neighborhood at night, not the candy haul, right? We also make our own treats, including Jack-O'-Lantern Cookies (page 386), Roasted Pumpkin Seeds (page 178), and Pumpkin Cider Latte (page 198).

SETTING YOUR PALEO TABLE

We all get into ruts with our meals. Cookbooks can help, but what is often left out is how to combine dishes for a complete meal.

In this section, we've strived to show you what some typical Paleo meals look like. Some of these meals we've identified as Phase 1; if you're in Phase 2 or Phase 3, like our family, these should be considered special meals that aren't for everyday. The rest of the meals show you how we normally eat and what we put together for parties or holidays.

Although we can personally say that the dishes in these meals taste wonderful together and we highly recommend re-creating the meals as outlined here, we also encourage you, as you get more comfortable with Paleo, to swap out some of the dishes for others and play with combinations in order to teach yourself how to create balanced Paleo meals.

COCONUT *or* ALMOND MILK
(p. 290)

HONEY NUT CEREAL
(p. 196)

QUICK BANANA-CHOCOLATE SOUFFLÉ CAKE
(p. 146)

MAKE-AHEAD BREAKFAST

TOTAL PREP-TO-TABLE TIME: 90 minutes · **FEEDS:** 4 to 6

RECIPES INCLUDED:

Quick Banana-Chocolate Soufflé Cake (page 146)

Honey Nut Cereal (page 196)

Coconut or Almond Milk (page 290)

WHY WE RECOMMEND THIS:

Make all the components on a weekend and you'll have cereal and cake for breakfast all week! If you miss the convenience of having cereal and muffins available, these recipes will do the trick.

MACRO- AND MICRONUTRIENTS:

This meal is relatively dominant in carbohydrates from the bananas and honey, but it contains significant protein and fat from the eggs and nuts as well.

MAKE AHEAD:

All of the components can and should be made ahead for an extremely quick and easy breakfast!

WHAT TO DO WITH LEFTOVERS:

Leftover cereal is perfect for dessert, or as a topping for yogurt or ice cream.

CHEF'S TIPS:

• The most important tip to making granola is to prevent it from burning. Be sure to stir the granola frequently while it bakes!

• If one of the components in our granola recipe is not your favorite, you may of course switch it out for something different. Or, if you'd prefer some dried fruit, stir that in once the granola has finished baking.

What else pairs well:

Fresh fruit with bacon or homemade sausage (page 164) would be a great replacement for the cake or the cereal.

Notes: This meal will be especially enjoyed by children, particularly those who are used to starting their day with a bowl of cereal.

**BLUEBERRY
SAGE
BREAKFAST
SAUSAGE**

(p. 164)

**SAUTÉED
APPLES**

(p. 274)

**CINNAMON
BREAD**

(p. 156)

BREAKFAST SNACK *for* COFFEE DRINKING *and* PAPER READING

TOTAL PREP-TO-TABLE TIME: Less than 30 minutes if the bread is made ahead of time; if not, 1 hour

FEEDS: 4 to 6

RECIPES INCLUDED:

Cinnamon Bread (page 156)

Sautéed Apples (page 274)

Blueberry Sage Breakfast Sausage (page 164)

WHY WE RECOMMEND THIS:

The flavors of cinnamon and fruit pair nicely in this meal, and the components are easily portable, making it a perfect meal for those who like a grazing-style breakfast. This breakfast is ideal for multitasking moments or perhaps for packing and taking to work with you.

MACRO- AND MICRONUTRIENTS:

This meal contains significant carbohydrate from the apples, blueberries, and raisins, but also fat and protein from the sausages and the almond butter in the bread.

MAKE AHEAD:

Definitely bake the bread ahead of time. It will save you much time, and the bread stores very well chilled for a week or so. The apples and sausage can also be made ahead to make this a quick reheat meal at home or at the office.

WHAT TO DO WITH LEFTOVERS:

- Leftover bread can be used in our Pumpkin Parfait (page 390) or saved for a weekend French toast indulgence.
- Leftover uncooked sausage can be used in our Sweet Potato Apple Hash (page 158).
- Apples can be ground up for applesauce or Apple Butter (page 112).

CHEF'S TIPS:

For effective sausage cooking, be sure to use the right amount of heat for the job. You need the outside to be browned but not blackened, while getting the inside cooked all the way through. On our gas burner, medium heat works best. On an electric stovetop, the right heat level may be lower. If this is tricky, you may want to consider cooking the sausage like Restaurant Steaks (page 346), browning both sides on the stovetop and finishing in the oven.

What else pairs well:

In place of the sausage, either of our other Breakfast Sausages (page 164) would be equally delicious.

An Iced Mocha (page 298) or Salted Caramel Frappé (page 296) in the summer or a Pumpkin Cider Latte (page 198) in the winter goes nicely.

Notes: If you're getting sick of egg-centric breakfasts, this meal is a good solution for you!

CHICKEN FINGERS
(p. 202)

COCONUT MILK
(p. 290)

ANTS ON A LOG *made with* **NUT BUTTER**
(p. 186)

HONEY MUSTARD
(p. 202)

KIDS' LUNCH

TOTAL PREP-TO-TABLE TIME: Less than 30 minutes if the coconut milk and nut butter are made ahead of time

FEEDS: 4 to 6

RECIPES INCLUDED:

Chicken Fingers with Honey Mustard (page 202)

Nut Butter of your choice (page 186)

Coconut Milk (page 290)

WHY WE RECOMMEND THIS:

Children often get attached to their favorite foods, and one of the most common attachments is to chicken fingers or nuggets. Re-creating these favorites will make your family's transition to Paleo smoother. But it's not only children who form attachments to food. Adults (us included!) do as well. Doesn't your inner child want a fried chicken finger with honey mustard, too?

MACRO- AND MICRONUTRIENTS:

You'll be getting a balance of carbohydrates from the apple butter and protein and fat from the chicken and honey mustard. Nonetheless, this is definitely a "treat" meal that is ideally followed by a veggie-rich dinner.

MAKE AHEAD:

Coconut milk and nut butters ought to be staples in your house, made ahead of time and kept in the fridge. The mayonnaise base for the Honey Mustard is also a weekly staple for us and makes quick work of this delicious dip.

WHAT TO DO WITH LEFTOVERS:

Honey mustard is great as a condiment on chicken of all sorts as well as on salads, though we don't think you'll have any leftovers!

CHEF'S TIPS:

Frying can certainly be dangerous! Hot oil is hotter than boiling water and baked goods coming out of the oven. We recommend that you use a heavy pot that will not tip over or an electric fryer with a breakaway electrical cord. Make sure that the sides are tall enough to minimize splatter. And once you have finished cooking, turn off the heat and allow the oil to cool completely before cleaning up! Strain and save the oil in a mason jar in the fridge or freezer. It should last for several uses before browning.

What else pairs well:

Instead of frying chicken, use the same batter to fry fish for an omega-3 boost!

Try using Apple Butter Barbecue Sauce (page 112) or even Ketchup (page 120) as your dipping sauce!

Notes: If frying seems arduous to you, try baking the battered chicken in a 350°F oven for 20 minutes instead.

KUNG
PAO
CHICKEN
(p. 322)

MONGOLIAN BEEF
(p. 320)

PLAIN CAULI-RICE
(p. 246)

CHINESE TAKE-OUT DINNER

TOTAL PREP-TO-TABLE TIME: 45 minutes · **FEEDS:** 4 to 6

RECIPES INCLUDED:

Mongolian Beef (page 320)

Kung Pao Chicken (page 322)

Plain Cauli-Rice (page 246)

WHY WE RECOMMEND THIS:

If you're avoiding the wheat-containing soy sauce prevalent in nearly all Chinese restaurant food, not to mention the MSG, you may want to consider taking on the challenge of making your own Chinese take-out meal like this one!

MACRO- AND MICRONUTRIENTS:

You've got fat and protein in the meat, especially the beef. Cauli-Rice adds nutrient-rich veggies in place of starch. The sweeteners in the sauce do add carbohydrates.

MAKE AHEAD:

Dice the vegetables and make the Cauli-Rice ahead of time. Keeping these things on hand will save you time!

WHAT TO DO WITH LEFTOVERS:

Only one thing is better than Chinese take-out: Chinese take-out leftovers for lunch the next day!

CHEF'S TIPS:

Be aware that regular soy sauce is not gluten-free. In fact, most brands these days list wheat as the first ingredient. Gluten-free alternatives include wheat-free tamari, which is simply fermented soybeans; coconut aminos; and other soy-free seasoning sauces, such as Naked Coconuts Sauce (see page 35 for more info).

What else pairs well:

Instead of Plain Cauli-Rice, consider making Thai Fried Cauli-Rice (page 247). Chinese Lettuce Cups (page 218) make an excellent appetizer.

Notes: These dishes work very well together as a Chinese-themed meal, so make it a special occasion. Call it "Chinese Night" and get the whole family involved.

STRAWBERRY STREUSEL MUFFINS
(p. 138)

ICED MOCHA
(p. 298)

SWEET POTATO APPLE HASH
(p. 158)

EASY PEASY PANCAKES
(p. 136)

EGGS STACY
(p. 152)

WEEKEND BRUNCH

TOTAL PREP-TO-TABLE TIME: 90 minutes

FEEDS: 4 (just poach a couple more eggs for the Eggs Stacy)

RECIPES INCLUDED:

Eggs Stacy (page 152)

Hollandaise Sauce (page 118)

Sweet Potato Apple Hash (page 158)

Easy Peasy Pancakes (page 136)

Strawberry Streusel Muffins (page 138)

Iced Mocha (page 298)

WHY WE RECOMMEND THIS:

Every Sunday, if we can, we make a huge breakfast feast featuring many of our favorite foods and interesting new experiments as well. We encourage you to do the same!

MACRO- AND MICRONUTRIENTS:

A good balance of macronutrients with fat and protein from the sausage, eggs, and hollandaise and carbohydrates from the muffins and pancakes. The great thing is that very little sweeteners are used!

MAKE AHEAD:

Make the raw sausage ahead of time. You can also premake the pancakes and reheat them before serving. Muffins are always good to make ahead.

WHAT TO DO WITH LEFTOVERS:

* Leftover pancakes can go in the freezer for a quick breakfast later.
* Sautéing leftover hash with greens like kale or spinach makes for a quick and simple lunch or dinner.
* Chill or freeze leftover muffins for snacks or breakfasts all week long or for the next Sunday feast.

CHEF'S TIPS:

Hollandaise is the component with the highest degree of difficulty here. Have patience, work slowly, and don't give up if you can't make it work on your first attempt! Perfecting hollandaise takes a lot of practice. We recommend practicing ahead of time so that you either have it on hand already or have the confidence to make it right before serving the meal.

What else pairs well:

Instead of the somewhat involved Eggs Stacy, make an Egg Pizza (page 162).

If pancakes aren't a favorite, try making Waffles (page 166).

Notes: Brunch is a great way to celebrate the holidays. Our family has specific brunch traditions for many holidays, from Christmas to Mother's Day.

VANILLA
CASHEW BUTTER
(p. 186)

TURKEY
CRANBERRY
BREAKFAST
SAUSAGE
(p. 164)

WAFFLES
(p. 166)

CC'S PERFECT
HASH BROWNS
(p. 142)

TURKEY 'N' WAFFLES

TOTAL PREP-TO-TABLE TIME: 45 minutes if making the waffles from scratch, 20 if the waffles are made ahead of time and frozen

FEEDS: 6 to 8

RECIPES INCLUDED:

Waffles (page 166)

Vanilla Cashew Butter (page 186)

Turkey Cranberry Breakfast Sausage (page 164)

CC's Perfect Hash Browns (page 142)

WHY WE RECOMMEND THIS:

Our waffles are truly outstanding and must be eaten to be believed! They're fruit-sweetened, freezable, and an absolute favorite for anyone who's tried them. Plus, this breakfast is quick to assemble and cook, even from scratch.

MACRO- AND MICRONUTRIENTS:

This meal is high in carbohydrates from the potatoes and waffles, but it includes some fat and protein from the sausage and the nuts in the waffles.

MAKE AHEAD:

- Premix the raw sausage so it's ready to fry when you are.
- Make the waffles ahead of time and freeze them. They reheat easily in the toaster.
- Store the nut butter chilled to eat as a snack all week.

WHAT TO DO WITH LEFTOVERS:

Leftover waffles are easily frozen for toaster reheating later. Simply put your frozen waffle in the toaster and toast until hot!

CHEF'S TIPS:

If you're not up for the lengthy task of pan-frying hash browns, they cook well in a waffle maker or sandwich press, believe it or not! Simply grease both the top and the bottom with lard, bacon fat, or butter, place the potatoes in a single layer in the bottom, and close the top. The hash browns will be done cooking in about 10 minutes.

What else pairs well:

Try Easy Peasy Pancakes (page 136) instead of Waffles or another of the sausages (page 164) instead of this turkey version.

Notes: What should you top your waffles with? The obvious choice, of course, is maple syrup, but many other choices remain. Try a Nut Butter (page 186), as pictured, or Coconut Butter (page 114), or maybe Whipped Coconut Cream (page 390) or our favorite, Apple or Pumpkin Butter (page 110).

EGGS *in* **A NEST**

(p. 144)

APPLE CINNAMON CRUMB CAKE

(p. 150)

STRAWBERRY MANGO SMOOTHIE

(p. 190)

FRUIT *and* EGGS TRANSFORMED

TOTAL PREP-TO-TABLE TIME: Less than 1 hour • **FEEDS:** 3 to 4

RECIPES INCLUDED:

Eggs in a Nest (page 144)

Apple Cinnamon Crumb Cake (page 150)

Strawberry Mango Smoothie (page 190)

WHY WE RECOMMEND THIS:

If you have a sweet tooth, a smoothie will certainly hit the spot, plus keep you going all morning with rich coconut milk. Add the vitamins and protein in the fried egg and you have a complete breakfast.

MACRO- AND MICRONUTRIENTS:

You'll consume a lot of healthy fat from the smoothie as well as carbohydrates from both the smoothie and the apple cake. You'll get protein from the nuts in the cake and the eggs. Plus, you'll get added nutrients from the spaghetti squash (a vegetable)!

MAKE AHEAD:

Bake the cake the day before, and preroast the spaghetti squash.

WHAT TO DO WITH LEFTOVERS:

Use the extra spaghetti squash to make a faux "pasta" dish for dinner. Freeze extra cake for a later date.

CHEF'S TIPS:

In cooking, there are many simple, everyday tasks that take a lifetime to master. There are some things that you're likely familiar with, like cooking a steak or roasting a chicken. But one of the less-mastered skills is frying an egg without burning the edges while making sure that the white is fully cooked and the yolk remains runny—all without breaking the yolk when flipping. Our no-flip steaming technique (page 144) will get you there, and your guests will love this stunning presentation.

What else pairs well:

Try Cranberry-Orange No-Bake Coconut Bars (page 172) in place of the muffins for a different fruity feel.

Notes: It goes without saying that smoothies are one of the quickest things you can prepare and consume if you need fuel fast. In fact, it's often our preworkout fuel on the days we go to the gym! Be sure to experiment with the many different smoothie flavors included on page 190! We like making our cake in individual ramekins for individual portion sizes.

LEMON
BLUEBERRY
BUNDT CAKE
(p. 396)

VEGGIE
LASAGNA
(p. 240)

CAESAR
SALAD
(p. 280)

GARLIC
BREADSTICKS
(p. 282)

ITALIAN LUNCH

TOTAL PREP-TO-TABLE TIME: About 1 hour • **FEEDS:** 4 to 6

RECIPES INCLUDED:

Veggie Lasagna (page 240)

Caesar Salad (page 280)

Garlic Breadsticks (page 282)

Lemon Blueberry Bundt Cake (page 396)

WHY WE RECOMMEND THIS:

This is a sneaky meal. It packs in a ton of vegetables without you even realizing it! Plus, if you add anchovies to the Caesar salad, it's a very palatable way to get extra seafood in.

MACRO- AND MICRONUTRIENTS:

A protein-light meal, the star is the transformed nutrient-rich veggies. Of course, you will get carbs from the cake and breadsticks—plus lovely omega-3 fats from the anchovies!

MAKE AHEAD:

Bake the cake and make the salad dressing ahead of time. Better yet, have the Cashew Cheese Sauce (page 126) ready and waiting as well!

WHAT TO DO WITH LEFTOVERS:

Leftover salad dressing will keep chilled for a week or more. The versatile base of the breadstick dough can be frozen or used to make gnocchi (page 260), slider "buns" (page 216), or the dumplings in Nona's Paprikosh (page 310).

CHEF'S TIPS:

If you don't have a special tool to slice foods thinly, we certainly recommend looking into it. A mandoline can be purchased for about $20, and you will find multiple ways to make use of it! Just make sure to follow the instructions; a mandoline is very sharp and can be dangerous if you're not careful.

What else pairs well:

Try a different salad if Caesar doesn't appeal, like Winter Salad (page 272) or Spinach, Walnut, and Bacon Salad (page 258).

Vegetarian friends? This meal will please them all if the salad is switched! Meat-eaters want more protein? Try our Butternut Squash Lasagna (page 362) instead of the veggie one.

FRIED SWEET
PLANTAINS
(p. 268)

PERUVIAN
CHICKEN
(p. 342)

CAULI-MASH
(p. 244)

PERUVIAN CHICKEN MEAL

TOTAL PREP-TO-TABLE TIME: 90 minutes · **FEEDS:** 4 to 6

RECIPES INCLUDED:

Peruvian Chicken (page 342)

Fried Sweet Plantains (page 268)

Cauli-Mash (page 244) or Yuca Fries (page 284)

WHY WE RECOMMEND THIS:

Pollo a la brasa, or Peruvian chicken, is rotisserie chicken with a crispy skin and juicy meat. It's the best way to consume chicken, in our opinion.

MACRO- AND MICRONUTRIENTS:

This meal is protein-rich from the chicken and heavy in carbohydrates from the plantains. The Cauli-Mash keeps it lower in fat than fried yuca, which is best immediately following a workout. For a special dinner, fry up some yuca!

MAKE AHEAD:

It's fine to make the chicken ahead of time and eat it cold with Mayonnaise (page 122).

WHAT TO DO WITH LEFTOVERS:

What can't you do with leftover chicken? Use it to make Stacy's Soup (page 312), Turkey Thai Basil (page 326), or Leftover Casserole (page 314).

CHEF'S TIPS:

This recipe makes use of vertical roasting in an attempt to mimic the all-over crispiness of rotisserie chicken. Although it is not quite the same, we're convinced that this is the best way to roast a whole chicken. Try it and you will not be disappointed!

What else pairs well:

Serve this with Mayonnaise (page 122) as a dipping sauce.

Notes: This is our favorite postworkout meal; expect to be satiated for quite a while! The Yuca Fries are the more traditional pairing.

KETCHUP
(p. 120)

MINI CORN
DOG MUFFINS
(p. 204)

ZUCCHINI
CAULIFLOWER
TOTS
(p. 206)

CORN DOGS *and* TOTS

TOTAL PREP-TO-TABLE TIME: About 45 minutes · **FEEDS:** 4 to 6

RECIPES INCLUDED:

Mini Corn Dog Muffins (page 204)

Zucchini Cauliflower Tots (page 206)

Ketchup (page 120)

WHY WE RECOMMEND THIS:

If there's one thing kids love when it comes to food, it's novelty. Who would have imagined a hot dog inside a mini muffin? The interesting presentation alone will fascinate them.

MACRO- AND MICRONUTRIENTS:

This meal is rich in protein and fat without a lot of emphasis on carbohydrates, despite having the appearance of bread.

MAKE AHEAD:

- Make the Ketchup ahead of time and always have it on hand.
- Bake the muffins and store them in the refrigerator.
- Shred the zucchini and steam the cauliflower in advance.

WHAT TO DO WITH LEFTOVERS:

- Leftover muffins can be stored in the fridge for a week or more or frozen. To reheat, defrost the muffins and then place them in a 350°F oven for 10 minutes.
- Ketchup is not only good on its own, but also useful as the base for a variety of sauces, like our Apple Butter BBQ Sauce (page 112).

CHEF'S TIPS:

Get your imagination going and try pairings that seem crazy. Hot dogs and muffins might seem outrageous, but this recipe actually works extremely well. It's like a corn dog, but one that is much easier to make and much healthier!

What else pairs well:

Lots of vegetables pair with the muffins, like Grilled Asparagus (page 270) or perhaps Citrus Broccoli (page 276) or Green Onion and Bacon Mac 'n' Cheese (page 238).

Notes: This meal was made to be a kids' classic, but quite a few adults have declared it perfect for on-the-go!

CITRUS BROCCOLI

(p. 276)

GREEN ONION *and*
BACON MAC 'N' CHEESE

(p. 238)

SAGE *and*
**CITRUS ROAST
CHICKEN**

(p. 306)

CHICKEN DINNER

TOTAL PREP-TO-TABLE TIME: 1 hour • **FEEDS:** 4 to 6

RECIPES INCLUDED:

Sage and Citrus Roast Chicken (page 306)

Citrus Broccoli (page 276)

Green Onion and Bacon Mac 'n' Cheese (page 238)

WHY WE RECOMMEND THIS:

A balanced meal with wide appeal, it's reminiscent of classic comfort food with much more pep and flavor. Incredibly flavorful, this is one of our weekly staples for its simplicity.

MACRO- AND MICRONUTRIENTS:

You'll get lots of protein from the chicken and carbohydrates from the butternut squash, with very moderate fats. The focus is on the squash, which adds a vegetable without tasting like one. The nutrient-rich broccoli is a perfect pairing, and high in vitamin C from the added citrus.

MAKE AHEAD:

Assemble the Green Onion and Bacon Mac 'n' Cheese ahead of time and bake it when you're ready.

WHAT TO DO WITH LEFTOVERS:

- The Mac 'n' Cheese will reheat well for lunch during the week.
- Shred the leftover chicken for Chicken Waldorf Salad (page 356) and use it for Stacy's Soup (page 312) later.

CHEF'S TIPS:

Knowing how to quickly steam and flavor vegetables is an immense time-saver! You'll get real nutrient value for little time commitment with broccoli florets, winter squash, carrots, or cauliflower.

What else pairs well:

Instead of chicken, switch to Restaurant Steaks (page 346), or replace the Mac 'n' Cheese with Yuca Fries (page 284) for more starch.

Notes: Leg quarters are some of the least expensive cuts of meat this side of offal. Organic family packs of six are often less than $6 at Whole Foods. It's hard to beat serving six people significant portions of meat for a dollar each!

WINTER SALAD
(p. 272)

MEATZA
(p. 208)

CREAMY COCONUT
CHOCOLATE CHIP MACAROONS
(p. 402)

MEATZA NIGHT

TOTAL PREP-TO-TABLE TIME: 45 minutes • **FEEDS:** 4

RECIPES INCLUDED:

Meatza (page 208; double the recipe to serve 4 people)

Winter Salad (page 272)

Creamy Coconut Chocolate Chip Macaroons (page 402)

WHY WE RECOMMEND THIS:

We fully understand how much a part of our culture pizza has become. It's hard to imagine life without it! With our Meatza, you can embrace pizza but not gluten. Adding a salad course and a dessert makes it a complete meal.

MACRO- AND MICRONUTRIENTS:

Very high in protein and fat, but low in carbohydrates. If you use pastured protein and veggies on the Meatza, this meal becomes not only filling, but also nutrient-rich!

MAKE AHEAD:

- Premix the salad and have it on hand in the fridge.
- Bake the cookies ahead of time; they will store well at room temperature for a week or more, although they taste best when reheated slightly.

WHAT TO DO WITH LEFTOVERS:

Leftover Meatza reheats well the next day, or chop it up and reimagine it as a stir-fry.

CHEF'S TIPS:

Don't feel limited to the toppings we suggest in this book. Any number of things can top your pizza. Try other traditional toppings, like ham and pineapple, or get crazy! Ever had a smoked salmon pizza? How about a fried egg pizza?

What else pairs well:

Any number of salads will work with the Meatza, especially a Caesar Salad (page 280).

Notes: Everyone loves pizza night! Make it a party by laying out a spread of topping options and allowing people to assemble their own pizzas.

THAI FRIED CAULI-RICE
(p. 247)

DRUNKEN CARROT NOODLES
(p. 324)

TURKEY THAI BASIL
(p. 326)

PANANG BEEF CURRY
(p. 328)

WANT *to* TRY SOME THAI?

TOTAL PREP-TO-TABLE TIME: 45 minutes · **FEEDS:** 4 to 6

RECIPES INCLUDED:

Panang Beef Curry (page 328)

Drunken Carrot Noodles (page 324)

Turkey Thai Basil (page 326)

Thai Fried Cauli-Rice (page 247) or Plain Cauli-Rice (page 246)

WHY WE RECOMMEND THIS:

Thai cuisine is very popular in the Paleo world because much of it is naturally gluten- and dairy-free. Use veggies to replace rice and it becomes grain-free as well!

MACRO- AND MICRONUTRIENTS:

There is plenty of protein in all of these dishes, plus fat from the coconut milk and moderate carbohydrates from the carrots and cauliflower.

MAKE AHEAD:

Use leftover turkey (or any protein) in the Turkey Thai Basil, and be sure to have Cauli-Rice on hand for such occasions.

WHAT TO DO WITH LEFTOVERS:

Just like take-out meals, these dishes are great to take to work or school for lunch the next day.

CHEF'S TIPS:

Fresh herbs are an important tool in your arsenal, so try growing your very own herb garden! You won't need a lot of space, and using the fresh stuff will add much more flavor than the more convenient dried versions. If you have a black thumb, we find the best prices and variety for herbs at our local Asian market. In these recipes, we use fresh Thai basil, which has a unique flavor that's awesome to have on hand for a variety of foods, but may be hard to find at your usual supermarket.

What else pairs well:

Have Plain Cauli-Rice on hand to serve with the curry. And try different curry pastes for different flavors!

Notes: Making food from different cultures is a fun experiment. If Thai doesn't appeal to you, or if you happen to be Thai, making this meal normal and boring, try making an Indian, Russian, or Brazilian meal. Or any of the thousands of cultures in this giant world!

EGG PIZZA
(p. 162)

BREAKFAST PUREE
(p. 242)

VEGGIE-HEAVY BREAKFAST

TOTAL PREP-TO-TABLE TIME: 45 minutes · **FEEDS:** 4 to 6

RECIPES INCLUDED:

Egg Pizza (page 162)

Breakfast Puree (page 242)

WHY WE RECOMMEND THIS:

Much of the time people go for meat- and egg-heavy breakfasts and skimp on nutrient-dense vegetables. Ideally, you should have both!

MACRO- AND MICRONUTRIENTS:

Carbohydrates from the butternut squash and some protein and fat from the egg pizza create a great balance to start the day.

MAKE AHEAD:

* Steam the squash the night before.
* Make the Egg Pizza beforehand and reheat it when you wish to eat it. Better yet, make both recipes ahead of time in a weekly cook-up, and they'll last you for days.

WHAT TO DO WITH LEFTOVERS:

* Egg Pizza can keep in the fridge all week and be reheated for breakfast.
* Puréed butternut squash can double as a dinner side dish.

CHEF'S TIPS:

We have a cultural idea of what constitutes "breakfast food" as opposed to "lunch food" or "dinner food." Break out of that habit and realize that all foods are just food; there's no actual quality of "breakfastness" that exists in some foods and not others. Eat stew for breakfast, pancakes for lunch, and a chicken salad for dinner if that's what you want!

What else pairs well:

Try any number of vegetable purees with this meal, including carrot and cauliflower.

Notes: For someone trying to cut back on calories and increase nutrients, replacing the daily breakfast meat with veggies is a great start to the day!

LAMB STEW *(p. 334)*
over
CAULI-MASH *(p. 244)*

HEARTY STEW MEAL

TOTAL PREP-TO-TABLE TIME: Several hours (but worth it!) · **FEEDS:** 4 to 6

RECIPES INCLUDED:

Lamb Stew (page 334)

Cauli-Mash (page 244)

WHY WE RECOMMEND THIS:

Hearty stew made with the most omega-3 rich of all the land animals will not only satisfy you, but also deliver a powerful serving of rich bone Stock (page 132).

MACRO- AND MICRONUTRIENTS:

A rich and balanced meal full of all the macronutrients, it also offers tremendous vitamin and mineral content from the vegetables and stock.

MAKE AHEAD:

You will need to have the Stock already made or it will take days to bring this meal to the table. We love to cook up a big batch once a week.

WHAT TO DO WITH LEFTOVERS:

When we make stew for dinner, stew then becomes the next day's breakfast!

CHEF'S TIPS:

Don't feel intimidated by longer preparations! Remember: You can usually turn a braising or stew recipe into a slow cooker recipe by changing the step "bring to a boil, and then simmer" to "place in a slow cooker and cook on low for 8 hours." These set-it-and-forget-it meals can be the time-saver you never knew about!

What else pairs well:

For a different take, try using a winter squash or turnip puree instead of cauliflower.

Notes: Lots of Americans don't prepare lamb. That's a shame, because it's a healthy meat that is almost always grass-fed. This stew is an easy way to add lamb to your dinner table.

GREEN SALAD
with
POACHED EGG *(p. 148)*

POACHED EGG SALAD

TOTAL PREP-TO-TABLE TIME: 30 minutes • **FEEDS:** 2

RECIPES INCLUDED:

Green Salad with Poached Egg (page 148)

WHY WE RECOMMEND THIS:

Getting extra Phase 3 nutrients doesn't have to be arduous. Poach an egg and set it on a bed of greens, and you have a delicious and nutritious lunch!

MACRO- AND MICRONUTRIENTS:

Fat is plentiful in the egg, plus you get vitamins and minerals from the yolk and greens.

MAKE AHEAD:

Poach the egg in the morning and keep it chilled until lunchtime.

WHAT TO DO WITH LEFTOVERS:

Extra poached eggs are great for breakfast! Make more than you need today, and then make Eggs Stacy tomorrow. Reheat poached eggs in a bowl of hot water until warm, but do not boil!

CHEF'S TIPS:

Try a variety of salad greens. These days, markets and grocery stores stock an amazing variety of lettuces, herbs, and tender greens that are perfect for lunchtime salads. Challenge yourself to try a different blend each time you shop. With fresh greens, a little olive oil and fresh citrus juice with salt and pepper is often all that is needed.

What else pairs well:

Try adding more vegetables to the salad, like carrots and zucchini!

Notes: Yes, you can certainly consider this meal portable, with refrigeration!

**GARDEN TUNA
SALAD**
(p. 354)

**PIZZA KALE
CHIPS**
(p. 174)

SNACK BALLS
(p. 170)

**CHICKEN
WALDORF
SALAD**
(p. 356)

COLLARD-WRAPPED LUNCH

TOTAL PREP-TO-TABLE TIME: 30 minutes, if the kale chips are made ahead of time

FEEDS: 4 to 6

RECIPES INCLUDED:

Chicken Waldorf Salad (page 356)

Garden Tuna Salad (page 354)

Pizza Kale Chips (page 174)

Snack Balls (page 170)

WHY WE RECOMMEND THIS:

This meal is a reminder that even if you give up grains, which means no bread, tortillas, or wraps, you can still embrace what's great about a sandwich. A packed lunch doesn't have to become impossible without those specific, minor ingredients!

MACRO- AND MICRONUTRIENTS:

You get tons of healthy fat and protein from the wraps filled with meat and salads and carbohydrates from the Snack Balls. With added veggies in and around the protein salads, this is an excellent afternoon meal!

MAKE AHEAD:

All of the components can be made ahead of time and assembled when you are ready.

WHAT TO DO WITH LEFTOVERS:

Save all your leftovers for tomorrow's lunch! We love snacking on tuna and carrots as well.

CHEF'S TIPS:

Tender young collard greens are perfect for this application because they're large and mild in flavor, but they're not the only thing that can make a wrap. Any large, flat green or lettuce leaf will do. Try red leaf lettuce or a chard leaf.

What else pairs well:

You can pack almost anything in your lunch box. Some of our other favorite portable foods are our Mini Corn Dog Muffins (page 204), Sweet Potato Chips (page 176), and Almond Meal Crackers (page 182). Or the simplest of all: Make a Nut Butter (page 186) wrap. You'd be surprised at how well they pair!

Notes: Don't be afraid to make Paleo-style lunch boxes for your children! And don't let a school try to tell you that a meal is incomplete without a sandwich. Whatever did people eat before Lord Sandwich invented portable meat?

CAULI-GNOCCHI *with*
BRUSSELS SPROUTS
and LEMON ZEST
(p. 260)

CARROT
MASH
(p. 278)

MACADAMIA-
CRUSTED
TILAPIA
(p. 316)

FISH DINNER

TOTAL PREP-TO-TABLE TIME: 1 hour · **FEEDS:** 4 to 6

RECIPES INCLUDED:

Macadamia-Crusted Tilapia (page 316)

Carrot Mash (page 278)

Cauli-Gnocchi with Brussels Sprouts and Lemon Zest (page 260)

WHY WE RECOMMEND THIS:

Fish is vital to your health; this fact cannot be overstated. With this meal, we tried to give you omega-3 rich fish in the most palatable way possible.

MACRO- AND MICRONUTRIENTS:

Fat and protein are in the fish and nuts, while carbohydrates are in the carrots and gnocchi. With three different vegetables, this is a very palatable way to eat the rainbow!

MAKE AHEAD:

Make the base of the gnocchi dough ahead of time.

WHAT TO DO WITH LEFTOVERS:

Leftover gnocchi dough can be used to make Garlic Breadsticks (page 282) or the dumplings for Nona's Paprikosh (page 310). Use leftover fish the next day as a protein in your lunch salad.

CHEF'S TIPS:

Fish cooks pretty fast and can go from underdone to overcooked even faster than chicken. It takes a lot of practice to get good at cooking fish, but once you do, you may discover that any aversion to fish you had was really just an aversion to poorly cooked fish.

What else pairs well:

Sub out the tilapia, an extremely mild fish, for something more robust, like trout, mahi mahi, or halibut.

Notes: Nut-crusted fish is one of those somewhat impressive dishes that is actually not difficult to make. Try it the next time you need to impress!

JUICY POT ROAST *(p. 308)*
over
CAULI-MASH *(p. 244)*

POT ROAST

TOTAL PREP-TO-TABLE TIME: 2½ hours · **FEEDS:** 4 to 6

RECIPES INCLUDED:

Juicy Pot Roast (page 308)

Cauli-Mash (page 244)

WHY WE RECOMMEND THIS:

This traditional and comforting meal combines many vegetables, braised meat in broth, and a ton of flavor!

MACRO- AND MICRONUTRIENTS:

This is a very balanced meal with protein and fat from the meat and carbohydrates from the starchy vegetables. With omega-3s from the beef and vitamins and minerals from the veggies, this one-pot meal is a win-win.

MAKE AHEAD:

Make sure to prepare the Stock ahead of time!

WHAT TO DO WITH LEFTOVERS:

Leftovers are awesome for lunch the following week, or the roast and mash can become a soup with the addition of bone Stock (page 132) and a little chopping and simmering.

CHEF'S TIPS:

The key to a good pot roast is controlling the quantity of liquid. You want enough to keep the meat braising the whole time without drying out, but not so much that you end up with a soup. Usually, halfway up the meat is sufficient. Once you master it, you'll be able to pot roast anything!

What else pairs well:

Instead of mash, go with Cauli-Rice (page 246)!

Notes: Chuck roast is usually a pretty cheap cut of beef and is often on sale. Look for opportunities to grab it cheap and pounce on it to fill your freezer!

STEAMED
MUSSELS *in*
TOMATO BROTH
(p. 232)

SAUTÉED
MUSHROOMS
and ONIONS
(p. 116)

CREAMED
KALE
(p. 254)

RESTAURANT
STEAKS
(p. 346)

BAKED
POTATO
SOUP
(p. 252)

RESTAURANT DINNER

TOTAL PREP-TO-TABLE TIME: 1 hour · **FEEDS:** 2 to 4

RECIPES INCLUDED:

Restaurant Steaks (page 346)

Sautéed Mushrooms and Onions (page 116)

Baked Potato Soup (page 252)

Creamed Kale (page 254)

Steamed Mussels in Tomato Broth (page 232)

WHY WE RECOMMEND THIS:

This full, three-course meal will convince a date that you're a restaurant-quality chef!

MACRO- AND MICRONUTRIENTS:

This is a well-balanced meal with proteins and fat from the steak and carbohydrates from the soup. It is surprisingly nutrient-rich from the grass-fed steak, kale, and mussels. This meal contains four of the Paleo superfoods.

MAKE AHEAD:

Make the Baked Potato Soup ahead of time and reheat.

WHAT TO DO WITH LEFTOVERS:

Leftover steak is a great topping for salad or addition to Panang Beef Curry (page 328).

CHEF'S TIPS:

Mussels and other shellfish are delicious when steamed in a flavorful liquid. Go ahead and experiment with that steaming liquid for mussels, clams, and other shellfish. We've made a curry-flavored version as well and know that you're going to have even more great ideas.

What else pairs well:

Instead of Baked Potato Soup, try making Butternut Bisque (page 264).

Notes: Freshly grated horseradish into Mayonnaise (page 122) makes an incredible replacement for sour cream or steak sauce on your steak.

EPIC
MEATLOAF
(p. 338)

SPINACH, WALNUT
and BACON SALAD
(p. 258)

EPIC MEATLOAF MEAL

TOTAL PREP-TO-TABLE TIME: 90 minutes · **FEEDS:** 6 to 8

RECIPES INCLUDED:

Epic Bacon Meatloaf (page 338)

Spinach, Walnut, and Bacon Salad (page 258)

WHY WE RECOMMEND THIS:

Our Epic Bacon Meatloaf packs an epic nutrient content, particularly when you "sneak" liver into it for an extra hit of nutrient density!

MACRO- AND MICRONUTRIENTS:

This protein-rich meal gets a huge micronutrient boost with the addition of liver. No one will even notice with all the delicious bacon!

MAKE AHEAD:

You can premake the meatloaf mix and press it into the loaf pan so it's ready when you're ready to bake it!

WHAT TO DO WITH LEFTOVERS:

We often chop up the Epic Bacon Meatloaf and simmer it in some stock for Stacy's Soup (page 312) the next day!

CHEF'S TIPS:

You definitely want to grind or chop up some liver and add it to your ground beef here. This is the perfect opportunity to add some offal to a dish without affecting the flavor in a noticeable way. We've served this dish to many people with liver added, and none of them have noticed a discernible liver flavor.

What else pairs well:

Try Winter Salad (page 272) or Caesar Salad (page 280) instead of the spinach salad.

Notes: Meatloaf is a great and fun dish to prepare with children on a weeknight. Have them mix the meatloaf by hand and then top it with the bacon!

PHASE 1 MEAL PLAN

SUNDAY

Breakfast

Egg Pizza (page 162)

Waffles (page 166) or gluten-free pancakes of your choice

Fresh fruit

Lunch

Mini Corn Dog Muffins (page 204)

Smoothie of your choice (page 190)

Dinner

Crispy Oven-Baked Chicken Wings (page 234)

Green Onion and Bacon Mac 'n' Cheese (page 238)

Snack

Chocolate Custard (page 406) with fresh fruit

Shortcuts, Tips, & Tricks
Make a double batch of Waffles and freeze the leftovers to eat later on weekdays when you're short on time! Also make Mayonnaise (page 122), Stock (page 132), Snack Balls (page 170), and Honey Nut Cereal (page 196) and Coconut or Almond Milk (page 290) if you want to try to get off of gluten-free cereal. Many dishes can be made ahead of time, like Mini Corn Dog Muffins (page 204) and Not Beanie Weenies (page 200), as well as baked goods like cookies and cake.

MONDAY

Breakfast

Quick Banana-Chocolate Soufflé Cake (page 146)

Bacon

Lunch

Leftover Green Onion and Bacon Mac 'n' Cheese

Leftover Mini Corn Dog Muffins

Dinner

Linguine with Baby Clams (page 340) served with spiral-sliced squash or your preferred gluten-free noodles

Garlic Breadsticks (page 282)

Green salad (see "Build Your Own Salad," page 50)

Snack

Snack Balls (page 170)

TUESDAY

Breakfast

Honey Nut Cereal (page 196) or gluten-free cereal of your choice

Coconut or other milk/ yogurt

Sliced banana or other fruit

Lunch

Garden Tuna Salad (page 354) on wrap or gluten-free bread

Sweet Potato Chips (page 176) or chip of your choice

Fresh fruit

Dinner

Slow-Roasted Pork Shoulder (page 332)

Apple Butter BBQ Sauce (page 112), Carolina-Style Sauce (page 234), or barbecue sauce of your choice

Roasted Rainbow Carrots (page 266)

Cauli-Mash (page 244) or mashed potatoes

Snack

Lemon Blueberry Bundt Cake (page 396)

Shortcuts, Tips, & Tricks
Double the recipe for Sweet Potato Chips for lunches later in the week.

Find a downloadable shopping list for this meal plan at paleoparents.com/downloads

WEDNESDAY

Breakfast

Leftover Quick Banana-Chocolate Soufflé Cake

Salted Caramel Frappé (page 296)

Lunch

Leftover Slow-Roasted Pork Shoulder with barbecue sauce on salad or gluten-free bread

Leftover Snack Balls

Ants on a Log with Nut Butter (page 186)

Dinner

Easy Peasy Pancakes (page 136) or gluten-free pancakes of your choice

Sweet Potato Apple Hash (page 158)

Shortcuts, Tips, & Tricks
Try eating your tuna salad with sliced veggies as the scooper. We love carrots, but any vegetable works!

Snack

Smoothie of your choice (page 190)

THURSDAY

Breakfast

Leftover dinner for breakfast

Lunch

Garden Tuna Salad (page 354) on wrap or gluten-free bread

Leftover Sweet Potato Chips or chip of your choice

Fresh fruit

Dinner

Peruvian Chicken (page 342)

Carrot Mash (page 278)

Spinach, Walnut, and Bacon Salad (page 258)

Snack

Jerky (page 180) or Energy Bars (page 188)

Shortcuts, Tips, & Tricks
Set aside 2 cups of diced cooked chicken from the Peruvian Chicken dinner for the Chicken Waldorf Salad that will be made the next day.

FRIDAY

Breakfast

Leftover Honey Nut Cereal or gluten-free cereal of your choice

Coconut (or other) milk/yogurt

Sliced banana or other fruit

Lunch

Chicken Waldorf Salad (page 356) made with leftover Peruvian Chicken on wraps or gluten-free bread

Leftover Sweet Potato Chips or chip of your choice

Leftover Snack Balls

Dinner

Meatza (page 208) or your favorite gluten-free pizza

Garlic Breadsticks (page 282) or your favorite gluten-free rolls

Snack

Leftover Lemon Blueberry Bundt Cake

SATURDAY

Breakfast

Blueberry Breakfast Cookies (page 140)

Blueberry Sage Breakfast Sausage (page 164)

Iced Mocha (page 298)

Lunch

Chicken Fingers with Honey Mustard (page 202)

Ants on a Log with leftover Nut Butter

Dinner

Panang Beef Curry (page 328)

Drunken Carrot Noodles (page 324)

Thai Fried Cauli-Rice (page 247) or Plain Cauli-Rice (page 246)

Snack

Leftover Jerky or Energy Bars

SUNDAY

Breakfast

Smoothie of your choice (page 190)

Lunch

Easy Peasy Pancakes (page 136)

Blueberry Sage Breakfast Sausage (page 164)

Egg Pizza (page 162)

Dinner

Green salad (see "Build Your Own Salad," page 50)

Garlic Breadsticks* (page 282)

Butternut Squash Lasagna (page 362)

Snack

Fresh fruit or Energy Bars (page 188)

Shortcuts, Tips, & Tricks

Make Stock (page 132), Energy Bars (page 188), Muffins (page 194), Apple Butter (page 110), and Kale Chips (page 174) over the weekend to have on hand all week.

*Double the batch of breadsticks and eat them later in the week with other meals.

MONDAY

Breakfast

Leftover Egg Pizza

Fresh fruit or Smoothie of your choice (page 190)

Lunch

Green salad (see "Build Your Own Salad," page 50)

Leftover Butternut Squash Lasagna

Dinner

Peruvian Chicken (page 342)

Cauli-Mash (page 244)

Fried Sweet Plantains (page 268)

Green salad (see "Build Your Own Salad," page 50)

Snack

Creamy Coconut Chocolate Chip Macaroons (page 402)

Shortcuts, Tips, & Tricks

Double the Peruvian Chicken recipe to make sure that you have enough leftover meat for lunch the next day and for making the Leftover Casserole. Double the base of the cookie dough, which also makes the Cranberry-Orange No-Bake Coconut Bars (page 172). Both will last a long time in the fridge!

TUESDAY

Breakfast

Chunky Monkey Muffins (page 194)

Leftover Blueberry Sage Breakfast Sausage

Lunch

Leftover Peruvian Chicken and Fried Sweet Plantains

Dinner

Leftover Casserole (page 314) made with leftover Peruvian Chicken

Snack

Cranberry-Orange No-Bake Coconut Bars (page 172)

Shortcuts, Tips, & Tricks

Save 4 cups of shredded cooked chicken from the Peruvian Chicken for the Leftover Casserole.

Find a downloadable shopping list for this meal plan at paleoparents.com/downloads

WEDNESDAY

Breakfast

Stacy's Soup (page 312) with leftover Leftover Casserole

Lunch

Green salad (see "Build Your Own Salad," page 50)

Canned salmon or other quick and easy protein

Dinner

Epic Bacon Meatloaf (page 338)

Garlic Breadsticks (page 282)

Snack

Leftover Creamy Coconut Chocolate Chip Macaroons

THURSDAY

Breakfast

Leftover Chunky Monkey Muffins

Energy Bars (page 188)

Lunch

Leftover Epic Bacon Meatloaf

Dinner

Sage and Citrus Roast Chicken (page 306)

Green Onion and Bacon Mac 'n' Cheese (page 238)

Citrus Broccoli (page 276)

Snack

Fresh fruit or Energy Bars (page 188)

Shortcuts, Tips, & Tricks
Use leftover chicken from dinner to make Chicken Waldorf Salad for tomorrow's lunch.

FRIDAY

Breakfast

Leftover Cranberry-Orange No-Bake Coconut Bars

Smoothie of your choice (page 190)

Lunch

Chicken Waldorf Salad (page 356)

Snack Balls (page 170)

Dinner

Apple Short Ribs (page 336)

Cauli-Mash (page 244)

Snack

Fresh fruit or Energy Bars (page 188)

SATURDAY

Breakfast

Eggs in a Nest (page 144)

Fresh fruit

Lunch

Leftover Apple Short Ribs over leftover spaghetti squash

Dinner

Chinese Take-Out Dinner (page 67)

Snack

Energy Bars (page 188)

SUNDAY

Breakfast

Breakfast Puree
(page 242)

Lunch

Breakfast Burritos
(page 160) with avocado

Dinner

Slow-Roasted Pork
Shoulder (page 332)

Roasted Rainbow
Carrots (page 266)

Winter Salad (page 272)

Snack

Gummy Snacks
(page 212)

Shortcuts, Tips, & Tricks
*Make Stock (page 132), Mayonnaise (page 122), and Slightly Sweet & Salty Snack Mix
(page 184) and a double batch of Kale Chips (page 174) for the week. Prep your salad greens
and dressing ahead so that you can have fresh premade salad throughout the week (but
remember to dress salads right before serving).*

MONDAY

Breakfast

Leftover Breakfast
Burritos

Lunch

Green Salad with
Poached Egg (page 148)

Leftover Breakfast Puree

Dinner

Leftover Casserole (page
314) made with leftover
Slow-Roasted Pork
Shoulder and leftover
Roasted Rainbow
Carrots

Leftover Winter Salad

Snack

Healthiest Ice Cream
Ever (page 384) topped
with Slight Sweet &
Salty Snack Mix
(page 184)

Shortcuts, Tips, & Tricks
*Double the butternut squash when
roasting it and then use it to make
Butternut Bisque (page 264) later in the
week.*

TUESDAY

Breakfast

Stacy's Soup (page 312)
made with leftover
Leftover Casserole

Lunch

Garden Tuna Salad (page
354) with carrot chips

Leftover Gummy Snacks

Pizza Kale Chips
(page 174)

Dinner

Beef Tongue Carnitas
(page 350)

Fiesta Caul-Rice
(page 247)

Tostadas (page 262)

Snack

Fresh fruit

*Find a downloadable shopping list for this meal
plan at paleoparents.com/downloads*

WEDNESDAY

Breakfast

Egg Pizza (page 162)

Lunch

Leftover Beef Tongue Carnitas with leftover Fried Cauli-Rice

Dinner

Crab Balls (page 318)

Tartar Sauce (page 122)

Green salad (see "Build Your Own Salad," page 50)

Snack

Leftover Gummy Snacks

THURSDAY

Breakfast

Butternut Bisque (page 264)

Lunch

Garden Tuna Salad (page 354) on mixed greens

Pizza Kale Chips (page 174)

Fresh fruit

Dinner

Brisket with Onion Jam (page 348)

Cauli-Mash (page 244)

Caesar Salad (page 280)

Shortcuts, Tips, & Tricks
Double the Cauli-Mash and save some for tomorrow's dinner.

Snack

Leftover Slight Sweet & Salty Snack Mix

FRIDAY

Breakfast

Leftover Egg Pizza

Leftover Caesar Salad

Lunch

Leftover Brisket with Onion Jam

Green salad (see "Build Your Own Salad," page 50)

Dinner

Juicy Pot Roast (page 308)

Leftover Cauli-Mash

Snack

Leftover Slightly Sweet & Salty Snack Mix

SATURDAY

Breakfast

Leftover Butternut Bisque

Lunch

Eastern Market Shrimp Salad (page 352)

Green salad (see "Build Your Own Salad," page 50)

Dinner

Restaurant Dinner (page 99)

Snack

Leftover Healthiest Ice Cream Ever

CONDIMENTS, SAUCES, AND DIPS

Most of the time, we think of condiments and sauces as things that you buy from an aisle in the grocery store. But everything from ketchup to ranch dressing was once a recipe that people made! Once you master the process of making these recipes, you'll never have to buy a junk-filled plastic bottle again.

	PHASE	PAGE #	UNDER 30 MIN	UNDER 5 INGREDIENTS	ONE POT	HOLIDAY	ON THE GO
Apple and Pumpkin Butters	2	110		YES		YES	
Apple Butter BBQ Sauce	2	112			YES		
Coconut Butter	2	114	YES	YES	YES		
Sautéed Mushrooms and Onions	2	116	YES	YES	YES		
Hollandaise Sauce	3	118	YES		YES	YES	
Ketchup	2	120			YES		
Mayonnaise and Mayo-Based Dips	3	122	YES	YES	YES		
Salad Dressings	3	124	YES		YES		
Cashew Cheese Sauce	2	126					
Pickled Onions	2	128		YES	YES		
Roasted Garlic	2	130		YES	YES		
Stock	3	132		YES	YES		

✔ Egg-Free
✔ Nut-Free
✔ Nightshade-Free

under 5
INGREDIENTS
HOLIDAY

Rather than slather our waffles and pancakes with high-fructose corn syrup–based jellies or syrups, we've taken to using apple or pumpkin butter that we make using only fruit and spices. It's sweet enough for even the pickiest sweet tooth but protects your liver and pancreas from a torrential sugar rush.

APPLE AND PUMPKIN BUTTERS

PREHEAT OVEN: 350°F · MAKES: ABOUT 2 CUPS EACH

Ingredients

Apple Butter

3 apples, peeled and sliced into eighths

1 cup apple cider

¼ teaspoon ground allspice

Pumpkin Butter

1 small pie pumpkin, ends removed, quartered, seeded, and peeled

1 cup apple cider

1 teaspoon ground cinnamon

¼ teaspoon ground nutmeg

¼ teaspoon ground allspice

SPECIAL TOOLS:

 OR

food processor   blender

1. Preheat the oven to 350°F.

2. Place the apples or pumpkin in a large baking dish and cover tightly with aluminum foil.

3. Place in the oven and bake for 1 hour or until completely soft. Allow to cool for 30 minutes.

4. Transfer to a food processor or blender and purée until smooth.

5. Add the remaining ingredients and pulse to incorporate.

6. Pour into a medium saucepan over low heat.

7. Cook, uncovered, stirring occasionally, until thickened to your preference (30 to 90 minutes, depending on the moisture content of the apples or pumpkin). Refrigerate in an airtight container for up to 2 weeks, or freeze for longer.

Note: These butters might look like they involve a lot of time and steps, but we promise that they're both simple and worthwhile. We recommend making a double batch, because you'll want them on everything and they keep for a long time!

Those who enjoy extra spicy barbecue sauce should not expect one at our table. Instead, we enjoy the tangy sweet sauce that we make using our own apple butter. This sauce is perfect for our Apple Short Ribs (page 336), of course, but we also use it on Slow-Roasted Pork Shoulder (page 332) and even on Crispy Oven-Baked Chicken Wings (page 234).

APPLE BUTTER BBQ SAUCE

MAKES: ABOUT 2 CUPS

Ingredients

- 1 cup Apple Butter (page 110)
- ½ cup Ketchup (page 120)
- 3 cloves garlic, minced
- 2 tablespoons maple syrup
- 1 tablespoon Worcestershire sauce
- 1 tablespoon apple cider vinegar
- 1 teaspoon onion powder
- 1 teaspoon dry mustard
- ½ teaspoon kosher or sea salt
- ⅛ teaspoon ground black pepper

1. In a medium saucepan over medium heat, whisk together all of the ingredients. Stir frequently until the sauce begins to bubble.

2. Reduce the heat to low and cover. Simmer for 20 minutes.

3. Although not necessary, we recommend making this sauce at least a day ahead of time to let the flavors really settle. Store chilled in an airtight container for up to 2 weeks.

Note: *We have found gluten-free, soy-free Worcestershire sauce at our local grocery store. If you can't find it, coconut aminos would work, too.*

- ✓ Egg-Free
- ✓ Nut-Free
- ✓ Nightshade-Free

UNDER 30 MIN

under 5 INGREDIENTS

ONE POT

You may have seen coconut butter labeled as many different things, like coconut cream concentrate or Coconut Manna. Once you figure out what it is, it's actually pretty simple to make at home with just a few easy-to-find ingredients. If you love the plain version but feel like trying some new, experiment with adding various flavors, like cacao powder and ground hazelnuts or pistachios, for your own custom treat. Eat it as a dip for fruit, in place of nut butter, or even by the spoonful, or blend it in coffee.

COCONUT BUTTER

MAKES: ABOUT 2 CUPS

Ingredients

- 2 cups unsweetened coconut flakes, shredded coconut, or dried coconut pulp left over from making Coconut Milk (page 290)
- 2 tablespoons coconut oil
- 1 teaspoon pure vanilla extract
- ¼ teaspoon kosher or sea salt

1. Place all of the ingredients in a blender or food processor and purée until a thick white butter forms, about 8 to 12 minutes.

Note: This recipe creates a thick, spreadable coconut butter that is traditionally spoonable (as pictured). To make coconut cream concentrate (for our Creamy Coconut Chocolate Chip Macaroons on page 402), which has a more viscous, almost liquid form, simply add 1 more tablespoon coconut oil and magic will happen!

SPECIAL TOOLS:

food processor OR blender

✓ Egg-Free
✓ Nut-Free
✓ Nightshade-Free

UNDER **30** MIN

under 5
INGREDIENTS

ONE POT

It may seem odd to list this as a condiment, but we believe that having sautéed mushrooms and onions in the fridge makes enhancing any meat dish an absolute breeze. We use this as a topping on our Restaurant Steaks (page 346) or chicken or even as a simple base for Stacy's Soup (page 312).

SAUTÉED MUSHROOMS AND ONIONS

MAKES: 1½ CUPS

Ingredients

1 tablespoon bacon fat or duck fat

½ cup diced yellow onion

1 cup sliced cremini mushrooms (baby portobella)

½ teaspoon kosher or sea salt

½ teaspoon garlic powder

⅛ teaspoon ground black pepper

1. Melt the fat in a medium skillet over medium heat.

2. Add the onion and mushrooms and sauté until the onion is translucent and the mushrooms are softened, about 7 minutes.

3. Add the salt, garlic powder, and pepper and stir to incorporate.

3

☐ Egg-Free
✓ Nut-Free
✓ Nightshade-Free

UNDER 30 MIN

ONE POT

HOLIDAY

Hollandaise sauce is a delicate emulsion of egg yolks and butter, and it requires your full attention. While it may seem intimidating at first, we have learned to make it at home, and we know that everyone else can learn to do it, too. Just dive right in and practice, and you will make it happen! We recommend serving it with Eggs Stacy (page 152) and Grilled Asparagus (page 270), but it's wonderful on just about anything.

HOLLANDAISE SAUCE

MAKES: ABOUT ½ CUP

Ingredients

4 large egg yolks, room temperature

1 tablespoon freshly squeezed lemon juice

½ cup melted butter or ghee

½ teaspoon kosher or sea salt

¼ teaspoon ground white pepper

⅛ teaspoon cayenne pepper (optional)

SPECIAL TOOLS:

Double boiler assembly

1. In the bottom of a double boiler or small saucepan, bring 1 cup of water to a simmer over medium heat.

2. In the top of the double boiler or a small, heatproof bowl that fits on top of the saucepan, whisk the egg yolks with the lemon juice until blended.

3. Place the bowl over the simmering water and gently whisk while the egg yolks warm. Make sure that the bottom of the bowl is not touching the water, or the eggs will scramble.

4. When the yolks are warm, about 3 minutes, slowly pour the melted butter into the yolks while whisking. Continue whisking until the butter is fully incorporated and the sauce is thick enough to coat the back of a spoon.

5. Immediately remove from the heat and whisk in the salt, pepper, and cayenne, if using. If you heat the sauce too long, the eggs will scramble and the sauce will break and cannot be recovered.

☑ Egg-Free
☑ Nut-Free
☐ Nightshade-Free

Anyone who has read the label on a ketchup bottle can tell you that one of the main ingredients in most commercial brands is high-fructose corn syrup. Our kids definitely noticed ketchup's absence when we stopped buying it, so we started to make our own. It took a few tries to replicate that store-bought flavor, but now they love this homemade version! You can even store it ketchup in a washed-out plastic ketchup bottle.

KETCHUP

MAKES: ABOUT 2 CUPS

Ingredients

- 2 tablespoons lard or fat of choice
- 1 medium Vidalia onion, diced
- 3 cloves garlic, minced
- 2 (6-ounce) cans tomato paste
- 1 teaspoon kosher or sea salt
- 2 teaspoons paprika
- ½ teaspoon dry mustard
- ¼ teaspoon ground cloves
- ¼ teaspoon ground black pepper
- ½ cup apple cider vinegar
- 2 tablespoons Worcestershire sauce or coconut aminos

1. In a large pot over medium heat, melt the lard. Sauté the onion and garlic in the lard for 8 minutes or until the onion starts to become translucent.

2. Add the tomato paste, salt, and spices and simmer for 15 minutes.

3. Add the vinegar and Worcestershire sauce, reduce the heat to medium-low, and simmer for 30 minutes.

4. Using a blender or an immersion blender, purée until smooth. Allow to cool for at least 20 minutes.

5. Transfer to a jar or squeeze bottle and store chilled for up to 2 weeks.

Note: If this ketchup is too thick for your liking, add water during cooking and whisk it in to achieve the desired consistency.

SPECIAL TOOLS:

 OR

blender   immersion blender

☐ Egg-Free
✓ Nut-Free
✓ Nightshade-Free

UNDER 30 MIN

under 5 INGREDIENTS

ONE POT

Mayonnaise is another one of those kitchen tricks that seems immensely difficult at first but does not have to be. Once you master the basic mayo recipe, you've opened up a whole new realm of sauces and dressings. The only real trick is to be absolutely patient. If you move too fast, you won't be able to make the magic happen.

MAYONNAISE AND MAYO-BASED DIPS

MAKES: ABOUT ½ CUP EACH

Ingredients

Mayonnaise

2 large pastured egg yolks

2 teaspoons freshly squeezed lemon juice

1 teaspoon apple cider vinegar

½ teaspoon Dijon mustard

Pinch of kosher or sea salt

¼ cup olive oil

½ cup avocado oil

Tartar Sauce

½ cup Mayonnaise (see above)

3 tablespoons sweet relish or finely diced bread-and-butter pickles

1 tablespoon chopped fresh dill

1 tablespoon freshly squeezed lemon juice

Garlic and Herb Aioli

½ cup Mayonnaise (see above)

1 teaspoon minced garlic

1 tablespoon chopped fresh parsley

1 tablespoon chopped fresh chives

Pinch of ground black pepper

To make mayonnaise:

1. Either by hand or using the whisk attachment on an electric mixer, whisk together the egg yolks, lemon juice, vinegar, mustard, and salt until well combined.

2. Slowly drizzle in the oils while whisking vigorously, about 5 minutes by hand or 2 minutes if using an electric mixer. The slower you incorporate the oils, the less likely your mayo will break.

3. Continue to whisk until the mayonnaise is the preferred consistency. This may take up to another 5 minutes if whisking by hand or 3 minutes with an electric mixer.

4. Transfer the mayonnaise to an airtight jar. It will thicken as it sets up in the fridge. Keep chilled for a few days or up to a week if made with high-quality, fresh eggs.

To make either of the mayo-based sauces/dips:

1. In a bowl, whisk together the mayonnaise with the additional ingredients. Store refrigerated for up to a week.

Note: If you have an immersion blender, this works extremely well in a mason jar, which can then serve as the storage container. A high-speed blender also works well. We use avocado oil for its neutral, buttery flavor. If it's too difficult to find or too expensive for you, using only olive oil also works.

Mayonnaise

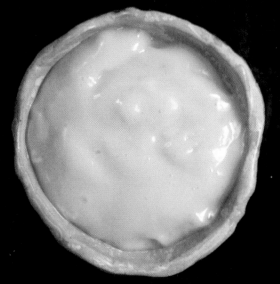

Tartar Sauce

Garlic and Herb Aioli

One of the biggest offenders when it comes to hidden refined sweeteners, processed oils, and chemicals is the very thing you smother your nutritious vegetables with—salad dressing. Although making homemade dressings can seem overwhelming and complicated at first, once you master making your own dressings you'll never want bottled again. And in a pinch, a drizzle of olive or avocado oil with a splash of vinegar or lemon juice and freshly cracked pepper and salt is always fantastic.

SALAD DRESSINGS

Ingredients

MAKES: ½ CUP TO 1 CUP EACH

☐ Egg-Free	☐ Egg-Free	☑ Egg-Free
☑ Nut-Free	☑ Nut-Free	☑ Nut-Free
☑ Nightshade-Free	☑ Nightshade-Free	☑ Nightshade-Free

Ranch Dressing	*Caesar Dressing*	*Berry Balsamic Dressing*
½ cup Mayonnaise (page 122)	½ cup Mayonnaise (page 122)	⅔ cup olive oil
¼ cup heavy cream or coconut cream from chilled full-fat coconut milk (see Note, page 252)	3 cloves garlic, minced	⅓ cup balsamic vinegar
1 teaspoon chopped fresh dill	1 tablespoon anchovy paste	1 tablespoon water
1 teaspoon chopped fresh parsley	1 teaspoon Dijon mustard	2 tablespoons strawberry or other berry puree (thaw from frozen or use very ripe berries for best results)
½ teaspoon garlic powder	⅛ teaspoon ground black pepper	½ teaspoon Dijon mustard
½ teaspoon kosher or sea salt		½ teaspoon minced garlic
⅛ teaspoon ground black pepper		

1. In a small bowl, whisk together all of the ingredients.

2. Transfer to an airtight container, such as a mason jar, and place in the fridge until ready to serve. These dressings will keep chilled for a few days.

3. Shake to re-emulsify the dressing before serving. Dress salads just before serving; once dressed, they will wilt over time.

Note: If taking a salad on the road, add dressing to bottom of container, then toss when ready to serve.

Caesar Dressing

Berry Balsamic Dressing

Ranch Dressing

If you have given up dairy and miss the taste of cheese, this sauce will change the way you cook forever. It has a thick consistency almost like that of sour cream and gives that distinct "cheesy" flavor to anything you add it to. It has revolutionized lasagna (pages 240 and 362) and pizza (see Meatza, page 208) for us and even inspired our Turkey Breasts Stuffed with "Cheese" and Cranberries (page 344) and creamy Leftover Casserole (page 314) that goes perfectly in Stacy's Soup (page 312). As a bonus, as noted in our recipe for Pizza Kale Chips (page 174), nutritional yeast has health benefits, so you can feel good about eating it. While the cheese sauce is easy to make, it's important to plan ahead and soak your cashews well before you need your sauce.

CASHEW CHEESE SAUCE

MAKES: ABOUT 1½ CUPS

Ingredients

1 cup raw cashews

¼ cup cauliflower florets

2½ tablespoons nutritional yeast

¼ cup water

Juice of ½ lemon

1 teaspoon kosher or sea salt

½ teaspoon ground black pepper

SPECIAL TOOLS:

food processor   blender

1. In a small bowl, cover the cashews with water and allow to soak for at least 2 hours or overnight.

2. Steam the cauliflower over boiling water or in a covered bowl in the microwave for 10 minutes until very soft and easily pierced with a fork. Remove to a food processor or blender and purée until smooth.

3. Drain the cashews and place in the food processor along with the remaining ingredients. Pulse until smooth, adding a tiny drizzle of water to achieve the desired consistency, if needed. You may need to tap the bowl against the countertop several times between pulses to release the air bubbles.

4. Keep chilled in an airtight container for up to several days, or store in the freezer.

Note: We highly suggest double or tripling this recipe when you make it and then saving the extra sauce for later. There isn't much that we don't enjoy slathering in this rich, delicious, nutrient-rich sauce.

☑ Egg-Free
☑ Nut-Free
☑ Nightshade-Free

under 5
INGREDIENTS

ONE POT

After trying these soft, pink onions for the first time at a Mediterranean-themed restaurant, we became addicted to pickled red onions and started filling our fridge with jars of them. We could not believe how simple it was to turn plain onions into a tasty treat. We add them to salads (page 50) and find that they go perfectly with pork!

PICKLED ONIONS

MAKES: 4 CUPS

Ingredients

2 red onions, sliced

1 cup apple cider vinegar

1 cup water

Juice of 1 lemon

2 teaspoons kosher or sea salt

1. Place the onions in a sealable quart jar.

2. In a bowl, whisk together the vinegar, water, lemon juice, and salt.

3. Pour the vinegar mixture into the jar over the onions. Push the onions down to completely submerge them.

4. Seal the jar and set on the counter overnight before placing in the refrigerator.

5. The onions will be ready to serve in 24 hours. Store leftovers refrigerated in the sealed jar for up to a month.

Note: Since pickled vegetables keep for a long time in the fridge, we highly recommend that you double or triple this recipe. That way, you only have to make them once a month.

✓ Egg-Free
✓ Nut-Free
✓ Nightshade-Free

Though a favorite on restaurant menus, roasted garlic need not be thought of as a complicated ingredient to be enjoyed only when dining out. We've found that making this delicious spreadable garlic to be anything but difficult. Rather than the sharp bite of a raw garlic clove, roasted garlic becomes almost sweet, and the roasted cloves are soft enough to spread like butter. We love to slice it thinly and add it to salads or Meatzas (page 208).

ROASTED GARLIC

PREHEAT OVEN: 400°F · MAKES: 1 HEAD

Ingredients

1 head garlic

1 tablespoon lard or fat of choice, melted

1. Preheat the oven to 400°F.

2. Slice off the top of the garlic head and brush the top with the lard.

3. With the remaining skin still on, wrap the garlic in aluminum foil and place in a muffin pan.

4. Roast in the oven for 30 minutes or until the cloves are very soft.

5. Let cool until easy to handle, and then remove the foil and peel the skin off of the garlic cloves.

6. Store the roasted cloves in an airtight container in the fridge for up to a week, and use in any recipe where garlic is needed or would be delicious.

Note: This recipe works well in batches, so make a dozen to fill your muffin pan and then, after roasting, remove the garlic peels and freeze the cloves in an airtight container until you are ready to use them.

3

☑ Egg-Free
☑ Nut-Free
☑ Nightshade-Free

under 5
INGREDIENTS

ONE POT

Whereas much of the Paleo community refers to this dish as "Bone Broth," the rest of the culinary world knows it as "Stock." Broth is made by boiling only meat and does not confer nearly the same health benefits of long-simmered bones used in the making of stock. Whatever you call it, this gelatinous superfood is collagen-rich and helps to heal the gut while imparting wonderful flavor to any dish you add it to.

Stacy is known in the community as the Soup Lady, and for good reason: Our family attributes the regular consumption of high-quality gelatinous stock made from humanely raised animals as a significant contributor to our health. Accordingly, you'll find this stock incorporated into many recipes in this cookbook. Buying a boxed version will not offer the same nutritional benefits or taste nearly as good!

STOCK (ALSO KNOWN AS "BONE BROTH")

MAKES: ABOUT 12 CUPS

Ingredients

5 pounds beef, pork, or lamb bones or 2 chicken carcasses

2 tablespoons apple cider vinegar

1 tablespoon kosher or sea salt

1 tablespoon black peppercorns

3 quarts water

1. Place the bones, vinegar, salt, and peppercorns in a stockpot. Pour in the water, making sure that the water level rises above the bones. (Add more water, if needed.)

2. Bring to a boil over high heat, and allow to boil for 3 minutes.

3. Cover and reduce the heat to low. If using beef or lamb bones, simmer for 24 to 48 hours or until the bones are very soft and easily broken by hand. If using chicken carcasses, simmer for 12 to 24 hours. If using pork bones, do a preboil before beginning the recipe: Boil the bones for 5 minutes, drain, and then proceed with Step 1, simmering for 24 to 48 hours. (This initial boiling prevents a bitter scum from rising to the top of the pot, which is particularly a problem with pork bones.)

4. Check the pot every few hours to ensure that it is still simmering and the solids are still covered by water. Skim any solids that rise to the top.

5. When the bones are soft, pour through a colander into a large bowl to remove the bones and peppercorns. Place the bowl in the refrigerator overnight.

6. Skim any fat from the top of the bowl. Pour the stock into a large, airtight storage container (such as a large mason jar) and seal. Once chilled, the stock may be semisolid and gelatinous from the collagen in the bones. Store in the refrigerator for up to 2 weeks, or freeze for later use.

BREAKFAST

As much as we'd love to have a leisurely breakfast every morning and spend time with our loved ones around a giant spread of breakfast foods, for most people this is all but a dream. What we do in our house is try to make the good foods—like frittatas, pancakes, and waffles—available throughout the week by preparing them ahead of time for later reheating. If you have more grab-and-go foods available to you in a quick, convenient form, you'll be set up for a successful start to the day! Over time, you may come to love leftover dinner as breakfast.

	PHASE	PAGE #	UNDER 30 MIN	under 5 INGREDIENTS	ONE POT	HOLIDAY	ON THE GO
Easy Peasy Pancakes	2	136	YES				
Strawberry Streusel Muffins	2	138					YES
Blueberry Breakfast Cookies	1	140					YES
CC's Perfect Hash Browns	2	142		YES		YES	
Eggs in a Nest	3	144		YES			
Quick Banana-Chocolate Soufflé Cake	2	146	YES				
Green Salad with Poached Egg	3	148	YES	YES			
Apple Cinnamon Crumb Cake	1	150					YES
Eggs Stacy	3	152				YES	
Pumpkin Pudding	1	154	YES				
Cinnamon Bread	1	156					YES
Sweet Potato Apple Hash	2	158	YES	YES	YES		
Breakfast Burritos	3	160					
Egg Pizza (Frittata)	2	162			YES	YES	YES
Breakfast Sausage	2	164	YES				
Waffles	2	166	YES				

Egg-Free

Nut-Free

✓ Nightshade-Free

UNDER 30 MIN

For years, we tried making the perfect Paleo pancakes. We were extremely picky about the batter needing to be light and fluffy and the pancakes needing to be easy to flip when cooking. Additionally, the finished pancakes had to have a crisp outer texture and a soft interior. It wasn't until we thought about how simple the batter is for regular pancakes—a mixture of flour, milk, eggs, fat or oil, and leavening—that it came together for us. This version replicates the simplicity of regular pancake batter by using banana as the starch (don't worry, the flavor is not overwhelming), but is otherwise classic and delicious!

EASY PEASY PANCAKES

SERVES: 6

Ingredients

1 medium banana, cut into chunks

4 large eggs

⅔ cup coconut milk (full-fat, canned or homemade, page 290) or Almond Milk (page 290)

2 cups blanched almond flour

1 teaspoon baking soda

½ teaspoon cream of tartar

Pinch of kosher or sea salt

1 teaspoon pure vanilla extract

2 tablespoons coconut oil, divided

Apple Butter (page 110) or fresh berries, for serving

1. In a food processor or blender, purée the banana, eggs, and milk until smooth.

2. Add the flour, baking soda, cream of tartar, salt, and vanilla and continue to process until the ingredients are thoroughly combined.

3. In a large skillet over medium heat, melt 1 tablespoon of the coconut oil.

4. Pour ¼-cup portions of the batter into the hot skillet to form pancakes about 4 inches in diameter.

5. Cook until all of the little bubbles on the top have popped and the bottom is golden brown and comes up from the pan intact, 3 to 5 minutes. Flip and cook the other side for about 3 minutes to get an even color.

6. Repeat until you have used up all of the batter. Between batches, you may need to add more coconut oil to the pan if it becomes dry.

7. Serve with apple butter or fresh berries.

Note: If you have leftovers, lay them flat on a tray in the freezer for a quick on-the-go snack in the future.

SPECIAL TOOLS:

food processor   OR   blender

These muffins were inspired by our desire to make something that could compare to the giant muffins found in coffee shops. So many people reach for a muffin thinking it's a healthier choice, not realizing that the muffin is more dense and full of sugar than even a doughnut. These muffins, on the other hand, are sweetened with fruit and contain protein and calcium from the almond flour—something you'd never find in those other treats. Of course, they are still sweet and should be enjoyed in moderation.

STRAWBERRY STREUSEL MUFFINS

PREHEAT OVEN: 350°F · MAKES: 1 DOZEN MUFFINS

1. Preheat the oven to 350°F. Line 12 cups of a muffin pan with paper liners.

2. In a food processor, pulse the topping ingredients until a crumbly mixture forms. Remove from the food processor and set aside. Rinse out the food processor.

3. Place the dates in the food processor and pulse until a thick paste forms.

4. Add the coconut oil, eggs, and vanilla and pulse to combine.

5. Add the flour, baking soda, and salt and process just until a thick batter forms, scraping the sides with a spatula.

6. Fold in the strawberries with juices, which will loosen the batter a bit.

7. Spoon ¼ cup of the batter into each lined muffin cup and evenly sprinkle on the topping.

8. Bake for 25 minutes, until the edges begin to brown. Let cool in the pan for 10 minutes before removing with a butter knife. Store leftovers in an airtight container in the refrigerator for up to a week.

Note: We recommend storing most baked treats in an airtight container at room temperature for no more than a few days, but recommend refrigerating them if they contain fresh fruit, like these muffins.

Ingredients

For the topping:

⅓ cup raw macadamia nuts

⅓ cup raw walnuts

1 tablespoon unrefined granulated palm, date, or maple sugar

1 tablespoon palm shortening or unsalted butter

1 tablespoon blanched almond flour

For the muffins:

1 cup soft Medjool dates, pitted

¼ cup coconut oil, melted

4 large eggs

1 tablespoon pure vanilla extract

2 cups blanched almond flour

1½ teaspoons baking soda

½ teaspoon kosher or sea salt

1 cup fresh or thawed frozen strawberries, chopped, with juices

SPECIAL TOOLS:

food processor

Egg-Free
Nut-Free
✓ Nightshade-Free

ON the GO

Cookies for breakfast? Seems crazy, but these little delights are low in sugar and full of the antioxidant power of blueberries. And all of the grain flours you might expect are replaced with ground seeds and nuts! Inspired to make breakfast for a friend, who can't eat almonds, these cookies are our take on a soft, earthy scone.

Ingredients

Coconut oil, for greasing the baking sheet (if not using parchment)

1 cup raw sunflower seeds

½ cup raw cashews

½ cup raw walnuts

⅓ cup lard, unsalted butter, or palm shortening

¼ cup unrefined granulated palm, date, or maple sugar

1 large egg

Grated zest of 1 lemon

2 tablespoons freshly squeezed lemon juice

2 tablespoons tapioca flour

1 teaspoon baking soda

½ teaspoon kosher or sea salt

1 cup blueberries

BLUEBERRY BREAKFAST COOKIES

PREHEAT OVEN: 350°F · MAKES: ABOUT 18 COOKIES

1. Preheat the oven to 350°F. Line a baking sheet with parchment paper or grease it with coconut oil.

2. In a food processor or high-speed blender, pulse the sunflower seeds, cashews, and walnuts to a fine flourlike consistency. Do not overblend, or a nut butter will form.

3. In a large mixing bowl, beat together the lard, sugar, egg, lemon zest, and lemon juice until thoroughly combined.

4. Stir the nut and seed flour, tapioca flour, baking soda, and salt into the wet ingredients until just combined.

5. Gently fold in the blueberries.

6. Drop large balls of the dough (about 2 tablespoons each) onto the prepared baking sheet, 1½ inches apart. Do not flatten; they will spread quite a bit.

7. Bake for 13 to 15 minutes or until golden brown on top.

8. Let the cookies cool on the baking sheet for 10 minutes, and then transfer them to a cooling rack to allow them to set up.

SPECIAL TOOLS:

food processor   blender

✓ Egg-Free
✓ Nut-Free
☐ Nightshade-Free

Every time Stacy's mother, the famous CC, visits us, we ask her to make these hash browns. While the original viewpoint in the Paleo community was to avoid eating white potatoes because they are very starchy and were thought to be void of nutrients, opinions have changed. We have now learned that the nutrient content of a white potato is actually greater than that of the recommended alternative, the sweet potato. Of course, if you do not eat white potatoes, sweet potatoes will work just as well in this recipe.

CC'S PERFECT HASH BROWNS

SERVES: 4 TO 6

1. Grate the potatoes into a large bowl. Season with salt and mix to evenly distribute.

2. Place the grated potatoes in a cheesecloth, fine-mesh strainer, or paper towel and press out as much water as you can. The more water that comes out, the better the hash browns will crisp and the more they will adhere together.

3. Melt the lard in a large skillet over medium heat.

4. Form the grated potatoes into 3-inch patties and fry in the lard. To ensure that you get crispy hash browns, do not overcrowd the pan. When the hash browns are golden brown on the bottom, about 5 minutes, flip with a spatula and fry on the other side. Press down on the patties a few times during cooking to flatten and allow as much of the surface to crisp as possible; this also helps them to hold together better.

5. When golden on both sides, remove to a paper towel–lined plate to drain off the excess fat. While warm, sprinkle with a pinch of salt, pepper, and paprika.

6. Repeat Steps 3 to 5 until all of the potatoes are cooked, adding more lard to the pan if it becomes dry.

Ingredients

1 pound baking potatoes, peeled

Salt to taste

3 tablespoons lard or bacon fat

Pepper to taste

Paprika to taste

SPECIAL TOOLS:

Food processor or grater; cheesecloth or fine-mesh strainer

food processor

cheesecloth   OR   strainer

Growing up, Stacy loved one of her mom's signature breakfasts: eggs in a nest. Essentially, it was an egg fried in the middle of a slice of bread. Without bread, you'd think this dish would be impossible to re-create. But then we realized that frying spaghetti squash around an egg would make a great substitute and add nutrients that you'd never find in regular old bread. A fun way to add veggies to your breakfast, we highly recommend that you pair this with bacon.

EGGS IN A NEST

PREHEAT OVEN: 350°F · SERVES: 6

Ingredients

1 small spaghetti squash (about 2 pounds)

2 tablespoons lard or fat of choice

6 large eggs

Salt and pepper to taste

For serving (optional):

Snipped fresh chives, for garnish

1. Preheat the oven to 350°F.

2. Halve the squash lengthwise, remove and discard the seeds, and place cut side down on a rimmed baking sheet with a small amount of water. Roast in the oven for 40 minutes, or until the flesh is easily pierced. Alternatively, microwave on high for 10 minutes.

3. Scoop out the soft flesh of the squash with a spoon or fork into a bowl. The flesh should come out in strands like spaghetti when scooped with the grain (lengthwise).

4. Melt the lard in a large skillet with a lid over medium heat.

5. Form the squash into 6 donut shapes about ½ inch tall and 4 inches across with a 2-inch-wide well in the middle. Place in the hot skillet. Crack an egg into each hole and sprinkle with a pinch of salt and pepper.

6. Fry for 1 minute, and then cover and reduce the heat to medium-low. Continue to fry for 7 minutes, or until all of the egg white is cooked through.

7. Serve warm and let the runny yolk flavor coat the pasta-like "noodles" of the spaghetti squash. Garnish with chives, if desired.

Note: This is our preferred method of frying eggs. The initial cooking phase gives you crispy edges, while the covered, lower-heat phase cooks the egg whites without overcooking the yolks.

Egg-Free
☑ Nut-Free
☑ Nightshade-Free

UNDER 30 MIN

We're always trying out new ways to serve a quick and easy breakfast. When this lovely, creamy cake came out of the oven, even we were shocked by how delicious it was. If you're not in the mood for chocolate, it's easy to make a vanilla version (see the variation).

QUICK BANANA-CHOCOLATE SOUFFLÉ CAKE

PREHEAT OVEN: 350°F · SERVES: 6 TO 8

Ingredients

½ cup coconut oil, softened, plus more for greasing the dish

4 medium bananas, cut into chunks

4 large eggs

¼ cup cacao powder

1 teaspoon pure vanilla extract

¼ teaspoon kosher or sea salt

1. Preheat the oven to 350°F. Grease the sides and bottom of a 1-quart soufflé dish with coconut oil. (A soufflé dish looks like a large ramekin with a fluted exterior.)

2. In a blender or food processor, purée all of the ingredients on high speed until fully incorporated. Watch for large banana chunks that do not purée completely.

3. Pour the batter into the soufflé dish and smooth the top with a spatula.

4. Bake for 20 to 30 minutes, until the cake is firm in the center. Cut into slices and serve. Store leftovers in an airtight container in the refrigerator for up to a week.

SPECIAL TOOLS:

food processor   OR   blender

Note: This cake can be made sweeter by using very ripe bananas. If your bananas are not yet ripe, you may want to add 1 to 2 tablespoons of honey.

Variation: Quick Banana Soufflé Cake
To make a vanilla version of this cake, replace the cacao powder with an equal amount of almond flour.

- Egg-Free
- ✓ Nut-Free
- ✓ Nightshade-Free

Having a green salad for breakfast may seem like an unusual idea, but with all the nutrients that leafy greens provide, it's a terrific way to start your day on the right foot. And if you haven't experienced the joy of using a runny egg yolk as part of your salad dressing, you're missing out!

GREEN SALAD WITH POACHED EGG

SERVES: 2

Ingredients

1 tablespoon apple cider vinegar

1 tablespoon kosher or sea salt

2 large eggs

3 cups mixed greens

1 tablespoon avocado or olive oil

1 tablespoon freshly squeezed lemon juice

Salt and pepper to taste

1. Fill a medium pot with water and add the vinegar and salt. Bring to a boil over high heat, and then reduce the heat to medium.

2. Carefully crack 1 egg into a bowl, leaving the yolk intact.

3. Holding the bowl close to the surface of the simmering water, gently slide the egg into the water, being careful not to break the yolk.

4. Poach the egg for 3 to 5 minutes, until the white is cooked. Gently remove with a slotted spoon and transfer to a plate.

5. Repeat Steps 2 to 4 with the second egg.

6. In a large bowl, toss together the mixed greens, oil, and lemon juice. Divide the salad between 2 serving bowls and top each with a poached egg. Sprinkle with salt and pepper.

7. To eat, break the eggs open and toss the salad with the runny yolks.

Note: When selecting greens for this simple salad, we favor an arugula mix to add a peppery flavor.

If you're the type of person who craves a doughnut or coffee cake with your morning routine, we suggest this tasty pastry to satisfy you without grains or refined sugars. Make it on Sunday to have with your coffee every day of the week. When making this recipe, we use a special pan made for cinnamon buns, which gives the illusion without the gluten.

APPLE CINNAMON CRUMB CAKE

PREHEAT OVEN: 350°F · MAKES: 8 PULL-APART PORTIONS

1. Preheat the oven to 350°F and grease your preferred pan.

2. In a medium mixing bowl, sift together the almond flour, arrowroot flour, cinnamon, and baking soda.

3. Using a food processor or an electric mixer, beat together the applesauce, honey, oil, and vanilla until smooth.

4. Stir in the dry ingredients until just combined.

5. Fold in apple pieces until well distributed.

6. Pour the batter into the pan, about two-thirds full.

7. In a small bowl, use a fork to combine the topping ingredients. Sprinkle the topping over the batter, distributing it evenly.

8. Bake for 30 minutes or until lightly browned. Let cool in the pan for 15 minutes before removing. Store in an airtight container at room temperature for up to a week.

9. If using coconut butter glaze, microwave in a small bowl for 30 seconds. Using a spoon, drizzle over the top of your cakes.

Note: Use your favorite type of apple. We love Honeycrisp and Gold Rush, but McIntosh and Gala apples have great flavor, too!

Variations: Apple Cinnamon Muffins with Crumb Topping and Apple Cinnamon Bread with Crumb Topping
To make muffins: Pour the batter into 12 greased or lined muffin cups or small ramekins, filling each cup two-thirds full. Top with the crumbly topping and bake at 350°F until a toothpick inserted in the center comes out clean, about 25 minutes. You can also make a quick bread with this recipe. Pour the batter into a 9-by-5-inch loaf pan and bake at 350°F for about 40 minutes, until a toothpick inserted in the center comes out clean.

Ingredients

For the cake:

1½ cups blanched almond flour

¼ cup arrowroot or tapioca flour

1 tablespoon ground cinnamon

1 teaspoon baking soda

½ cup applesauce

⅓ cup honey

⅓ cup coconut oil

1 tablespoon pure vanilla extract

1 large apple, peeled, cored, and diced

For the topping (optional):

½ cup blanched almond flour

½ cup slivered almonds

3 tablespoons unrefined granulated palm, date, or maple sugar

1 tablespoon ground cinnamon

For the glaze (optional)

¼ cup Coconut Butter (page 114)

SPECIAL TOOLS:
Food processor or electric mixer (optional)

food processor

A classic, fancy breakfast dish, eggs Benedict used to be Stacy's favorite to order when dining out for brunch. Traditionally, it consists of an English muffin and Canadian bacon topped with a poached egg and hollandaise sauce. Instead of going that route, we came up with our own version that we named after our inspiration, the spinach-loving lady herself!

EGGS STACY

PREHEAT OVEN: 350°F · SERVES: 2

Ingredients

For serving (optional):

1 batch Hollandaise Sauce (page 118)

For the sausage:

½ pound Traditional Beef Breakfast Sausage (page 164) or bulk pork breakfast sausage

For the poached eggs:

2 teaspoons kosher or sea salt

1 tablespoon apple cider vinegar

2 large eggs

For the spinach:

2 tablespoons bacon fat or lard

2 cups baby spinach

¼ teaspoon garlic powder

Salt and pepper to taste

1. If using hollandaise to finish this dish, make it first and set it aside over a bowl of warm water.

2. Preheat the oven to 350°F. Form the sausage into four 3-inch-wide patties and place in a glass baking dish. Bake until the sausages are cooked through, about 20 minutes for patties 3 inches in diameter and 1 inch thick.

3. To make the poached eggs: Fill a medium pot with water and add the salt. Bring to a boil over high heat.

4. Meanwhile, cook the spinach: Melt the bacon fat in a medium skillet over medium heat. Add the baby spinach, garlic powder, and salt and pepper and sauté until the greens are softened and wilted. Set aside.

5. When the water for the eggs is boiling, add the vinegar and stir. Turn down the heat to medium.

6. Carefully crack an egg into a small bowl, leaving the yolk intact. Holding the bowl close to the surface of the simmering water, gently slide the egg into the water, being careful not to break the yolk.

7. Poach the egg for 3 to 5 minutes, until the white is cooked. Gently remove with a slotted spoon and transfer to a plate.

8. Repeat Steps 6 and 7 with the second egg.

9. To assemble, create a base with half of the spinach, place 2 sausage patties on top, and then gently top each patty with an egg. Smother it in hollandaise sauce, if using. Repeat with the remaining spinach, sausage patties, eggs, and hollandaise, if using.

Egg-Free
Nut-Free
Nightshade-Free

UNDER 30 MIN

You may be able to find lots of boxes of pudding on grocery store shelves, but you'll never find pudding this delicious. Infused with the flavors of fall and without any unpronounceable ingredients, this pudding is low in sweeteners and sure to please your taste buds. It works wonderfully in our Pumpkin Parfait (page 390).

PUMPKIN PUDDING

SERVES: 6

Ingredients

2 cups coconut milk (full-fat, canned or homemade, page 290), room temperature

1 cup pumpkin puree, room temperature

½ cup boiling water

1 tablespoon gelatin powder

⅓ cup maple syrup

2 teaspoons ground cinnamon

½ teaspoon ground nutmeg

½ teaspoon ground allspice

¼ teaspoon ginger powder

½ teaspoon kosher or sea salt

For serving (optional):

Slightly Sweet & Salty Snack Mix (page 184), chopped nuts of choice, or Whipped Coconut Cream (page 390)

SPECIAL TOOLS:

 OR

food processor   blender

1. In a blender or food processor, pulse the coconut milk and pumpkin purée until combined.

2. In a small bowl, pour the boiling water over the gelatin powder and stir with a fork until the gelatin powder has completely dissolved. Do not let the gelatin cool.

3. Add the gelatin mixture to the coconut milk and pumpkin puree. Turn on the blender or food processor and add the remaining pudding ingredients.

4. When the mixture is thoroughly combined, pour into 6 small bowls and let the pudding set in the refrigerator for at least an hour.

5. To prevent a stiff skin from forming, press plastic wrap directly onto the surface of the pudding before chilling. Store chilled for up to several days.

6. Serve cold topped with Slightly Sweet & Salty Snack Mix, chopped nuts, or whipped coconut cream, if desired.

For many people, the biggest hurdle to this dietary change is losing bread. Unfortunately, there is no perfect alternative to bread made from wheat flour. This cinnamon bread, however, is a great alternative to the cinnamon bread found on many breakfast plates. We've even used it for bread puddings, French toast, and our Pumpkin Parfait (page 390) with great success.

CINNAMON BREAD

PREHEAT OVEN: 350°F · MAKES: 1 (9-BY-5-INCH) LOAF

Ingredients

Coconut oil, for greasing the pan

1 (16-ounce) jar almond butter or 2 cups Almond Butter (page 186)

1½ cups blanched almond flour

4 large eggs

¼ cup maple syrup

1 teaspoon baking soda

1 tablespoon ground cinnamon

½ teaspoon ground nutmeg

½ teaspoon kosher or sea salt

¾ cup raisins (optional)

SPECIAL TOOLS:

food processor

1. Preheat the oven to 350°F. Grease a 9-by-5-inch loaf pan with coconut oil.

2. Place all of the ingredients except the raisins in a food processor and pulse until combined. If the dough is dry and crumbly, add a thin drizzle of melted coconut oil until the batter is thick and smooth.

3. Fold in the raisins, if using, with a spatula.

4. Scrape the dough into the prepared loaf pan with the spatula. Smooth the top.

5. Bake for 45 minutes to an hour, until the top is slightly golden brown and a toothpick inserted in the center comes out clean. (Begin checking the bread at the 45-minute mark, and continue to check it every 5 minutes. The cooking time will depend on the humidity, the amount of oil in the nut butter, and many other variants.) The bread will continue to cook slightly as it cools. Do not overbake, or it will become tough and hard.

6. Let cool on a cooling rack for about an hour, and then remove from the pan. Slice and store in an airtight container for up to a week.

✓ Egg-Free
✓ Nut-Free
☐ Nightshade-Free

UNDER 30 MIN

under 5 INGREDIENTS

ONE POT

The first time we made this recipe, it was in a cabin on a lake and we were running low on food options. When your larder runs low, you improvise! Thus was born this combination of sausage, sweet potato, and apple. It remains a go-to dish in our repertoire to this day.

SWEET POTATO APPLE HASH

SERVES: 4 TO 6

Ingredients

2 tablespoons lard or fat of choice

2 medium sweet potatoes, peeled and diced

1 large yellow onion, diced

1 pound Traditional Beef Breakfast Sausage (page 164) or store-bought breakfast sausage

2 medium green apples, peeled and diced

Salt and pepper to taste

1. In a large cast-iron skillet over medium heat, melt the lard.

2. Sauté the sweet potatoes and onion, stirring frequently, until the sweet potatoes just begin to soften and the onion is translucent but not browned.

3. Add the sausage and apples and continue to stir and cook until the sausage has browned. As you cook, break up the larger pieces of sausage with a spatula.

4. Season with salt and pepper, stir to incorporate, and serve.

Note: You can use this recipe as a guide for many other variations on hash. Try butternut or acorn squash with pears.

■ Egg-Free
✓ Nut-Free
■ Nightshade-Free

In our house, we prefer to eat burritos for breakfast rather than dinner any day of the week. There is something especially tasty about a spicy red enchilada sauce combined with sausage and eggs. Although these burritos require a bit of work, this recipe can easily be doubled and frozen for later— trust us, you'll want to! It is truly a special treat.

Ingredients

For the wrappers:

¼ cup kosher or sea salt

1 head green cabbage, core removed

For the filling:

1 pound Traditional Beef Breakfast Sausage (page 164) or other breakfast sausage or chorizo

6 large eggs

¼ cup coconut milk (full-fat, canned or homemade, page 290) or Almond Milk (page 290)

Salt and pepper to taste

For the enchilada sauce:

2 tablespoons lard or fat of choice

1 tablespoon arrowroot or tapioca flour

3 tablespoons chili powder

1 teaspoon ground cumin

½ teaspoon garlic powder

½ teaspoon dried oregano leaves

½ teaspoon kosher or sea salt

1 cup Stock, beef recommended (page 132)

6 ounces tomato paste

For serving:

Your favorite burrito toppings, such as sliced avocado or salsa verde

BREAKFAST BURRITOS

PREHEAT OVEN: 350°F · MAKES: 6 TO 8 BURRITOS

1. Fill a large pot with water and add the salt. Bring to a boil, and then remove from the heat. Submerge the cabbage head in the water, cover the pot, and let sit for 15 minutes.

2. While waiting for the cabbage to soften, make the filling: In a large skillet over medium heat, brown the sausage, using a spatula to break up the chunks as it cooks. When fully cooked, remove the sausage from the pan and drain off all but 2 tablespoons of fat.

3. In a medium bowl, whisk the eggs with the milk until frothy. Add the salt and pepper.

4. Pour the eggs into the pan in which the sausage was cooked and set over medium heat. Slowly shift the eggs in the pan every 30 to 60 seconds until they are no longer liquid-y and the large folds and chunks are broken up. Since they will be cooked in the oven, do not overcook or completely dry out the scrambled eggs; they are most flavorful when still slightly loose. Remove from the heat and set aside.

5. Make the sauce: Melt the lard in a medium saucepan over high heat. Add the flour, spices, and salt and cook until aromatic, about 30 seconds. Whisk in the stock and tomato paste and bring to a boil. Reduce the heat to low and simmer until the tomato paste is incorporated and the sauce coats the back of a spoon, about 15 minutes. Set aside.

6. After the cabbage has rested in the hot water for 15 minutes, remove it from the pot and gently peel back and remove the softened leaves. Be careful to remove each leaf whole.

7. Preheat the oven to 350°F.

8. Assemble the burritos in a 13-by-9-inch baking dish. Spread ¼ cup of the enchilada sauce on the bottom of the dish (to prevent sticking). Then spoon about ⅓ cup of the sausage, ⅓ cup of the eggs, and 1 to 2 tablespoons of the sauce into the center of a cabbage leaf. Fold in the sides first, then roll it up, and finally place the burrito fold side down in the sauced dish. Repeat until you have used up all of the sausage and eggs.

9. Set aside about ½ cup of the sauce for serving, and then pour the remaining sauce over the top of the burritos and bake for 20 minutes. Serve with the reserved sauce and your favorite toppings—we love fresh avocado and salsa verde!

☐ Egg-Free
☑ Nut-Free
☑ Nightshade-Free

ONE POT
HOLIDAY
ON the GO

Some people have that one-handed omelet flip down pat. This recipe is for the rest of us who enjoy having our eggs with a veggie filling but just can't seem to master the flip. Our boys took to calling this Egg Pizza, as the result is a slice of pie on your plate. Serve your "pizza" over a bed of arugula and spinach greens for a complete breakfast. This is a perfect make-ahead dish that can be served as leftovers or for breakfast all week long.

EGG PIZZA (FRITTATA)

PREHEAT OVEN: 400°F · SERVES: 6 TO 8

Ingredients

2 tablespoons bacon fat

½ cup diced red onion

½ cup diced asparagus

½ cup diced mushrooms

8 large eggs

½ cup coconut milk (full-fat, canned or homemade, page 290)

¼ cup coconut flour

1 teaspoon dried oregano leaves

Salt and pepper to taste

1. Preheat the oven to 400°F.

2. In a large ovenproof skillet, melt the bacon fat over medium heat.

3. Add the vegetables and sauté until soft, about 8 minutes.

4. Meanwhile, scramble the eggs with a whisk until the yolks are fully incorporated. Add the milk, flour, oregano, and salt and pepper and whisk to combine.

5. Pour the eggs into the skillet and place in the oven. Bake for 15 to 20 minutes or until the liquid has solidified and the top has started to brown. Cut into wedges and serve. Store in the fridge and reheat in the microwave on high for 45 seconds.

Note: Just like with regular pizza, changing your toppings is very much encouraged! Any number of vegetables can replace the ones called for here.

UNDER 30 MIN

Ingredients

Blueberry Sage

☑ Egg-Free
☑ Nut-Free
☑ Nightshade-Free

1 pound ground pork
2 teaspoons kosher or sea salt
1 teaspoon dried ground sage
¼ teaspoon ground black pepper
¼ cup dried blueberries
1 teaspoon maple syrup

Turkey Cranberry

☑ Egg-Free
☑ Nut-Free
☑ Nightshade-Free

1 pound ground turkey
2 teaspoons kosher or sea salt
1½ teaspoons dried rosemary
1 teaspoon dried thyme leaves
½ teaspoon dried ground sage
⅛ teaspoon ground black pepper
¼ cup dried cranberries

Traditional Beef

☑ Egg-Free
☑ Nut-Free
▣ Nightshade-Free

1 pound ground beef
2 teaspoons kosher or sea salt
1 teaspoon fennel seeds
½ teaspoon paprika
½ teaspoon dried oregano leaves
⅛ teaspoon ground black pepper

Once you realize how easy it is to make your own breakfast sausage, you'll never go back to buying it from a store. These are some standard recipes that we always turn to, but sausage is very customizable, so go wild with your imagination!

BREAKFAST SAUSAGE

SERVES: 4

1. In a small bowl, combine the meat and spices.

2. Using your hands, work the spices evenly into the meat by massaging them thoroughly.

3. When the spices are uniformly distributed, work any add-ins, like dried fruit or maple syrup, into the meat mixture. Let sit for as long as you are able; an hour or more will allow flavors to develop, but it can be cooked immediately if preferred.

4. Preheat a large skillet over medium heat.

5. If not making as loose, crumbled sausage, form by hand into 2-inch-diameter patties, ½ inch thick.

6. Fry for about 5 minutes until the bottoms are browned. Flip and cook the other side for 5 minutes or until thoroughly cooked. Alternatively, if loose sausage is desired, simply cook over medium heat, constantly stirring and breaking up the large chunks, until browned, about 8 to 10 minutes.

Note: For a Phase 3 upgrade, why not grind some organ meat into your sausage?

For nightshade-free beef sausage, use ground cumin instead of paprika.

Traditional Beef Sausage

Turkey Cranberry Sausage

Blueberry Sage Sausage

Our family loves brunch. On Sunday mornings we like to be lazy and cook big meals together. Although those meals almost always include a frittata (see Egg Pizza, page 162) and homemade sausage (page 164), we also love to add something bread-like. One morning, upon our children's request, we attempted to make waffles. We wanted them to be fruit-sweetened so the kids could freeze them and have leftovers during the school week. Five hours, four hands thrown up in frustration, three hungry children, two frazzled adults, and one overworked waffle iron later, we had created this amazing recipe. It's one of our fan favorites and beloved to this day. Our favorite way to enjoy them these days is with chicken for a true Southern tradition.

WAFFLES

MAKES: ABOUT 8 LARGE WAFFLES

Ingredients

Melted coconut oil for greasing the waffle iron

1 medium apple, peeled and cored

1 medium banana, cut into chunks

1 cup Almond Butter (page 186) or sunflower seed butter

2 large eggs

1 tablespoon arrowroot flour

1 teaspoon pure vanilla extract

½ teaspoon baking soda

SPECIAL TOOLS:

Waffle iron; food processor; electric mixer

food processor

1. Brush the grids of the waffle iron with melted coconut oil and preheat to medium high.

2. Purée the apple and banana in a food processor until completely smooth.

3. Using the whisk attachment on an electric mixer, whip the almond butter on high for 2 to 3 minutes until smooth and fluffed.

4. Add the fruit puree and the remaining ingredients to the whipped almond butter and continue to whip until combined.

5. Regrease the hot waffle iron.

6. Use a ladle to pour about ⅓ cup of batter per 8-by-4-inch waffle onto the hot waffle grid. Do not fill the entire waffle iron; instead, leave about 40 percent unfilled so that the batter can spread. Cook for 3 to 5 minutes, until browned. If your waffle is soft or floppy, it's not ready yet—keep cooking for another minute or two.

Note: While you'll probably want to eat all of the waffles immediately, we like to make a double or triple batch so that we can have more for later. Store flat in the freezer and reheat in the toaster for a fast and easy breakfast.

SNACKS AND ON-THE-GO

While we've found that switching to a Paleo diet has eliminated most of our between meal cravings, there will always be a desire for something you can pack in a bag and have available to you throughout the day. Rather than finding yourself in a convenience store, we recommend that you spend a little time making your own convenience foods with these terrific snack recipes.

	PHASE	PAGE #	UNDER 30 MIN	under 5 INGREDIENTS	ONE POT	HOLIDAY	ON the GO
Snack Balls	2	170	YES	YES	YES		YES
Cranberry-Orange No-Bake Coconut Bars	2	172					YES
Kale Chips—Two Ways	3	174	YES				YES
Sweet Potato Chips	2	176		YES			YES
Roasted Pumpkin Seeds	2	178	YES	YES		YES	YES
Jerky	3	180					YES
Almond Meal Crackers	2	182		YES			YES
Slightly Sweet & Salty Snack Mix	2	184	YES	YES	YES		YES
Nut Butter	2	186		YES	YES		
Energy Bars	2	188					YES
Smoothies	2	190	YES	YES	YES		YES

SPECIAL TOOLS:

food processor

There is a brand of date-based fruit and nut bars that we really enjoy as a snack. Unfortunately, at two dollars or more per bar, frequent consumption would be outrageous. Lucky for all of us, they're not that difficult to re-create. This recipe includes four variations to keep your snacks interesting.

SNACK BALLS

Ingredients

MAKES: ABOUT 2 DOZEN BALLS

☑ Egg-Free	☑ Egg-Free	☑ Egg-Free	☑ Egg-Free
☑ Nut-Free	☑ Nut-Free	▣ Nut-Free	▣ Nut-Free
☑ Nightshade-Free	☑ Nightshade-Free	☑ Nightshade-Free	☑ Nightshade-Free

Apple Pie

- 1 cup soft Medjool dates, pitted
- 1 cup crunchy cinnamon apple chips, such as Brothers-All-Natural
- 1 cup unsweetened coconut flakes
- 1 cup dried, soft cinnamon apple rings (purchase from a store like Whole Foods or dehydrate yourself)
- ¾ cup raisins

Banana Bread

- 1 cup soft Medjool dates, pitted
- 1 cup unsweetened banana chips
- 1 cup unsweetened coconut flakes
- 1 cup dried soft whole bananas, cut into 2-inch pieces

Coconut Cream

- 1 cup soft Medjool dates, pitted
- 1 cup raw cashews
- 1 cup unsweetened coconut flakes

Chocolate Chip Cookie

- 1 cup soft Medjool dates, pitted
- 1 cup raw macadamia nuts
- ¼ cup unsweetened coconut flakes
- ¼ cup chocolate chips

For the coating (for 1 recipe):

- ½ cup unsweetened shredded coconut or finely chopped raw nuts of choice

Note: The sky is the limit on your choices here! Experiment with your own flavors, keeping the ratio of dates and other dried fruit to dry nuts at 1:1. If you can't find soft, plump Medjool dates, you can use harder and drier dates and rehydrate them by soaking them in hot water for 10 to 20 minutes. Before buying dried fruit, check out our brand recommendations on page 24.

1. In a food processor, purée the dates until a thick ball of paste forms. This is the glue that will hold everything together.

2. Using a spoon, break up the date ball, and then add the chips (except the chocolate chips) or nuts and coconut. Pulse to distribute and combine into a coarse meal.

3. Finally, add any soft dried fruit or chocolate chips and pulse just to incorporate. Putting this in last will keep it from being chopped completely, thus leaving little bits intact to enjoy.

4. Scoop out a 2-tablespoon portion of the mixture and roll by hand into a ball. Roll the ball in the shredded coconut or finely chopped nuts until coated. Repeat with the remaining mixture and coating.

2

☑ Egg-Free

☐ Nut-Free

☑ Nightshade-Free

ON the GO

It's hard to believe, but these quick and easily assembled bars require zero baking and very little sweetener and will set on their own without the addition of gelatin powder due to the fruit's natural pectin. They're also constructed of perfectly contrasting flavors and textures: a crunchy walnut crust, a creamy coconut layer followed by a tangy cranberry layer, and finally an aromatic orange zest topping.

CRANBERRY-ORANGE NO-BAKE COCONUT BARS

MAKES: 16 (2-INCH) BARS

Ingredients

¾ cup soft Medjool dates, pitted

1½ cups raw walnuts

1 cup unsweetened coconut flakes

¼ cup honey

1 cup coconut cream concentrate, or 1 cup Coconut Butter (page 114) blended with 1 tablespoon coconut oil until loose and almost liquid

3 cups fresh cranberries

1 cup freshly squeezed orange juice

Zest of 1 orange

SPECIAL TOOLS:

food processor

1. In a food processor, pulse the dates and walnuts until a thick paste forms. Press into an 8-by-8-inch baking dish by hand to form an even crust layer at the bottom.

2. In a small mixing bowl, fold the coconut flakes into the honey and coconut cream concentrate until fully incorporated. Press this mixture on top of the crust.

3. In a medium saucepan over medium heat, stir together the cranberries and orange juice. Bring to a simmer while stirring frequently. The cranberries will begin to "pop" and release their juices.

4. When all the cranberries have popped and a thick jelly forms, about 10 minutes, pour over the top of the coconut layer and smooth the top with a spatula. Top with the orange zest.

5. Refrigerate for 1 hour to set the cranberry jelly before cutting into squares and serving.

Note: If you're not able to obtain fresh cranberries, you can use any fruit (strawberries work wonderfully), but add a dash of gelatin powder. As with the cranberries, heat the fruit and orange juice together until thickened.

SPECIAL TOOLS:

blender

Ingredients

Pizza Kale Chips

☑ Egg-Free

▪ Nut-Free

▪ Nightshade-Free

⅓ cup raw cashews

1 bunch kale

2 tablespoons olive oil

1 tablespoon nutritional yeast (see Note)

1 tablespoon tomato paste

1 teaspoon dried oregano leaves

1 teaspoon kosher or sea salt

⅛ teaspoon ground black pepper

Salt and Vinegar Kale Chips

☑ Egg-Free

☑ Nut-Free

☑ Nightshade-Free

1 bunch kale

2 tablespoons apple cider vinegar

2 tablespoons melted lard or fat of choice

1 teaspoon kosher or sea salt

While kale has become known as a powerful superfood, few people have found ways to really enjoy it. Here, we offer two variations on the classic kale chip. The first, made with nutritional yeast, an ingredient we discovered only recently, has a cheesy pizza flavor. After doing our research, we firmly believe that nutritional yeast, popular with vegans, is a powerful nutritional source for everyone. Packed with vitamins and essential amino acids, nutritional yeast is most notable for imparting the flavor that our brains think of as "cheesy." The second variation is a classic and beloved potato chip flavor: salt and vinegar. Something about this combination has always appealed to us, so we've kept true to the flavor of the traditional chips but upgraded them by making them out of kale. They're crispy, salty, sour—just like the original!

KALE CHIPS—TWO WAYS

PREHEAT OVEN: 350°F · SERVES: 2 TO 4

To make Pizza Kale Chips:

1. Place the cashews in a bowl. Cover them with water and let soak for 2 hours. Drain and rinse thoroughly.

2. Preheat the oven to 350°F.

3. Remove the stems (including the thick ribs, which can be bitter) from the kale leaves and tear the leaves into chip-sized pieces. You should have about 4 cups.

4. In a blender, purée the cashews, olive oil, nutritional yeast, tomato paste, oregano, salt, and pepper until a paste forms.

5. On a rimmed baking sheet, toss the kale leaves with the puréed mixture until every leaf is thoroughly coated. Spread out the leaves in a single layer, with no leaves overlapping.

6. Place on the lowest rack of the oven for 5 minutes. After 5 minutes, remove from the oven and toss the leaves. Return to the oven for 5 minutes. Repeat as necessary until the leaves are crispy but not blackened, a process that will take between 15 and 25 minutes.

To make Salt and Vinegar Kale Chips:

1. Preheat the oven to 350°F.

2. Remove the stems (including the thick ribs) from the kale leaves and tear the leaves into chip-sized pieces. You should have about 4 cups.

3. On a rimmed baking sheet, toss the kale leaves, vinegar, lard, and salt until every leaf is thoroughly coated. Spread out the leaves in a single layer, with no leaves overlapping.

4. Place in the oven and bake for 15 to 20 minutes, tossing every 5 minutes.

Note: We recommend beet-derived
nutritional yeast.

- ✓ Egg-Free
- ✓ Nut-Free
- ✓ Nightshade-Free

under 5 INGREDIENTS

ON *the* GO

The legend says that chips were invented by an annoyed chef as revenge against a complaining customer. Sick of remaking fries in thinner and thinner shapes, the chef simply sliced the potatoes as thin as he could and invented the dish we now know as potato chips or crisps. Although attention intensive, chips are extremely easy to make, and these sweet potato chips fried in coconut oil go very well with our Garden Tuna Salad (page 354), Spinach and Artichoke Dip (page 226), or Braunschweiger Burger Sliders (page 216). For a unique twist, dust the warm chips with cinnamon and a pinch of nutmeg instead of salt.

SWEET POTATO CHIPS

PREHEAT OVEN: 350°F · SERVES: 4 TO 6

1. Using a knife, mandoline, or food slicer, slice the sweet potatoes very thinly, ⅛ inch or thinner. Set on a paper towel to dry any excess moisture as the oil comes to temperature.

2. Heat the oil in an electric deep-fryer or deep, heavy-bottomed pot to 350°F over medium heat. Watch the temperature so that it stays as close to 350°F as possible, reducing the heat if needed.

3. Fry the sweet potatoes in a single layer without overlaps for about 4 minutes, or until they turn golden brown in places.

4. Remove from the oil and set on a paper towel–lined cooling rack to drain the excess oil. Sprinkle each batch with salt while it's still hot. To turn up the flavor, toss with other flavorings when warm out of the fryer, such as Roasted Garlic (page 130) and minced fresh rosemary.

5. Although best served warm, these chips keep well at room temperature for several days.

Ingredients

3 medium sweet potatoes, peeled

3 cups coconut oil or fat of choice

Kosher or sea salt to taste

SPECIAL TOOLS:

Deep-fryer or deep, heavy-bottomed pot

fryer

Note: Try this recipe with a variety of sweet potatoes. Our family loves white sweet potatoes and purple, too. Each color has a different variation on flavor and nutrients—the more variety, the better!

☑ Egg-Free
☑ Nut-Free
☑ Nightshade-Free

Growing up, Matt and his brothers looked forward to the yearly tradition of roasting and eating the seeds from jack-o'-lanterns. Now, as an adult, he still loves to snack on them and can appreciate using all the parts of the pumpkin to reduce food waste. Pumpkin seeds are so good that they shouldn't be considered seasonal—we like to roast all of our winter squash seeds so they don't go to waste. We almost always have some on our shelf, as they make a great movie-time replacement for popcorn.

ROASTED PUMPKIN SEEDS

PREHEAT OVEN: 400°F · MAKES: 2 CUPS

Ingredients

2 tablespoons coconut oil or fat of choice, melted, plus more for greasing the baking sheet

2 cups pumpkin seeds or seeds of any winter squash

1½ teaspoons kosher or sea salt

1. Preheat the oven to 400°F. Grease a rimmed baking sheet with the coconut oil.

2. Rinse the pumpkin seeds in cold water to remove any extra pumpkin flesh or membranes.

3. Bring a large pot of water to a boil over high heat. Blanch the seeds for 5 minutes, and then transfer them to a bowl of ice water to stop the cooking.

4. Set the seeds on a paper towel and pat dry.

5. Lay the pumpkin seeds out on the prepared baking sheet, tossing to moisten them slightly with the oil. Sprinkle with the salt and toss to coat.

6. Place in the oven and roast for 5 to 10 minutes. Flip the seeds by shaking the pan, and then return to the oven to roast for another 5 to 10 minutes—the larger the seeds, the longer they need to cook. The seeds should be dry, lightly browned, and easily cracked open when done.

Note: After you scoop the seeds from a squash, you can keep them in an airtight container in the refrigerator for a few days if you're not ready to clean and roast them right away.

SPECIAL TOOLS:

dehydrator

From the earliest hunter-gatherer times, people have been laying out strips of meat in the sun to dry, which both preserved the meat and made it portable. To this day, dehydrating is the best way to have some protein on the go. And using organ meats in these recipes will make them much more palatable to even the least adventurous among us. We often make a mixed batch of all three cuts to get the benefits of each version.

JERKY

Ingredients

MAKES: ABOUT 1 POUND

✓ Egg-Free	✓ Egg-Free	✓ Egg-Free
✓ Nut-Free	✓ Nut-Free	✓ Nut-Free
✓ Nightshade-Free	■ Nightshade-Free	✓ Nightshade-Free

Sweet Heart Jerky

1 beef heart, trimmed

For the marinade:
¾ cup pineapple juice
½ cup water
2 tablespoons fish sauce
1 tablespoon apple cider vinegar
1 tablespoon yellow curry powder
½ teaspoon ground black pepper

Note: If you don't have top round for the Teriyaki Jerky, any lean cut of meat will work great. Order in advance and ask your butcher to slice it for you!

Superfood Jerky

2 pounds beef liver

For the marinade:
½ cup coconut aminos or tamari
½ cup water
4 cloves garlic, smashed with the side of a knife
1 tablespoon chili powder
1 teaspoon paprika
1 teaspoon ginger powder
½ teaspoon ground black pepper

Teriyaki Jerky

2 pounds top round

For the marinade:
½ cup coconut aminos or tamari
½ cup water
2 tablespoons honey
1 tablespoon grated fresh ginger (optional; adds heat)
3 cloves garlic, grated
½ teaspoon ground black pepper
2 teaspoons ground cumin
1 teaspoon ground cinnamon
1 teaspoon untoasted, cold-pressed sesame oil

1. If the meat is frozen, allow it to thaw in the refrigerator for several hours to make slicing easier. If the meat is fresh, place it in the freezer for 2 hours so that it is stiff when you are ready to slice it.

2. Slice the meat into ¼-inch-thick slices, discarding slices with thick, tough white tissue or excess fat. This is most easily accomplished with a meat slicer or mandoline, but can be done with a sharp knife as well. The slices should be no longer or wider than 3 inches.

3. In a sealable, microwaveable container, whisk together the ingredients for the marinade. Place the marinade in the microwave and heat for 1 minute.

4. Place the meat slices in the marinade, pushing them down until completely submerged.

5. Seal and store in the fridge for 4 hours or overnight.

6. Dehydrate in a dehydrator on high (155°F) for 6 hours. Alternatively, you can cook them in the oven at the lowest temperature until the jerky is dry but still flexible. Be sure to rotate the trays and flip the pieces when they begin to dry.

☑ Egg-Free
☐ Nut-Free
☑ Nightshade-Free

After making Almond Milk (page 290), you'll find yourself with a ton of pulp that seems destined for the trashcan. How wasteful! This is the best way we have found to use this leftover pulp. The crackers that result are easy to make and full of flavor. Top them with nutrient-rich smoked salmon or our Spinach and Artichoke Dip (page 226).

ALMOND MEAL CRACKERS

PREHEAT OVEN: 275°F · MAKES: 16 CRACKERS

Ingredients

2 cups almond pulp left over from making Almond Milk (page 290)

2 tablespoons olive oil

2 teaspoons dried tarragon leaves

1 teaspoon kosher or sea salt

Grated zest of 1 lemon

1 tablespoon freshly squeezed lemon juice

SPECIAL TOOLS:

  OR

cheesecloth   strainer

1. Place leftover almond pulp in a cheesecloth or strainer and squeeze or press any remaining moisture from the pulp.

2. Preheat the oven to 275°F. Line a rimmed baking sheet with parchment paper.

3. In a medium mixing bowl, knead together all of the ingredients.

4. Press out the dough on the prepared baking sheet until it reaches a uniform thickness of ⅛ to ¼ inch.

5. Bake for 1 hour, until no longer moist in the center and slightly golden brown on the edges.

6. Remove from the oven and increase the oven temperature to 350°F.

7. Cut the cooked dough into 2-inch squares with a pizza cutter or knife. Separate and return to the oven for 10 to 15 minutes to crisp the crackers.

8. Let cool on the baking sheet for 15 minutes before transferring to an airtight container. The crackers will keep for up to a week.

Note: These crackers will get crispy once cooled, so remove them from the oven when lightly browned. Don't overcook, or they will be more likely to fall apart.

✓ Egg-Free
■ Nut-Free
✓ Nightshade-Free

UNDER 30 MIN

under 5 INGREDIENTS

ONE POT

ON the GO

Originally conceived as a sugarless ice cream topping, we've found that this crunchy toasted combo of almonds and coconut is perfect anytime. Place it in a to-go container and use it as a simple yet tasty trail mix, or eat it while you watch a movie. We like to add it to Pumpkin Pudding (page 154), Healthiest Ice Cream Ever (page 384), and Chocolate Custard (page 406).

SLIGHTLY SWEET & SALTY SNACK MIX

MAKES: ABOUT ½ CUP

Ingredients

¼ cup unsweetened coconut chips

¼ cup sliced raw almonds

1 teaspoon kosher or sea salt

1 teaspoon ground cinnamon

½ teaspoon ground nutmeg (freshly grated preferred)

1. Toast the coconut chips and almonds in a small skillet over medium-high heat, stirring often, until the fragrance of the nuts and coconut comes out and a light brown color develops, about 4 minutes.

2. Add the remaining ingredients to the skillet and toss the coconut chips and almonds in the spices until each piece is coated.

3. Serve on top of ice cream or as a snack on its own. Store in an airtight container at room temperature for up to several weeks.

Note: This recipe is very scalable and keeps for a long time in an airtight container, so feel free to make as much or as little as you'd like.

✓ Egg-Free
■ Nut-Free
✓ Nightshade-Free

under 5
INGREDIENTS

ONE POT

Peanut butter is a staple in the American diet, but, unfortunately, peanuts are actually legumes (not nuts) and are problematic for many, many people. Luckily, making butter out of other nuts is simple and can lead to so much creativity. We give you two variations to get you started.

NUT BUTTER

MAKES: ABOUT 2 CUPS

Ingredients

Vanilla Cashew Butter

2 cups raw whole cashews

Seeds scraped from 1 vanilla bean

Salted Caramel Almond Butter *

3 cups raw whole almonds

6 soft Medjool dates, pitted

2 teaspoons kosher or sea salt

3 tablespoons coconut milk (full-fat, canned or homemade, page 290)

1. In a food processor or high-speed blender, grind the nuts on high speed until they become dry and crumbly, about 8 minutes.

2. If making the Vanilla Cashew Butter, add the vanilla bean seeds.

   or

3. If making the Salted Caramel Almond Butter, add the dates. Continue to process either mixture until the oils release and the texture begins to resemble that of nut butter (another few minutes). Then add the remaining ingredients for the Salted Caramel Almond Butter.

4. After the ingredients are fully combined and the nut butter has the desired texture, stop the processor and transfer to an airtight container. Store chilled, but allow it to come to room temperature before using for the best flavor and texture. Store in the refrigerator for up to 2 weeks.

Note: *If you're sensitive to nuts, try soaking them overnight before making nut butter. Soaking can help to remove inflammatory antinutrient properties from the nuts, making for a healthier butter. If you're allergic to nuts, we don't recommend these nut butters, but this technique can be used on sunflower seeds, sesame seeds, and more for a similar taste and texture.*

*Variation: Almond Butter
To make regular almond butter for use in recipes, follow the directions but omit the salt and dates.

SPECIAL TOOLS:

food processor   OR   blender

We got the idea that ground meat could be dehydrated while writing our first book, *Eat Like a Dinosaur,* but we didn't realize the full potential of this technique until we realized how portable, affordable, and filling ground-meat jerky can be. Lean ground meat can be shaped into snack bars that you can take with you anywhere, and so much flavor can be added to them!

ENERGY BARS

MAKES: 8 BARS

Ingredients

½ cup raw cashews

½ cup dried cranberries, divided

1 pound ground red meat, at least 95% lean

2 teaspoons kosher or sea salt

1 teaspoon ginger powder

1 teaspoon dried ground sage

¼ teaspoon ground black pepper

1. In a food processor or blender, purée the cashews and ¼ cup of the dried cranberries until a paste forms and the cashews are tiny bits.

2. In a medium mixing bowl, incorporate the cashew-cranberry paste into the meat by hand until evenly mixed.

3. Add the spices and the remaining dried cranberries and mix thoroughly.

4. Form into eight ¼-inch-thick rectangular bars, about 1½ by 4 inches, and place in a dehydrator.

5. Dehydrate on high (155°F) for 5 to 6 hours, until brown all the way through and firm to the touch. If the bars are thicker than ½ inch, additional time may be needed. To ensure that the bars are done, press the center of a bar with your finger; there should be no give.

6. Store at room temperature for a day or two (these work perfectly in lunch boxes), or chill or freeze for longer periods.

SPECIAL TOOLS:

food processor   dehydrator

✓ Egg-Free
✓ Nut-Free
✓ Nightshade-Free

UNDER 30 MIN

under 5 INGREDIENTS

ONE POT

ON the GO

On those days when you have nothing prepared, no time to prepare it, and a deadline on the horizon, how can you possibly fuel yourself for breakfast or a midday snack? In our house, we load up with these quick smoothies, especially when our boys' appetites seem unsatisfiable. No matter your situation, a smoothie, with just a few ingredients, will hit the spot.

SMOOTHIES

Ingredients

MAKES: 2 TO 4 (8-OUNCE) SERVINGS

Blueberry

1 cup frozen blueberries

2 bananas, cut into chunks and frozen

1 (13½-ounce) can full-fat coconut milk or 1¾ cups homemade (page 290)

2 tablespoons cold-water-soluble gelatin powder (optional)

Strawberry Mango

1 (13½-ounce) can full-fat coconut milk or 1¾ cups homemade (page 290)

1 cup diced mango, frozen

½ cup diced strawberries, frozen

1 banana, cut into chunks and frozen

2 tablespoons cold-water-soluble gelatin powder (optional)

PB&J

1 banana, cut into chunks and frozen

½ cup diced strawberries, frozen

2 cups coconut milk (full-fat, canned or homemade, page 290) or Almond Milk (page 290)

2 tablespoons sunflower seed butter or Almond Butter (page 186)

2 tablespoons cold-water-soluble gelatin powder (optional)

The Elvis Presley

1 banana, cut into chunks and frozen

2 cups coconut milk (full-fat, canned or homemade, page 290) or Almond Milk (page 290)

2 tablespoons sunflower seed butter or Almond Butter (page 186)

2 tablespoons cacao powder

2 tablespoons cold-water-soluble gelatin powder (optional)

SPECIAL TOOLS:

blender

1. In a blender, combine all of the ingredients and purée until smooth.

2. For added nutrients, stir in the gelatin powder. Though not necessary, we recommend that you try it, because gelatin is flavorless. It's almost as nutritious as drinking a rich broth.

Note: We recommend the Natural Value brand of canned coconut milk. You can freeze leftover smoothies into popsicles.

CHILDHOOD FAVORITES

Those foods that remind us of our childhoods stick with us all throughout our lives. Who are we to tell you that your comfort foods are off-limits forever? Instead, we'd prefer to help you keep them in your life in a healthier, Paleo style!

	PHASE	PAGE #	UNDER 30 MIN	under 5 INGREDIENTS	ONE POT	HOLIDAY	ON the GO
Chunky Monkey Muffins	2	194	YES				YES
Honey Nut Cereal	1	196					YES
Pumpkin Cider Latte	2	198	YES	YES		YES	
Not Beanie Weenies	2	200	YES		YES		
Chicken Fingers with Honey Mustard	2	202	YES				
Mini Corn Dog Muffins	1	204	YES				YES
Zucchini Cauliflower Tots	2	206		YES			
Meatza	2	208			YES		
Monkey Bread	1	210				YES	
Gummy Snacks	3	212		YES			YES

✓ Egg-Free
✓ Nut-Free
✓ Nightshade-Free

Definitely inspired by a certain ice cream flavor, these muffins have become a fan favorite recipe of ours. If you're avoiding grains, eggs, and nuts, even attempting to make a bread-like sweet treat will certainly seem impossible. These muffins are not only egg- and nut-free, but also fruit-sweetened and still absolutely delicious and moist. These are always our go-to treat for the boys' classrooms because they work for so many people. An added bonus: You can choose whether you want to make vanilla- or chocolate-flavored muffins.

CHUNKY MONKEY MUFFINS

PREHEAT OVEN: 350°F · MAKES: 1 DOZEN MUFFINS

1. Preheat the oven to 350°F. Line 12 cups of a muffin pan with paper liners.

2. In a food processor, purée the bananas and dates until smooth.

3. Add the almond butter, coconut flour, cacao powder or tapioca flour, coconut oil, palm shortening, baking soda, vanilla, and salt to the food processor. Pulse until a thick batter forms, stopping the machine a couple of times to scrape down the sides. Do not overblend.

4. Spoon the batter into the lined muffin cups, filling them two-thirds full.

5. In a small bowl, toss together the topping ingredients. Sprinkle on top of each muffin, pressing gently to get the topping to "stick."

6. Bake for 16 to 18 minutes, until a toothpick inserted in the center comes out clean. Let cool in the pan for 15 minutes, and then remove the muffins with a butter knife. Store in an airtight container for up to a week.

Note: As noted on page 33, using sunflower seed butter causes a chemical reaction involving chlorophyll, which will make the muffins turn green—an awesome science experiment!

Ingredients

2 ripe bananas

1 cup soft Medjool dates, pitted

½ cup Almond Butter (page 186) or sunflower seed butter

½ cup coconut flour

2 tablespoons cacao powder (for chocolate muffins) or tapioca flour (for vanilla muffins)

¼ cup coconut oil, melted

¼ cup palm shortening or unsalted butter, softened

2 teaspoons baking soda

1 teaspoon pure vanilla extract

½ teaspoon kosher or sea salt

For the topping (optional):

½ cup chocolate chips

½ cup raw walnuts, chopped

SPECIAL TOOLS:

food processor

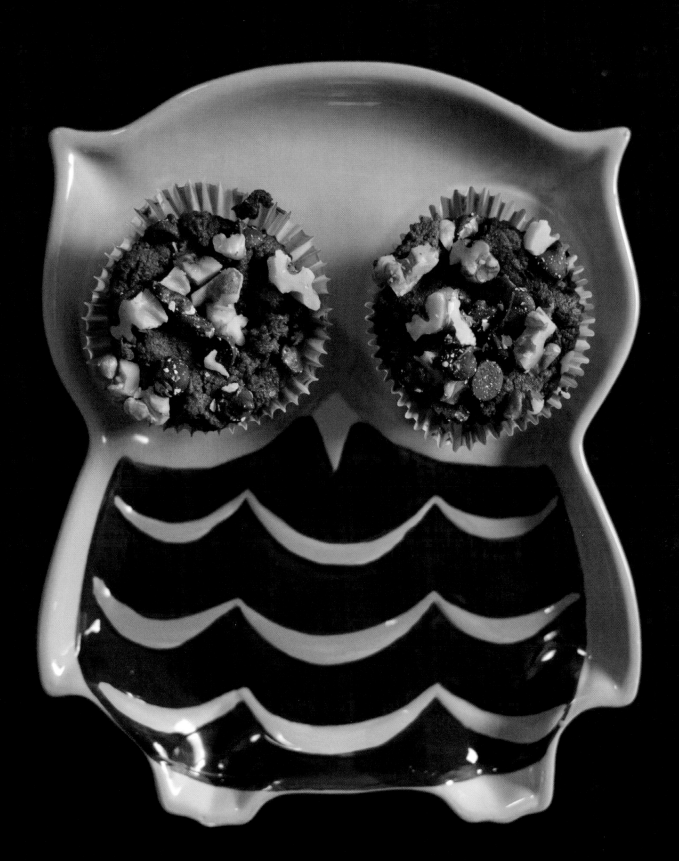

At a certain point in the previous century, people forgot how to make breakfast due to the amazing convenience of boxed cereal. You can't compete with the simplicity of "pour milk over it and consume." Although we've come to love a warm breakfast now, we still sometimes miss the flavor and convenience of the boxed stuff. We use this grain-free granola to replace the junk-filled version, and the kids are thrilled when it's offered.

HONEY NUT CEREAL

PREHEAT OVEN: 275°F · MAKES: ABOUT 5 CUPS

Ingredients

½ cup coconut oil, melted, plus more for greasing the baking sheet

1½ cups unsweetened coconut flakes

1½ cups sliced almonds

1 cup raw walnuts, finely chopped

1 cup raw pecans, finely chopped

⅓ cup honey

1 teaspoon kosher or sea salt

For serving:

Almond Milk (page 290) or coconut milk (full-fat, canned or homemade, page 290)

Fruit of choice

1. Preheat the oven to 275°F. Lightly grease a rimmed baking sheet with coconut oil.

2. Combine the coconut flakes and nuts in a bowl.

3. In a medium saucepan over medium heat, whisk together the oil, honey, and salt until it just begins to bubble. Remove from the heat.

4. Pour the oil-honey-salt mixture over the nut mixture, and stir with a spatula to coat the nuts and coconut flakes.

5. Spread into a single layer on the prepared baking sheet.

6. Bake for 1 hour, stirring every 15 minutes to prevent burning.

7. Serve with almond or coconut milk and your favorite fruit. Allow to cool before storing in an airtight container, such as a mason jar. Store at room temperature for up to 2 weeks.

✓ Egg-Free
✓ Nut-Free
✓ Nightshade-Free

UNDER 30 MIN

under 5
INGREDIENTS

HOLIDAY

On cool fall days, nothing hits the spot like a warm, rich beverage. For some people, it's a cup of hot cocoa or coffee. But for us, it's this seasonal latte, developed for the whole family to enjoy. It's infused with the delicious flavors of autumn but sweetened with nothing but fruit and vegetables.

PUMPKIN CIDER LATTE

MAKES: 2 (8-OUNCE) SERVINGS

Ingredients

1 cup pumpkin puree

1 cup pure apple juice

1 cup coconut milk (full-fat, canned or homemade, page 290) or Almond Milk (page 290)

1 teaspoon ground cinnamon

¼ teaspoon ground nutmeg

1. In a medium saucepan over medium heat, whisk together the pumpkin puree, apple juice, and milk until it just begins to boil, stirring constantly, about 10 minutes.

2. Whisk in the cinnamon and nutmeg until combined and remove from the heat.

3. Pour through a small fine-mesh strainer lined with cheesecloth into 2 coffee mugs. Press all the liquid through the strainer. Serve warm.

Note: We recommend throwing a tea party with your lattes and some Jack-O'-Lantern Cookies (page 386).

✓ **Egg-Free**
✓ **Nut-Free**
◼ **Nightshade-Free**

UNDER 30 MIN

ONE POT

One of the staples of childhood in many homes is cooking slices of hot dogs in baked beans. These days, the thought of those sugary, gut-damaging beans is enough to make us shiver. We came up with this replacement so that we could share our experience with beanie weenies with our kids in a healthier way.

NOT BEANIE WEENIES

Ingredients

1 tablespoon lard or fat of choice

½ onion, diced

1 large sweet potato, peeled and diced

1 teaspoon kosher or sea salt

½ teaspoon garlic powder

½ teaspoon ground cumin

½ teaspoon chili powder

2 tablespoons tomato paste

1 tablespoon blackstrap molasses (optional)

1 (14-ounce) can diced tomatoes

½ cup water

3 uncured hot dogs, sliced

SERVES: 4

1. In a large saucepan, melt the lard over medium heat. Add the onion and sweet potato and sauté for 7 to 10 minutes or until the onion is translucent and the sweet potato begins to soften.

2. Add the salt, spices, tomato paste, and molasses, if using, and stir for 3 minutes. The result at this point will be a thick sauce.

3. Pour in the tomatoes with their juices and water and reduce the heat to medium-low. Simmer, covered, for 15 minutes until the "bean" sauce thickens and the sweet potatoes are tender.

4. Add the hot dog slices and cook for 5 minutes, until heated through. Spoon into bowls and serve. This dish keeps well chilled and reheats perfectly for lunches all week long!

Note: If the sauce gets too thick before the sweet potatoes are cooked through, add ¼ cup of water at a time until you achieve the desired consistency. If the sauce is too watery, remove the lid and let it cook down to the desired consistency.

Who doesn't love chicken nuggets? They're crispy on the outside, tender on the inside, and perfect for pairing with dips or sauces. We were determined to come up with a chicken tender so good you'll forget all about the drive-thru window, and we know we've succeeded with this recipe!

CHICKEN FINGERS WITH HONEY MUSTARD

PREHEAT FRYER: 350°F · SERVES: 4 TO 6

Ingredients

2 cups lard, coconut oil, or fat of choice for frying

2 pounds chicken tenderloins or boneless, skinless breasts, sliced into 1-inch-wide strips

½ cup blanched almond flour

½ cup tapioca flour

2 large eggs

½ teaspoon dry mustard

½ teaspoon turmeric powder

1 teaspoon kosher or sea salt

⅛ teaspoon ground black pepper

For the Honey Mustard:

½ cup Mayonnaise (page 122)

2 tablespoons honey

2 tablespoons prepared yellow mustard

¼ teaspoon garlic powder

SPECIAL TOOLS:

Deep-fryer or deep, heavy-bottomed pot

fryer

1. Heat the lard in an electric deep-fryer or deep, heavy-bottomed pot to 350°F over medium-high heat.

2. Pat the chicken strips dry with a paper towel. The drier the chicken is, the better the batter will adhere.

3. In a wide-bottomed bowl, whisk together the flours, eggs, dry mustard, turmeric, salt, and pepper until a thick batter forms, being careful to break up any lumps.

4. Coat each chicken strip in the batter, rotating to coat completely.

5. Deep-fry for about 5 minutes or until the chicken is cooked through and the outside is slightly browned.

6. Remove to a paper towel–lined rack to drain the excess oil and allow to crisp.

7. Serve warm with Honey Mustard, if desired.

Note: This recipe also works great for a hearty fish like cod or swai, paired with Tartar Sauce (page 122). If you prefer, dip the Chicken Fingers in Ranch Dressing (page 124) instead of Honey Mustard.

To make the Honey Mustard:

1. In a bowl, whisk together the Mayonnaise with the remaining ingredients. Store refrigerated for up to a week.

We know it may seem like a strange idea to put hot dogs in muffins, but it absolutely works, trust us! These tiny bites of goodness will certainly please the corn dog lover in your life. They taste great at room temperature, so make them ahead and include them in lunch boxes.

MINI CORN DOG MUFFINS

PREHEAT OVEN: 350°F · MAKES: 36 MINI MUFFINS

Ingredients

- 2 cups blanched almond flour
- ½ cup tapioca flour
- 1 teaspoon kosher or sea salt
- 1 teaspoon baking soda
- 1 cup coconut milk (full-fat, canned or homemade, page 290)
- 3 large eggs
- ¼ cup coconut oil, melted
- 1 tablespoon apple cider vinegar
- 6 hot dogs, sliced crosswise into 1-inch pieces

1. Preheat the oven to 350°F. Grease 36 cups of 2 mini muffin pans, or line the cups with paper liners.

2. In a medium mixing bowl, sift together the flours, salt, and baking soda.

3. In a large bowl, whisk together the coconut milk, eggs, coconut oil, and vinegar, making sure that the yolks are broken and incorporated.

4. Slowly whisk the dry ingredients into the wet ingredients until a batter forms.

5. Spoon about 1 tablespoon of the batter into each muffin cup, and then press a slice of hot dog into each muffin.

6. Bake for 15 to 20 minutes or until the tops just begin to brown. Allow to cool in the pans for 10 minutes before turning out onto a plate. Store refrigerated in an airtight container for up to a week.

Egg-Free

Nut-Free

✓ Nightshade-Free

under 5
INGREDIENTS

In our house, we had to impose a seven-tot limit on these tasty nuggets of veggie goodness because the boys were eating us out of house and home! They're so delectable, restraint is difficult to come by! If you're looking to get your children to eat more vegetables, we recommend making a double batch of these and having them for lunch and dinner all week long.

ZUCCHINI CAULIFLOWER TOTS

PREHEAT OVEN: 350°F · SERVES: 6 TO 8

Ingredients

Coconut oil, for greasing the baking sheet (if not using parchment)

2 cups cauliflower florets

½ cup blanched almond flour

½ cup tapioca flour

2 large eggs

½ teaspoon kosher or sea salt

⅛ teaspoon ground black pepper

2 cups shredded zucchini

SPECIAL TOOLS:

food processor

1. Preheat the oven to 350°F. Lightly grease a rimmed baking sheet with coconut oil or line it with parchment paper.

2. Steam the cauliflower over boiling water until easily pierced with a fork, about 10 minutes.

3. Purée the cauliflower in a food processor until smooth. Add the flours, eggs, salt, and pepper and pulse to combine.

4. Fold in the shredded zucchini by hand.

5. Form tablespoons of the batter into "tot" shapes, roughly cylinders, and place on the prepared baking sheet.

6. Bake for 20 minutes, flipping the tots halfway through. Allow to cool for 5 minutes before serving.

7. Store chilled for up to several days, or freeze to have on hand for the next side-dish-in-a-hurry emergency.

Note: We recommend thawing any frozen tots before reheating them in a 350°F oven for 10 minutes.

2

ONE POT

■ Egg-Free
■ Nut-Free
✓ Nightshade-Free

It's nearly impossible to make a truly satisfying chewy pizza crust without special high-gluten wheat flour. So rather than make the inevitably lackluster attempt, we prefer to make a Meatza, a pizza with a ground meat crust reminiscent of the flavors of sausage topping. With this recipe, we give you two topping combinations to get you started, but they are merely suggestions. The reality is that you are limited only by your imagination.

MEATZA

PREHEAT OVEN: 325°F · SERVES: 4 TO 6

Ingredients

■ Egg-Free	■ Egg-Free
■ Nut-Free	■ Nut-Free
✓ Nightshade-Free	■ Nightshade-Free

For the crust:

1 pound ground pork
1 pound ground beef
½ cup tapioca flour
2 large eggs
1 teaspoon fennel seeds
1 teaspoon dried oregano leaves
1 teaspoon kosher or sea salt
½ teaspoon garlic powder
¼ teaspoon ground black pepper

For the sauce:

½ cup Cashew Cheese Sauce (page 126)

Prosciutto, arugula, and pear

1 pear, cored and sliced
Roasted Garlic (page 130), thinly sliced
4 ounces prosciutto
Arugula leaves (add after cooking)

Supreme

Tomato sauce
Tomato slices
Bell pepper slices
Sliced mushrooms
Sliced black olives
Roasted Garlic (page 130), thinly sliced
Fresh basil, chiffonaded (add after cooking)

1. Preheat the oven to 325°F.

2. In a medium mixing bowl, combine the crust ingredients. Using your hands, mix until fully incorporated.

3. Divide the mixture in half and form into two 10-inch circles with slightly thicker rims on 2 rimmed baking sheets.

4. Bake for 15 minutes or until thoroughly cooked.

5. Let cool for 10 minutes, and then add about ¼ cup of the cheese sauce over each crust.

6. Add the toppings of your choice (or use the suggested prosciutto, arugula, and pear or supreme toppings) and return to the oven for another 15 minutes.

SPECIAL TOOLS:

food processor

Ingredients

½ cup coconut oil, softened, plus more for greasing the pan

⅔ cup soft Medjool dates, pitted

2 tablespoons honey

1 tablespoon pure vanilla extract

2½ cups blanched almond flour, divided

1 cup tapioca flour

3 tablespoons arrowroot flour

1 teaspoon baking soda

¼ teaspoon cream of tartar

¼ teaspoon kosher or sea salt

3 large egg whites

⅓ cup raw walnuts, chopped

6 tablespoons palm shortening or unsalted butter, softened, divided

½ cup plus 3 tablespoons unrefined granulated palm, date, or cane sugar, divided

1 tablespoon ground cinnamon

Note: To reheat leftovers, place in a 350°F oven for 10 minutes.

Growing up, Stacy's Christmas tradition was to enjoy "monkey bread," a pull-apart sweet bread that her family assembled with pop-can biscuits, sugar, and butter. When we went Paleo the first year and it wasn't set out on the table on Christmas morning, the extended family was outraged and made us promise to come up with a grain-free option. For years now the family has been eating this version, which is the most anticipated food we make when we host Christmas brunch every year. Though it is a labor of love, the result is truly something special.

MONKEY BREAD

PREHEAT OVEN: 375°F · SERVES: 6 TO 8

1. Preheat the oven to 375°F. Lightly grease a 12-cup Bundt pan with coconut oil.

2. In a food processor, purée the dates. Add the oil, honey, and vanilla and pulse until combined. Transfer the mixture to a large bowl.

3. In a separate bowl, sift 1½ cups of the almond flour, the tapioca flour, arrowroot flour, baking soda, cream of tartar, and salt and stir to evenly distribute.

4. Add the dry ingredients to the wet ingredients and whisk until a thick dough forms. Set aside.

5. Whip the egg whites to soft peaks. (This can take 15 minutes or more, so doing it in a stand mixer or with a hand-held electric mixer is preferable.)

6. Gently fold the egg whites into the dough until incorporated.

7. Gently mix in the remaining 1 cup of almond flour, ¼ cup at a time, until the dough becomes very sticky. Set aside.

8. In a small bowl, mix the walnuts, 1½ tablespoons of the palm shortening, and 3 tablespoons of the sugar. Sprinkle this mixture in the bottom of the prepared Bundt pan.

9. With a fork, mix together the remaining ½ cup of sugar and the cinnamon in a small bowl.

10. Drop tablespoons of the dough into the cinnamon sugar and roll around to coat; add the sugared balls to the Bundt pan.

11. When all of the dough is in the pan, sprinkle the top with the remaining 4½ tablespoons of shortening and the remaining cinnamon sugar.

12. Place in the oven and bake for 30 minutes, until the top is golden brown.

13. Let cool in the pan for at least 20 minutes, and then turn out onto a serving platter. Enjoy warm. Store leftovers in an airtight container at room temperature for up to a week.

☑ Egg-Free
☑ Nut-Free
☑ Nightshade-Free

Gummy snacks are often considered to be candy, but they really don't have to be. This recipe is enhanced with the healing powers of gelatin and is sweetened by fruit alone. Now you can enjoy a dense, jiggly snack without feeding the sugar monster.

GUMMY SNACKS

SERVES: 2 TO 4

1. In a food processor or blender, purée the fruit and water until smooth.

2. Pour the puree into a medium saucepan over medium heat. Add the lemon juice, and then slowly add the gelatin while stirring constantly. Continue stirring to dissolve the gelatin. When all of the gelatin has dissolved, remove from the heat.

3. Pour this mixture into individual molds or a 9-by-9-inch glass baking dish (no need to oil or flour) and transfer to the refrigerator.

4. Chill for at least an hour, preferably overnight. Then unmold, or cut into 1-inch squares, to serve and enjoy. Keep chilled until ready to serve.

Notes: We've heard that sour is the favorite flavor for these gummy snacks, hence the lemon juice in this version. We love to make ours with strawberries (they taste like strawberry lemonade) or fresh, juicy mango—but any combination works well. If you have an adventurous palate, try pear gummy snacks spiced with grated fresh ginger!

The molds we prefer are the soft silicone molds found in baking and craft stores and sold as candy molds. They can also be found on Amazon or other online retailers.

Ingredients

1 cup roughly chopped ripe fresh fruit

½ cup water

1 tablespoon freshly squeezed lemon juice

¼ cup gelatin powder, about 4 (1-ounce) packets

SPECIAL TOOLS:

food processor   blender

APPETIZERS

Amuse your mouth with these small teaser dishes that you can serve at parties or just for yourself. Who wouldn't prefer to get started on dinner early, even if it means giving up dessert?

	PHASE	PAGE #	UNDER 30 MIN	under 5 INGREDIENTS	ONE POT	HOLIDAY	ON the GO
Braunschweiger Burger Sliders	3	216	YES				
Chinese Lettuce Cups	2	218	YES		YES		
Chicken Liver Mousse	3	220					
Prosciutto-Wrapped Pears	2	222	YES		YES		YES
Pork Belly Bites with Arugula	2	224					
Spinach and Artichoke Dip	2	226	YES				
Stuffed Mushrooms	2	228					
Meatballs—Three Ways	3	230					
Steamed Mussels in Tomato Broth	3	232					
Crispy Oven-Baked Chicken Wings	2	234		YES			

Egg-Free
Nut-Free
✓ Nightshade-Free

UNDER 30 MIN

Of all of our recommendations for Phase 3, perhaps the most difficult is to incorporate organ meats, especially liver, into your diet. Even for us, sautéed liver doesn't hold much appeal. What is helpful, though, is to transform your offal into something more palatable. These sliders include plenty of liver, whether you use Braunschweiger or mix up a beef and liver mixture of your own, and will please the palate, too, because the dominant flavor will be bacon. They pair wonderfully with Sautéed Mushrooms and Onions (page 116).

BRAUNSCHWEIGER BURGER SLIDERS

PREHEAT OVEN: 350°F · MAKES: 12 SLIDERS

Ingredients

For the burgers:

1 pound beef bacon

1 pound Braunschweiger or 60/40 mix of ground beef and liver

1 teaspoon ground cumin

1 teaspoon kosher or sea salt

½ teaspoon ground black pepper

For the "buns" (optional):

Cauli-Gnocchi dough (page 260)

For serving (optional):

Greens

Ketchup (page 120)

Mustard

Mayonnaise (page 122)

1. Grind the beef bacon in a meat grinder or chop in a food processor until it resembles ground meat.

2. In a large bowl, mix the ground bacon with the Braunschweiger, cumin, salt, and pepper by hand until evenly incorporated.

3. If making the "buns," preheat the oven to 350°F and have on hand a 12-cup muffin pan.

4. Form the ground meat into 2-inch-round, 1-inch-thick patties, slightly less wide than the size of a muffin cup.

5. If not making the optional "buns," cook the patties in a large skillet over medium-high heat to medium doneness, about 4 minutes per side. The outsides will get browned and crispy while the insides stay tender.

   or

6. If making the "buns," spoon 1½ tablespoons of the bun dough into each muffin cup. Add an uncooked patty to each cup and top with another 1½ tablespoons of the dough. Bake for 20 minutes, or until the dough is slightly golden and the meat reaches the internal temperature for the desired doneness (see page 412 for a cooking temperature chart).

7. Serve warm, ideally with greens and homemade ketchup, mustard, and mayonnaise.

Note: Because the burgers will be moist, the bottom part of the "buns" may become soggy, depending on the percentage of fat of your ground meat. The burgers are just as delicious when served over arugula or other greens.

SPECIAL TOOLS:

  OR

food processor   meat grinder

✓ Egg-Free
✓ Nut-Free
✓ Nightshade-Free

One of our most loved restaurant meals is an appetizer served in a chain of Chinese restaurants. This is our Paleo riff on that dish. The combination of crisp lettuce and savory chicken filling is a great way to start any meal. We highly recommend it paired with Kung Pao Chicken (page 322), Mongolian Beef (page 320), and Cauli-Rice (page 246).

CHINESE LETTUCE CUPS

SERVES: 2 TO 4

Ingredients

2 tablespoons lard or fat of choice

1 cup diced raw skinless chicken breast or thigh meat

½ cup diced onion

½ cup diced celery

½ cup diced water chestnuts

½ cup diced mushrooms

2 cloves garlic, minced

1 tablespoon honey

1 tablespoon coconut aminos or tamari

2 teaspoons untoasted, cold-pressed sesame oil

2 teaspoons rice wine vinegar

1 teaspoon ginger powder

2 green onions, sliced

4 to 8 crisp iceberg lettuce leaves

Condiments (optional):

Gluten-free hoisin sauce

Coconut aminos

Roasted chili paste

Sliced green onions

1. In a large skillet or wok over medium-high heat, melt the lard.

2. Add the chicken, diced onion, celery, water chestnuts, mushrooms, and garlic and stir-fry until the chicken is browned, about 5 minutes.

3. Meanwhile, in a separate bowl, whisk together the honey, coconut aminos, oil, vinegar, and ginger powder.

4. Add the sauce to the wok and stir to coat. Continue to cook for another 5 minutes.

5. Remove from the heat and stir in the green onions.

6. Serve warm alongside the lettuce leaves. Top with hoisin sauce, coconut aminos, roasted chili paste, and/or more green onions, if desired.

Once a week or so, we make a batch of this rich and creamy dip. Found in many upscale restaurants around the world as an unctuous high-end starter, we find that this is the best way to get health-strengthening liver into our lives. We recommend using a tart apple for dipping to make this a tasty treat, but it could pair with carrot sticks or Almond Meal Crackers (page 182), too!

CHICKEN LIVER MOUSSE

MAKES: ABOUT 2½ CUPS

Ingredients

2 tablespoons unsalted butter or lard

1 pound chicken livers, drained

1 shallot or small onion, finely diced

⅓ cup white wine, brandy, or tequila

¼ cup heavy cream or Coconut Milk (page 290)

1 teaspoon kosher or sea salt

1 teaspoon fresh thyme leaves

3 black peppercorns

3 allspice berries

½ cup unsalted butter or lard, melted

1. In a cast-iron skillet, melt the 2 tablespoons of the butter over medium heat.

2. Sauté the livers with the shallot for about 90 seconds per side. The insides of the livers will still be pink.

3. Transfer the livers and shallot to a blender. Pour in the wine and cream and add the salt, thyme, peppercorns, and allspice. Blend on high until completely smooth.

4. Pour in the melted butter and pulse to combine.

5. Pour into two 16-ounce mason jars or other storage containers and chill for 2 hours or until cold. When served, it should have a pink undertone and the texture of softened ice cream.

Note: This is one of only a few recipes in this book in which we specifically recommend dairy (other than butter). The reason is twofold. Grass-fed cream and butter have an incredible amount of nutrients that are wonderful for those who are able to tolerate them and, since this dish was created for the purpose of being a healing food, we wanted to pack in as much of a nutritional punch as possible. In addition, the rich, buttery flavor of cream covers up the taste and texture of liver better than the dairy-free version.

SPECIAL TOOLS:

blender

✓ Egg-Free
✓ Nut-Free
✓ Nightshade-Free

In the deli section in a typical grocery store, your best option for lunch meat is often prosciutto since it's made with just two ingredients: pork and salt. Of course, they leave out the six-month curing time on that ingredient list, which makes prosciutto fairly pricey. Luckily, a tiny bit can go a long way, and pairing the tasty salt pork with sweet fruit and sour-brined veggies will really do the pork justice.

PROSCIUTTO-WRAPPED PEARS

MAKES: 8 WRAPS

Ingredients

2½ cups arugula

1 cup Pickled Onions (page 128)

1 tablespoon freshly squeezed lemon juice

1 tablespoon olive oil or avocado oil

Salt and pepper to taste

8 slices prosciutto

1 pear, sliced into 8 wedges

1. In a medium mixing bowl, toss together the arugula, pickled onions, lemon juice, oil, and salt and pepper.

2. Spread out each slice of prosciutto and place a pear wedge on top of each.

3. Add ½ cup of the salad to each prosciutto slice.

4. Roll up the prosciutto slices into bundles.

While most people are quite familiar with bacon, what we learned when we wrote *Beyond Bacon* is that we much prefer to cook uncured, fresh pork belly. The skin gets crispy while the meat underneath remains very tender. Small squares of belly make an excellent appetizer that you won't want to share.

PORK BELLY BITES WITH ARUGULA

PREHEAT OVEN: 325°F · SERVES: 6 TO 8

Ingredients

2 teaspoons kosher or sea salt

1 teaspoon garlic powder

1 teaspoon ground cumin

1 teaspoon ground coriander

½ teaspoon ground cinnamon

½ teaspoon ground nutmeg

⅛ teaspoon ground black pepper

3 pounds pork belly

2½ cups arugula

1 cup Pickled Onions (page 128)

1 tablespoon freshly squeezed lemon juice

1 tablespoon olive oil or avocado oil

Salt and pepper to taste

1. Preheat the oven to 325°F.

2. In a small bowl, combine salt and spices with a fork to create a rub. Set aside.

3. With a sharp knife, score the pork belly in a diagonal crosshatch pattern, with the slices about 1 inch apart. Penetrate just the skin with your knife and no deeper.

4. Coat each side of the belly with the rub. Place on a rimmed baking sheet.

5. Place in the oven and bake for 1 hour or until the belly is cooked through and the skin is crisped.

6. When the pork belly is done, toss together the arugula, pickled onions, lemon juice, oil, and salt and pepper in a bowl.

7. Slice the pork belly along the crosshatches into 1-inch-square pieces. Serve over the salad.

Note: You can also serve this pork belly as a main dish.
Cut it into 1-inch slices and serve with cooked greens.

Artichokes are a difficult vegetable to eat, as they are thorny, hard plants with little meat inside. But the delicious hearts are a secret treat. Making them into a dip with spinach and garlic will make you a believer, too.

SPINACH AND ARTICHOKE DIP

MAKES: ABOUT 3 CUPS

Ingredients

2 tablespoons lard or fat of choice

1 yellow onion, diced

2 cloves garlic, minced

2 cup baby spinach, fresh or thawed frozen

1½ cups artichoke hearts, thawed from frozen

1 cup coconut milk (full-fat, canned or homemade, page 290)

Salt and pepper to taste

For serving:

Sweet Potato Chips (page 176), carrots, or plantain chips

1. Melt the lard in a large sauté pan over medium heat.

2. Add the onion and garlic and sauté for about 5 minutes, until the onion is translucent.

3. Add the spinach and toss with the onion and garlic until completely wilted.

4. Add the artichoke hearts and toss to combine.

5. Pour in the coconut milk and reduce the heat to medium-low. Simmer for 10 minutes.

6. Pour into a food processor and pulse to chop to the desired consistency. Season with salt and pepper and pulse once more to combine.

7. Serve warm with sweet potato chips, carrots, or plantain chips.

Note: If you'd like an extra cheesy flavor, mix in 1 cup of Cashew Cheese Sauce (page 126) in Step 5, toward the end of simmering, to heat through.

SPECIAL TOOLS:

food processor

☑ Egg-Free
☐ Nut-Free
☑ Nightshade-Free

In our house, mushrooms are the most fought-over food items. The children in particular can't get enough of them from our soups, stews, and pot roasts. When we came up with this recipe to honor their favorite food, they were over-the-moon ecstatic. Of course, most kids don't love mushrooms like ours do, so perhaps you could serve it as a fun finger food at a Paleo party.

STUFFED MUSHROOMS

PREHEAT OVEN: 350°F · SERVES: 4 TO 6

Ingredients

Coconut oil, for greasing the baking sheet (if not using parchment)

1 cup fresh parsley

½ cup cranberries

½ cup raw walnuts

2 cloves garlic, minced

Juice of ½ lemon

1 teaspoon kosher or sea salt

½ teaspoon ground black pepper

¼ cup olive oil

18 medium mushrooms

1. Preheat the oven to 350°F. Line a rimmed baking sheet with parchment paper or grease it with coconut oil.

2. In a food processor or blender, pulse the parsley, cranberries, walnuts, garlic, and lemon juice until chopped into small pieces.

3. Add the salt and pepper and, with the processor running, pour in the oil.

4. Wipe the mushrooms clean with a wet cloth. Remove the stems and place the mushroom caps on the baking sheet.

5. Press about a tablespoon of the parsley mixture into each mushroom cap. They should be filled but not overflowing.

6. Place in the oven and bake for 30 minutes, or until the mushrooms are soft and the top of the stuffing is browned.

SPECIAL TOOLS:

food processor   blender

3

When it comes to party appetizers, meatballs may be king. Instead of making typical meatballs simmering in tomato sauce, we enjoy experimenting with different types of meat and different spice combinations. These recipes are our favorite discoveries, but we encourage you to try your own!

MEATBALLS—THREE WAYS

PREHEAT OVEN: 350°F · SERVES: 10 TO 12 (MINT LAMB) OR 6 TO 8 (PIG BLANKET AND ORANGE SESAME)

Ingredients

☐ Egg-Free
✓ Nut-Free
✓ Nightshade-Free

☐ Egg-Free
✓ Nut-Free
☐ Nightshade-Free

☐ Egg-Free
☐ Nut-Free
✓ Nightshade-Free

Mint Lamb Meatballs

4 pounds ground lamb
2 large eggs
½ cup blanched almond flour
1 teaspoon garam masala
1 teaspoon ground coriander
1 teaspoon ground cardamom
½ teaspoon garlic powder
½ teaspoon ground cinnamon
½ teaspoon ground cumin
¼ teaspoon ground nutmeg
¼ teaspoon ginger powder
¼ teaspoon dried ground sage
⅛ teaspoon ground cloves
½ teaspoon kosher or sea salt
¼ teaspoon ground black pepper
¾ cup fresh mint leaves (about 35), finely chopped
Fresh mint leaves, for garnish (optional)

Note: Meatballs are a great way to add nutrient-dense organ meats like liver and kidney to your diet! Simply grind the raw organ meat with a meat grinder or food processor and use it to replace some of the ground meat.

Meatballs in a Pig Blanket

2 pounds ground bison, beef, or venison (see Note)
2 large eggs
½ cup blanched almond flour
2 teaspoons chili powder
1 teaspoon garlic powder
½ teaspoon ground black pepper
About 1 pound bacon (depending on size of meatballs)

Orange Sesame Meatballs

2 pounds ground pork
2 large eggs
½ cup blanched almond flour
1 tablespoon grated orange zest
2 tablespoons freshly squeezed orange juice
2 tablespoons white sesame seeds
1 teaspoon kosher or sea salt
½ teaspoon garlic power

1. Preheat the oven to 350°F.

2. Mix the meat, eggs, and flour (if needed) by hand until thoroughly combined.

3. Add the spices, herbs, salt, and pepper and continue to mix until fully incorporated.

4. Roll rounded tablespoons of the mixture into balls and place on a rimmed baking sheet.

5. If making the Meatballs in a Pig Blanket, slice the bacon strips in half, then wrap a half around each meatball. Secure the bacon by piercing each meatball with a skewer or toothpick.

6. Place in the oven and bake for 25 to 30 minutes, until the meatballs reach the desired doneness.

7. Serve warm on toothpicks. Garnish the lamb meatballs with mint leaves, if desired.

☑ Egg-Free
☑ Nut-Free
☐ Nightshade-Free

This dish is an interpretation of our son Cole's favorite food: the mussels served as an appetizer at a local restaurant. He loves them so much that he'll order a whole appetizer for himself and eat all of it. Our kids fell in love with shellfish when we made it at home for the first time. Instead of talking about death, we focused on why it was cooked that way and how we could tell it was working. They've been hooked on helping with this dish ever since.

STEAMED MUSSELS IN TOMATO BROTH

SERVES: 4 TO 6

Ingredients

¼ cup olive oil

1 yellow onion, diced

4 cloves garlic, minced

¼ cup fresh parsley, chopped, plus more for garnish (optional)

¼ cup white wine

1 (28-ounce) can diced tomatoes, drained

2 pounds fresh mussels, scrubbed and debearded (see Note)

1. In a large pot, heat the oil over medium heat.

2. Add the onion and garlic and sauté until softened, about 5 minutes.

3. Stir in the parsley and wine and simmer for 1 minute.

4. Pour in the tomatoes and reduce the heat to medium-low. Simmer, covered, for 20 minutes.

5. Add the mussels, stir, and cover. Increase the heat to high and cook for 3 minutes.

6. Transfer the cooked mussels to a serving bowl, leaving any that did not open in the pot. Cover and cook for 1 more minute. Remove the lid and transfer any mussels that have opened to the serving bowl. Repeat as necessary for up to 6 minutes. Throw away any mussels that remain closed.

7. Pour the tomato broth over the mussels in the serving bowl. Garnish with chopped parsley, if desired, and serve.

Note: The mussels will be alive when you buy them, so make sure to leave them in a container that has air and plan to cook them within a day or two. Before cooking, pick over the mussels and discard any that are open and do not shut tight when tapped (which indicates that they have died). Unfortunately, this dish can't be made ahead or frozen for later. It is, however, a wonderful way to introduce your children to something different in the kitchen.

This is by far the absolute best method for making crispy chicken wings in the oven. There are a zillion recommended ways out there, but we can tell you that this is the one to try. Baking at a high temperature for a long time is the secret. No fryer is needed—we promise! With this method, chewy, soft wings will be a thing of the past, and your friends will beg you to tell them your secret.

CRISPY OVEN-BAKED CHICKEN WINGS

PREHEAT OVEN: 400°F · SERVES: 4 TO 6

Ingredients

	☑ Egg-Free ☑ Nut-Free ☑ Nightshade-Free	☑ Egg-Free ☑ Nut-Free ☐ Nightshade-Free	☑ Egg-Free ☑ Nut-Free ☐ Nightshade-Free
Basic Ingredients	*Lemon Garlic Sauce*	*Carolina-Style Sauce*	*Spicy Sauce*
20 chicken wing pieces (drumettes and wings), tips removed	½ cup lard or unsalted butter, melted	¼ cup unsalted butter, melted	½ cup Ketchup (page 120)
Salt and pepper to taste	2 teaspoons minced garlic	½ cup apple cider vinegar	1 tablespoon chili powder
	1 teaspoon grated lemon zest	1 tablespoon chili powder	1 teaspoon garlic powder
☑ Egg-Free ☑ Nut-Free ☐ Nightshade-Free	1 tablespoon freshly squeezed lemon juice	1 clove garlic, minced	1 teaspoon onion powder
Sweet BBQ Sauce		1 tablespoon prepared yellow mustard	1 teaspoon hot pepper sauce (such as Tabasco or Tessemae's Hot Sauce)
1 cup Apple Butter BBQ Sauce (page 112)			

Note: If you're in a hurry and don't want to make your own sauce, the salt and pepper base version of these wings are fantastic on their own. You can also toss them in your favorite store-bought hot sauce; we like Tessemae's products.

1. Preheat the oven to 400°F.

2. Using a paper towel, dry the chicken pieces thoroughly.

3. Place a rack inside a rimmed baking sheet and lay the chicken pieces in a single layer on the rack. Generously sprinkle with salt and pepper.

4. Place in the oven and roast for 1 hour.

5. Meanwhile, whisk together the ingredients for the sauce of your choice.

6. Toss the baked chicken pieces with the sauce in a large bowl and serve.

SIDES

Making vegetables interesting is often the biggest challenge for home cooks. We can certainly relate! How to make them interesting *and tasty,* even to children, is even more difficult. These dishes are some of our favorite ways to round out a meal. Pay close attention, and you may even find some unique ideas that will please the most anti-green members of your family.

	PHASE	PAGE #	UNDER 30 MIN	UNDER 5 INGREDIENTS	ONE POT	HOLIDAY	ON THE GO
Green Onion and Bacon Mac 'n' Cheese	3	238					
Veggie Lasagna	2	240					
Breakfast Puree	3	242	YES				
Cauli-Mash	3	244	YES	YES			
Cauli-Rice	3	246	YES	YES			
Green Bean Casserole	3	248				YES	
Biscuits	2	250				YES	YES
Baked Potato Soup	3	252			YES		
Creamed Kale	3	254	YES		YES		
Cucumber Salad	3	256	YES	YES	YES		
Spinach, Walnut, and Bacon Salad	3	258	YES	YES	YES		
Cauli-Gnocchi with Brussels Sprouts and Lemon Zest	3	260					
Tostadas	2	262					
Butternut Bisque	3	264					
Roasted Rainbow Carrots	3	266	YES	YES	YES		
Fried Sweet Plantains	2	268	YES	YES	YES		
Grilled Asparagus	3	270	YES	YES	YES		
Winter Salad	3	272	YES	YES	YES		
Sautéed Apples	2	274	YES	YES	YES		
Citrus Broccoli	3	276	YES	YES	YES		
Carrot Mash	3	278	YES	YES			
Caesar Salad	3	280	YES	YES	YES		
Garlic Breadsticks	2	282				YES	YES
Yuca Fries	2	284			YES		
Pickled Onion and Arugula Salad	3	286	YES	YES	YES		

We used to joke that the only meal we couldn't re-create using Paleo-friendly ingredients was macaroni and cheese. While this recipe includes neither mac nor cheese, it certainly reminds us of that childhood staple we never thought we could make again . . . until now.

GREEN ONION AND BACON MAC 'N' CHEESE

PREHEAT OVEN: 350°F · SERVES: 4 TO 6

Ingredients

1 medium butternut squash (about 1½ pounds), peeled, seeded, and shredded

2 large eggs

¼ cup blanched almond flour

1 tablespoon nutritional yeast

1 teaspoon dry mustard

1 teaspoon kosher or sea salt

¼ teaspoon ground black pepper

For the topping:

5 strips bacon, diced

3 green onions, sliced

½ cup blanched almond flour

¼ cup lard or fat of choice

1. Preheat the oven to 350°F.

2. In a bowl, combine the squash, eggs, almond flour, nutritional yeast, dry mustard, salt, and pepper and mix thoroughly by hand with a wooden spoon.

3. Press the mixture into the bottom of an 8-by-8-inch baking dish.

4. Make the topping: Fry the bacon in a skillet over medium heat until crispy. Transfer the bacon to a bowl. Add the green onions, almond flour, and lard and mix until crumbly.

5. Sprinkle the topping mixture over the top of the squash mixture.

6. Place in the oven and bake for 30 minutes, or until the top begins to brown.

Note: This recipe makes quite a bit of mac 'n' cheese, but it's great as leftovers and freezes well!

☑ Egg-Free

■ Nut-Free

■ Nightshade-Free

Whenever we have the opportunity to replace grain-based products with nutrient-dense vegetables, we take it! Veggie noodles make a surprisingly perfect substitute for lasagna noodles, and this carrot and zucchini lasagna is absolutely delicious without the wheat.

VEGGIE LASAGNA

PREHEAT OVEN: 350°F · SERVES: 4 TO 6

Ingredients

2 medium zucchini

4 carrots (as thick as you can find), peeled

2 cups tomato sauce, divided

2 cups Cashew Cheese Sauce (page 126)

2 tablespoons chopped fresh parsley

1. Preheat the oven to 350°F.

2. Cut off the ends of the zucchini and carrots. Using a mandoline, food slicer, vegetable peeler, or careful knife work, slice the zucchini and carrots lengthwise into very thin planks.

3. Blanch the zucchini and carrot "noodles" separately in boiling water for about 90 seconds each. Remove the noodles to a bowl of ice water to stop the cooking.

4. Set aside ¼ cup of the tomato sauce for the top, and then spread ¼ cup of the tomato sauce over the bottom of an 8-by-8-inch baking dish or 2-quart casserole dish.

5. Lay down a layer of the noodles, alternating carrots and zucchini.

6. Spread ¼ cup of the tomato sauce over the noodle layer.

7. Dollop several spoonfuls of the cheese sauce on top of the tomato sauce and spread it as evenly as possible.

8. Repeat with a layer of tomato sauce, noodles, and cheese sauce, until you have used all of the sauce and noodles. Finish with the reserved tomato sauce, and then sprinkle the parsley on top.

9. Place in the oven and bake for 30 minutes, until the top is browned slightly.

3

✓ Egg-Free
✓ Nut-Free
✓ Nightshade-Free

UNDER 30 MIN

If you want a change from eggs for breakfast, we recommend that you try soup or this veggie puree. The sweetness of the carrots and squash will remind you of pudding, but the nutrient-rich vegetables paired with protein, like bacon or Breakfast Sausage (page 164), will nourish your body for a busy day. Of course, it also makes a great side for dinner.

BREAKFAST PUREE

SERVES: 4

Ingredients

- 5 medium carrots, peeled and cut into 2-inch lengths
- 1 medium butternut squash (about 1½ pounds), peeled, seeded, and cubed
- ½ cup coconut milk (full-fat, canned or homemade, page 290)
- 3 tablespoons lard, ghee, or unsalted butter
- 1 tablespoon ground cinnamon
- 2 teaspoons kosher or sea salt
- ½ teaspoon ground nutmeg
- ¼ teaspoon ground black pepper

1. Steam the carrots and squash in a steaming basket over boiling water for 10 minutes, or until easily pierced with a fork.

2. Transfer the vegetables to a food processor and pulse to a lumpy mashed potato consistency, or purée until smooth if preferred. Alternatively, mash the vegetables by hand using a potato masher.

3. Add the rest of the ingredients and pulse or mash until fully combined. Serve warm in bowls.

Note: It is always preferable to steam your vegetables rather than boil them since boiling leaches the nutrients into the water instead of your body. For convenience, we use a special clay tagine in our microwave for steaming. You could also use a steamer or a steaming basket over boiling water. If you boil the vegetables, place the carrots and squash in a stockpot, cover with water, and bring to a boil over high heat. Boil, covered, for 10 minutes, and then drain and rinse with cold water.

SPECIAL TOOLS:

food processor (optional)　steaming basket (optional)

✓ Egg-Free
✓ Nut-Free
✓ Nightshade-Free

UNDER 30 MIN

under 5 INGREDIENTS

Once you know how to make a creamy, tasty vegetable puree or mash (see Make Paleo Mashes and Rices on page 50), you'll be serving one at every meal. We use mashes as bases for stews or braises or as side dishes by themselves several times a week. Super simple and versatile, they are quick and easy to pull together!

CAULI-MASH

SERVES: 4 TO 6

Ingredients

1 head cauliflower, cored, stems removed, and cut into florets

2 tablespoons bacon fat, ghee, lard, or unsalted butter

¼ cup coconut milk (full-fat, canned or homemade, page 290)

Salt and pepper to taste

SPECIAL TOOLS:

food processor

1. Steam the cauliflower for 10 minutes, or until it is easily pierced with a fork. You can either use a steaming basket over boiling water or microwave the florets in a covered microwave-safe bowl with a couple tablespoons of water. We recommend and use a clay tagine for microwaving.

2. Place the steamed cauliflower in a food processor and purée for 1 minute.

3. Add the fat, milk, and salt and pepper as the machine is running. When the mash reaches the desired consistency, stop the processor. Transfer to a serving bowl and serve warm, or store in an airtight container in the refrigerator for up to several days.

Note: Cauliflower is not great for creating a good lumpy mash like you may be used to from potatoes. If you desire a chunky texture, try half cauliflower and half turnip, or even half parsnip and turnip. Turnips and parsnips have a much more potato-like texture than cauliflower.

Cauliflower is the perfect replacement for rice; we use it all the time. Even if you still eat rice as a part of your personal Paleo template, adding Cauli-Rice to your table is an easy way to add more veggies to your diet.

CAULI-RICE

SERVES: 4 TO 6

Ingredients

☑ Egg-Free	☑ Egg-Free	◼ Egg-Free
☑ Nut-Free	☑ Nut-Free	☑ Nut-Free
☑ Nightshade-Free	◼ Nightshade-Free	☑ Nightshade-Free

Basic Ingredients	*Plain*	*Fiesta*	*Thai Fried*
½ medium head cauliflower, cored, stems removed, and cut into small florets	3 cups riced cauliflower (from basic ingredients)	2 tablespoons lard or fat of choice	2 tablespoons lard or fat of choice
		½ cup diced yellow bell pepper	1 pound (21 to 30) large shrimp, peeled and deveined
		½ cup diced red bell pepper	⅓ cup diced carrots
SPECIAL TOOLS:		1 jalapeño, seeds removed and finely chopped (optional)	⅓ cup diced onion
		½ cup diced red onion	3 cups riced cauliflower (from basic ingredients)
food processor		1 cup canned diced tomatoes, strained	2 large eggs
		3 cups riced cauliflower (from basic ingredients)	1 tablespoon coconut aminos or tamari
		Salt and pepper to taste	1½ tablespoons fish sauce
			1 teaspoon untoasted, cold-pressed sesame oil
			1 cup pineapple chunks
			20 fresh Thai basil leaves, sliced

1. To make riced cauliflower, place the cauliflower florets in a food processor and pulse until chopped into tiny grains. You should have 3 cups of riced cauliflower. It can be steamed to make Plain Cauli-Rice or used to make Fiesta Cauli-Rice or Thai Fried Cauli-Rice.

To make Plain Cauli-Rice:

1. Place the riced cauliflower in a microwaveable bowl with 2 tablespoons of water and cover. Microwave for 6 minutes, until easily pierced with a fork. Alternatively, use a cheesecloth-lined steaming basket and steam over a pot of boiling water for 6 minutes.

To make Fiesta Cauli-Rice:

1. In a medium saucepan, melt the lard over medium heat.

2. When hot, add the bell peppers, jalapeño, and onion and sauté until soft, about 6 minutes.

3. Add the tomatoes and stir to combine. Simmer for 5 minutes to reduce the liquid.

4. Add the riced cauliflower and stir to combine. Continue to simmer for 10 minutes, stirring frequently, until the rice is tender.

To make Thai Fried Cauli-Rice:

1. In a large skillet or wok, melt the lard over medium-high heat.

2. Add the shrimp and sauté until pink. Using a slotted spoon, remove the shrimp from the skillet and set aside.

3. Add the carrots and onion to the skillet and sauté over medium-high heat until softened, about 4 minutes. Add the riced cauliflower and continue to sauté for 1 minute.

4. Push the vegetables to the sides of the skillet to create a well in the center. Crack the eggs into the well and scramble until cooked. Toss the cooked eggs into the rest of the rice.

5. Add the coconut aminos, fish sauce, sesame oil, and pineapple and toss until heated through. Remove from the heat and stir in the basil leaves.

Before you ask about beans in a Paleo book, allow us to set your mind at ease. Rest assured that green beans are a legitimate vegetable. Not only are they low in the problematic phytates, but they're also nutrient-packed, with lots of vitamin C, vitamin K, and folate.

GREEN BEAN CASSEROLE

PREHEAT OVEN: 350°F · SERVES: 4 TO 6

Ingredients

- 2 pounds green beans, washed and trimmed
- 2 tablespoons lard or fat of choice
- ½ cup diced shallots
- 1 cup diced mushrooms
- 2 cloves garlic, minced
- 1 cup coconut milk (full-fat, canned or homemade, page 290)

1. Preheat the oven to 350°F.

2. In a pot of boiling water, boil the green beans for 90 seconds. Immediately drain in a colander and rinse with cold water to stop the cooking. Drain well.

3. In a large skillet, melt the lard over medium heat. Add the diced shallots and mushrooms and sauté until softened, about 5 minutes.

4. Add the garlic and sauté for 1 minute.

5. Pour in the coconut milk, reduce the heat to medium-low, and simmer for about 10 minutes, until thickened.

6. Add the green beans to the skillet and toss to coat in the sauce. Transfer the contents of the skillet to a 9-inch-square baking dish. Bake for 30 minutes, or until the top is slightly browned.

Note: A great classic dish for the holidays, Green Bean Casserole is incredibly comforting at any time of year.

We first made these biscuits for a Thanksgiving feast and have continued to serve them at every special occasion since then. Wonderful paired with soups and stews, like this paprikosh (page 310), they also work on the brunch table with Apple and Pumpkin Butters (page 110).

BISCUITS

PREHEAT OVEN: 450°F · MAKES: 6 BISCUITS

Ingredients

- ½ cup lard
- 1 cup blanched almond flour
- ½ cup tapioca flour
- ⅓ cup coconut flour
- 1 teaspoon baking soda
- ½ teaspoon kosher or sea salt
- ⅔ cup coconut milk (full-fat, canned or homemade, page 290)
- 2 tablespoons honey
- 1 large egg white

1. Preheat the oven to 450°F. Line a baking sheet with parchment paper.

2. Form a square-shaped, ½-inch-thick mound with the lard. Place it on wax paper, and put it in the freezer for at least 15 minutes to chill.

3. Meanwhile, in a large mixing bowl, sift the flours, baking soda, and salt and whisk to evenly distribute.

4. Dice the very cold lard into small pieces. Work quickly and avoid touching it so that it doesn't warm from your hands. If the lard is no longer cold after cutting, put it back in the freezer for a few minutes.

5. Cut the lard into the dry ingredients with a pastry cutter or fork until crumbly, but will stick if pinched with fingers.

6. Combine the coconut milk and honey in a separate bowl and pour over the dry ingredients. Mix with a rubber spatula until smooth and completely wet.

7. In a separate small bowl, whip the egg white until soft peaks form. For ease, use an electric hand-held mixer or a stand mixer.

8. Fold the egg whites into the dough with a spatula until well combined.

9. Scoop out ⅓ cup of the dough at a time and form into rounds by hand. Or, if perfect biscuits are desired, flour the work surface and a rolling pin lightly with tapioca flour and roll out the dough to ½ inch thick. Cut into biscuits using a round biscuit cutter. Gather up the scraps of dough, reroll, and cut the remaining biscuits.

10. Place the biscuits, 2 inches apart, on the prepared baking sheet. Place in the oven and bake for 12 minutes, until golden brown. Let cool on the sheet for 10 minutes before serving. Store at room temperature in an airtight container for up to a week.

✓ Egg-Free
✓ Nut-Free
✓ Nightshade-Free

ONE POT

Traditional baked potato soup is a thick cream-based soup with potato fixings: bacon, chives, sour cream . . . deliciousness. Missing this incredible treat from our favorite steakhouse, we set out to create our own version. Our trick to this creamy soup is using vegetables as the thickener. In place of potatoes, we use turnips, their better, buttery-tasting cousins, with a bit of creamy cauliflower puree. We find that this nutrient-dense soup with bacon and chives is popular even with those who don't like veggies. It's so creamy, you'll never know that it's missing dairy!

BAKED POTATO SOUP

SERVES: 4 TO 6

Ingredients

5 strips bacon, diced

4 turnips (about 1½ pounds), peeled and cubed, divided

½ pound cauliflower, cut into small florets

1 yellow onion, diced

8 cups Stock, chicken recommended (page 132)

½ cup coconut cream from chilled full-fat coconut milk (see Note)

2 tablespoons chopped fresh chives

SPECIAL TOOLS:

blender · OR · immersion blender

1. In a stockpot, fry the bacon pieces over medium heat until crispy. Using a slotted spoon, remove the bacon to a paper towel–lined plate to drain.

2. Pour off all but about 2 tablespoons of the bacon fat and return the skillet to medium heat.

3. Sauté half of the turnip pieces, the cauliflower, and the onion in the hot bacon fat for 10 minutes, stirring frequently.

4. Pour in the stock and stir. Bring to a boil over high heat.

5. After it boils for 3 minutes, reduce the heat to medium-low and simmer for 5 minutes.

6. Using an immersion blender, or in a regular blender in batches, purée the cooked turnips, cauliflower, and onion until smooth, and then return to the pot.

7. Add the remaining turnips and coconut cream and continue to simmer until the turnips are easily pierced with a fork, about 20 minutes.

8. Serve topped with the bacon and chives.

Note: *To extract coconut cream from full-fat coconut milk, place the can(s) of coconut milk in the refrigerator the night before you plan to use the cream. Open the can and skim off the thick cream that has risen to the top. To get the ½ cup of coconut cream needed for this recipe, you will need 1 (13½-ounce) can of full-fat coconut milk.*

✓ Egg-Free
✓ Nut-Free
✓ Nightshade-Free

UNDER 30 MIN
ONE POT

Kale may be a fad food these days, but there is a very good reason for its popularity. This humble leaf is one of the most nutrient-packed vegetables you can find in the supermarket. Not only does it have comparable calcium as a glass of milk, but it's also a good source of vitamins K and A.

CREAMED KALE

SERVES: 4 TO 6

Ingredients

2 tablespoons lard or fat of choice

1 bunch kale (about 1 pound), stems removed, cut into 2-inch pieces (about 4 cups)

½ teaspoon kosher or sea salt

½ teaspoon garlic powder

½ teaspoon ground nutmeg

⅛ teaspoon ground black pepper

1 cup coconut milk (full-fat, canned or homemade, page 290)

1. Melt the lard in a large skillet (we use our cast-iron skillet) over medium heat.

2. Add the kale and sauté until it begins to soften, about 6 minutes.

3. Add the salt and spices and stir to coat the kale pieces.

4. Pour in the coconut milk and stir to incorporate.

5. Simmer for 10 minutes, stirring occasionally to prevent burning.

6. When the kale is completely wilted and the coconut milk has thickened and coats the back of a spoon, remove from the heat and serve.

Note: Because greens cook down so much, we recommend serving this dish with another side during a meal or doubling the recipe; however, you'll need a very large pan to cook 8 cups of kale.

☑ Egg-Free
☑ Nut-Free
☑ Nightshade-Free

Cucumbers are often a player in salads all over the world, but they deserve the spotlight from time to time. Sweet cucumber paired with tangy vinegar makes a delicious and easy salad. A great make-ahead dish that gets better with time, we love to serve this with our Eastern Market Shrimp Salad (page 352).

Ingredients

4 cups (¼-inch-thick) cucumber slices

1 red onion, diced

⅓ cup apple cider vinegar

¼ cup olive oil or avocado oil

Salt and pepper to taste

CUCUMBER SALAD

SERVES: 4 TO 6

1. Toss together all of the ingredients in a serving bowl. Serve chilled.

Note: We like to use thin-skinned English cucumbers, which allows us to leave the peel on. If you use traditional garden-variety cucumbers, we recommend peeling off most of the skin and leaving just a small percentage on for a pop of color and texture.

☑ Egg-Free
■ Nut-Free
☑ Nightshade-Free

UNDER 30 MIN

under 5 INGREDIENTS

ONE POT

Having written a book called *Beyond Bacon,* we're quite familiar with the ins and outs of bacon preparation. But strangely, this kind of hot and cold salad never occurred to us before. This is an excellent way to ease extra vegetables into your diet with the ever-popular bacon, the duct tape of the kitchen.

SPINACH, WALNUT, AND BACON SALAD

SERVES: 2 TO 4

Ingredients

5 strips bacon

1 pound baby spinach, washed and dried

½ cup raw walnut halves, coarsely chopped

For the dressing:

Your favorite salad dressing (see page 124 for ideas) or a good-quality oil and vinegar

1. Cut the bacon crosswise into ¼-inch-wide strips (aka lardons).

2. In a large skillet over medium heat, fry the bacon until brown and crispy, stirring frequently. Remove from the pan to a paper towel–lined plate to drain briefly.

3. In a bowl, quickly toss the raw baby spinach with the hot bacon, walnuts, and your favorite salad dressing. Or simply dress the salad with a drizzle of avocado oil or olive oil and a splash of vinegar.

Note: Use your imagination to enhance this salad. We loved to add diced dates, dried cranberries, or sliced strawberries and toss it with our Berry Balsamic Dressing (page 124).

Gnocchi are tiny pasta balls that are boiled and often pan-fried. In a gluten-free world, this is very difficult to replicate. But you'll find this versatile cauliflower-based dough perfect for a variety of uses, including Braunschweiger Burger Sliders (page 216) and Nona's Paprikosh (page 310). Want to make this a main dish? Instead of Brussels sprouts, these would also be good in marinara sauce with sausage (page 164).

CAULI-GNOCCHI WITH BRUSSELS SPROUTS AND LEMON ZEST

Ingredients

For the cauli-gnocchi dough:

1 cup cauliflower florets, steamed and puréed

2 cups tapioca flour

2 cups blanched almond flour

2 large eggs

1 teaspoon garlic powder

1 teaspoon kosher or sea salt

½ teaspoon ground black pepper

12 Brussels sprouts

2 tablespoons lard or fat of choice

Grated zest of 1 lemon

1 tablespoon freshly squeezed lemon juice

SERVES: 4 TO 6

1. Make the Cauli-Gnocchi dough: In a food processor or blender, blend all of the ingredients until a smooth dough forms.

2. Bring a pot of water to a boil.

3. To form the gnocchi: Using your hands, form the dough into cylindrical shapes, about 1 inch long and ½ inch wide. Drop the gnocchi into the boiling water and cook for 2 to 3 minutes, or until they float to the surface.

4. Using a slotted spoon, remove the cooked gnocchi to a paper towel to dry.

5. Meanwhile, to prepare the Brussels sprouts: Cut the stems off the sprouts and separate the leaves.

6. In a large skillet, melt the lard over medium heat.

7. Fry the gnocchi in the lard until browned on all sides. Add the Brussels sprout leaves and sauté until softened, about 3 to 5 minutes.

8. Remove from the heat and add the lemon zest and juice.

SPECIAL TOOLS:

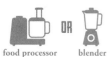

food processor   **OR**   blender

Yes, you can make a wrap with gluten-free flours. Well, okay, they won't be stretchy, but they will be delicious! We love these tasty flatbreads, akin to traditional tostadas, and find that they are great for a variety of uses, especially with our Beef Tongue Carnitas (page 350). Though pliable, no gluten-free dough is perfect. Have patience and pinch them back together if they crack.

TOSTADAS

MAKES: ABOUT 1 DOZEN TOSTADAS

Ingredients

1 cup blanched almond flour

1 cup tapioca flour, plus more to dust the dough

¾ cup coconut flour

1 teaspoon baking soda

1 teaspoon white vinegar

6 tablespoons lard or palm shortening

1 cup warm water

1. In a stand mixer fitted with a paddle attachment, cut together the flours, baking soda, and vinegar with the lard.

2. When you have a crumbly mixture, add the water and mix until a sticky dough forms. Allow the dough to rest for 10 minutes.

3. Preheat a dry, well-seasoned cast-iron skillet over medium heat.

4. Scoop ¼ cup of the dough and form by hand into a disk shape.

5. Flour the dough with tapioca flour and place it between 2 sheets of parchment paper. Roll it out into a 4-inch-wide, ⅛-inch-thick circle, turning it 45 degrees as you go to roll it out evenly.

6. Carefully transfer your tostadas to the skillet (see the Note below for guidance). Cook for 1 minute, and then flip. Cook for another minute and then remove to a plate.

7. Repeat Steps 4 to 6 until you have used all of the dough. If the tostadas crack and break, they're still tasty. And the more you make them, the more you'll get used to perfecting the size and temperature to keep them firm and together as they cook.

Note: The hardest part of this recipe is getting the tostadas into and out of the pan. Peel off one sheet of the parchment paper and then flop the tostada from upside down into the pan. When turning, use a large spatula to help prevent the tostada from breaking.

During the late fall months, butternut squash begins to appear on supermarket shelves. There is no better way to weather October cold spells than with a thick and rich soup topped with crispy bacon crumbles.

BUTTERNUT BISQUE

SERVES: 4 TO 6

Ingredients

2 tablespoons lard or fat of choice

1 medium butternut squash (about 1½ pounds), peeled, seeded, and cubed

1 medium head cauliflower, cored, stems removed, and cut into florets

1 yellow onion, sliced

¼ cup white wine or apple juice

4 cups Stock, beef recommended (page 132)

2 cups water

1 teaspoon kosher or sea salt

2 teaspoons ground cinnamon

1 teaspoon ground nutmeg

¾ teaspoon ginger powder

¼ teaspoon ground cloves

¼ teaspoon ground white pepper

8 strips bacon

SPECIAL TOOLS:

blender   OR   immersion blender

1. In a stockpot, melt the lard over medium heat.

2. Add the squash, cauliflower, and onion and sweat until slightly softened, stirring occasionally, about 8 minutes.

3. Add the wine to deglaze the pan. Simmer for 3 minutes.

4. Add the stock and water and bring to a boil over high heat.

5. Reduce the heat to medium-low and cover. Simmer for 60 minutes or until the vegetables are very soft.

6. Remove the cover and use an immersion blender to purée the soup until smooth. Alternatively, you can purée it in batches in a regular blender or food processor.

7. Add the salt and spices and continue to simmer while you cook the bacon.

8. Fry the bacon in a cast-iron skillet over medium heat for about 10 minutes, flipping halfway through. When crispy, remove to a paper towel–lined plate to drain.

9. Serve the soup in bowls and crumble the bacon over the top.

Note: If you're short on time, almost all grocery stores sell prepackaged peeled and cubed raw butternut squash in the produce section.

✓ Egg-Free
✓ Nut-Free
✓ Nightshade-Free

UNDER 30 MIN

under 5 **INGREDIENTS**

ONE POT

If there is one thing nature is superb at, it's creating beautiful variety. Roasted carrots can be an elegant side dish, particularly when you use the rainbow of hues that carrots come in to full advantage. Of course, regular orange carrots will work, too. However, not only do rainbow carrots offer additional beauty, but the variety in color means variations in nutrients.

ROASTED RAINBOW CARROTS

PREHEAT OVEN: 350°F · SERVES: 2 TO 4

Ingredients

- 1 dozen medium rainbow carrots, stems on preferred
- 2 tablespoons melted lard or fat of choice
- ½ teaspoon ground cumin
- ½ teaspoon kosher or sea salt
- ⅛ teaspoon ground black pepper

1. Preheat the oven to 350°F.

2. Chop off most of the carrot stems, leaving about 1 inch on the end. Peel the carrots.

3. Toss the carrots with the melted lard, cumin, salt, and pepper until coated.

4. Lay the carrots in a single layer in a medium baking dish.

5. Place in the oven and roast for about 25 minutes, or until the carrots are soft to the touch and begin to turn brown and caramelize.

Note: Use this technique and recipe to enhance the sweetness of any vegetable. We love all root vegetables roasted, but Brussels sprouts are a family favorite. Trust us, the kids beg for roasted Brussels sprouts!

✓ Egg-Free
✓ Nut-Free
✓ Nightshade-Free

UNDER 30 MIN

under 5 INGREDIENTS

ONE POT

If you're not familiar with them, plantains might strike you as odd bananas that aren't even all that sweet. But they are so much more than that! These starchy fruits are wonderful when fried and make a more interesting carbohydrate than your typical root vegetable. Although it is fantastic with our Peruvian Chicken (page 342), this dish goes great with almost anything.

FRIED SWEET PLANTAINS

SERVES: 4 TO 6

Ingredients

½ to 1 cup avocado oil or coconut oil

2 ripe yellow plantains

1 teaspoon kosher or sea salt

1 teaspoon ground cinnamon (optional)

1. Heat the oil in a wide, deep cast-iron skillet over medium heat. The oil should be deep enough to come halfway up the sides of the plantain slices.

2. Cut each plantain into thirds, and then slice each piece in half lengthwise.

3. Fry each piece until brown and soft, about 4 minutes per side. Remove from the oil and place on a paper towel–lined plate. Sprinkle with the salt and cinnamon, if using. Serve hot.

Note: Sweet plantains are prepared when the plantains have turned completely yellow and have just begun to brown. They are akin to the overripe bananas often called for in banana breads.

✓ Egg-Free
✓ Nut-Free
✓ Nightshade-Free

When our nephew stayed with us, we never realized that asparagus, his favorite vegetable, would appear so often on our plates. We quickly identified the best and easiest ways to prepare the green spears, including using them as a side in our summer grilling exploits. This dish is perfect for weeknight dinners but can be made fancy with our Hollandaise Sauce (page 118).

GRILLED ASPARAGUS

PREHEAT GRILL: MEDIUM · SERVES: 4 TO 6

1. Preheat the grill to medium.

2. Snap off the tough ends of each asparagus spear and lay on a 24-inch-long sheet of aluminum foil. Turn up the edges of the foil to form a rim.

3. Toss the asparagus spears with the oil and salt and pepper. Spread out the spears on the foil in a single layer, leaving several inches of foil empty on each end.

4. Cover with a second piece of foil and roll over the edges on all sides to seal.

5. Place on the highest rack on the grill and roast for about 20 minutes, until the spears are tender but still have a bite to them.

Note: Alternatively, you can make this dish in the oven. Simply lay the asparagus on a baking sheet and follow the same step of coating with oil and seasoning with salt and pepper. Then roast at 350°F for 20 minutes.

Ingredients

2 pounds asparagus (2 bunches)

2 tablespoons olive oil or avocado oil

Salt and pepper to taste

SPECIAL TOOLS:

grill

✓ Egg-Free
■ Nut-Free
✓ Nightshade-Free

Sometimes you just want something new and different from a traditional green salad. Occasionally, we add diced, roasted winter squash, such as acorn or butternut squash, to add a bit of bright color and interesting flavor. This Winter Salad is certainly a mishmash, but sometimes combining disparate flavors delivers impressive results.

WINTER SALAD

SERVES: 2 TO 4

Ingredients

1 cup each baby spinach, baby arugula, and baby radicchio or other greens of choice

½ cup diced and roasted butternut squash

3 mandarin oranges, sectioned

⅓ cup raw almonds, sliced

¼ cup Berry Balsamic Dressing (page 124) or dressing of choice

1. Toss together the spinach, arugula, radicchio, squash, oranges, and almonds and top with the dressing. If taking this salad on the go, pour the dressing in the bottom of the bowl and toss just before serving.

Note: The "culinary" thing to do with the orange sections is to supreme them—that is, to remove the whitish membrane from around the "meat" of the orange. You may, of course, do this and will likely prefer the oranges that way.

✓ Egg-Free
✓ Nut-Free
✓ Nightshade-Free

UNDER 30 MIN

under 5 INGREDIENTS

ONE POT

Pork is often served with apples, and when this recipe is paired with our Blueberry Sage Breakfast Sausage (page 164), it is our breakfast take on this classic flavor combination. Sautéed in flavorful fat, these apples have the perfect texture to accompany the meat and will in no way remind you of baby food. This dish also pairs perfectly with our Slow-Roasted Pork Shoulder (page 332).

SAUTÉED APPLES

SERVES: 2 TO 4

Ingredients

2 tablespoons coconut oil, ghee, or unsalted butter

2 apples, peeled, cored, and sliced into 8 wedges each

1 teaspoon ground cinnamon

½ teaspoon kosher or sea salt

1. Melt the coconut oil in a large skillet over medium heat.

2. Add the apples and toss to coat in the oil. Sauté, stirring frequently, until completely softened, about 10 minutes.

3. Transfer to a serving dish and toss with the cinnamon and salt. These apples are best served warm.

✓ Egg-Free
✓ Nut-Free
✓ Nightshade-Free

UNDER **30** MIN

under 5
INGREDIENTS

ONE POT

Back in 1990, George Bush the elder, president at the time, declared that he didn't like broccoli and would never eat it again. At the time, this was extremely confusing to a young Matt, who considered broccoli to be the best of all the vegetables. The president may or may not have received a handwritten letter to this effect. Perhaps President Bush just needed to try this version, which pairs well with our Sage and Citrus Roast Chicken (page 306).

CITRUS BROCCOLI

SERVES: 2 TO 4

1. Steam the broccoli until tender but not mushy, about 8 minutes. You can either use a steaming basket over boiling water or microwave the broccoli in a covered microwave-safe bowl with a couple tablespoons of water. We recommend and use a clay tagine for microwaving.

2. Drain and toss with the remaining ingredients.

Ingredients

1 pound broccoli spears (about 1 head)

1 tablespoon olive or avocado oil

Grated zest of 1 lemon

Juice of 1 lemon

½ teaspoon kosher or sea salt

⅛ teaspoon ground black pepper

SPECIAL TOOLS:

steaming
basket
(optional)

3

✓ Egg-Free
✓ Nut-Free
✓ Nightshade-Free

UNDER 30 MIN

under 5
INGREDIENTS

Carrots are one of our family's favorite vegetables. A large bag of organic carrots is one of the most affordable produce items we buy, so they are usually on our table at least once a week. Making them into a mash is a great way to change it up a bit. If you think of carrots only as a portable snack to munch on, mashing them with coconut milk and spices will change your mind.

CARROT MASH

SERVES: 4 TO 6

Ingredients

- 2 pounds carrots, peeled and cut into large chunks
- ¼ cup coconut milk (full-fat, canned or homemade, page 290)
- 2 tablespoons lard or fat of choice
- 1 teaspoon ground nutmeg
- ½ teaspoon kosher or sea salt
- ⅛ teaspoon ground black pepper

1. Steam the carrots until soft and easily pierced with a fork, about 10 minutes. You can either use a steaming basket over boiling water or microwave the carrots in a covered microwave-safe bowl with a couple tablespoons of water. We recommend and use a clay tagine for microwaving.

2. In a large bowl, mash the carrots to the desired consistency. Alternatively, place them in a food processor and purée until smooth.

3. Add the remaining ingredients and stir to incorporate.

SPECIAL TOOLS:

steaming basket (optional)

food processor (optional)

Egg-Free
☑ Nut-Free
☑ Nightshade-Free

UNDER 30 MIN

under 5 INGREDIENTS

ONE POT

We once went on a cruise ship and spent a week being able to eat anything we wanted off of a vast menu. While the kitchen staff went out of their way to provide us with Paleo-friendly options, they weren't very varied after a couple of days on the ship. But there was one dish they made for us that we ate over and over again and still love to this day: Caesar salad, hold the croutons, extra anchovies!

CAESAR SALAD

SERVES: 2 TO 4

Ingredients

1 romaine heart, sliced into ½-inch strips

½ cup shredded carrots

1 (4½-ounce) can anchovies in oil, drain and rinsed (see Note)

Sprinkle of nutritional yeast (see page 174)

¼ to ½ cup Caesar Dressing (page 124)

1. In a serving bowl, toss together all of the ingredients, ensuring that all of the lettuce leaves get an even coat of dressing.

2. Serve immediately, as the dressed salad will wilt over time. If you'd like to take this salad to a party, add the dressing to the bottom of the bowl and then, upon your arrival, add the remaining ingredients, toss, and serve.

Note: Although you may think that you don't like anchovies, these salty fish pack a big nutritional punch and are definitely worth trying. Just cut them up into little pieces and they'll be like salty bites of heaven.

Now that we've taught you to make lasagna (pages 240 and 362) and pasta (page 340), you're going to want breadsticks to go with them, right? This simple dough makes exactly the breadstick you never thought you'd eat again. The big surprise? It's made with cauliflower! When you serve these breadsticks with tomato sauce (we love Middle Earth Organics), you'll feel like you're eating a real Italian appetizer.

GARLIC BREADSTICKS

PREHEAT OVEN: 350°F · SERVES: 6 TO 8

1. Preheat the oven to 350°F. Line a baking sheet with parchment paper.

2. In a food processor, combine the cauliflower puree, flours, baking soda, eggs, garlic powder, salt, and pepper until a dough forms.

3. Place the dough in a pastry bag fitted with a ½-inch-wide circular tip or in a plastic zip-top bag with a corner cut off.

4. Squeeze out the dough into 4-by-½-inch breadsticks (or your desired shape) onto the prepared baking sheet.

5. Brush the tops of the breadsticks with the melted butter, ghee, or lard. Place in the oven and bake for 15 minutes or until the tops are golden brown. Serve warm. Store in an airtight container in the refrigerator for up to a week.

Note: For extra garlic flavor, work some slivered Roasted Garlic (page 130) into the dough in the food processor. For a cheesy flavor, sprinkle the buttered dough with a very light dusting of nutritional yeast before baking.

Ingredients

- 1 cup cauliflower florets, steamed and puréed
- 2 cups tapioca flour
- 2 cups blanched almond flour
- 1 teaspoon baking soda
- 2 large eggs
- 1 teaspoon garlic powder
- 1 teaspoon kosher or sea salt
- ½ teaspoon ground black pepper
- 2 tablespoons unsalted butter, ghee, or lard, melted

SPECIAL TOOLS:

food processor

Move over, white potatoes; yuca fries are more interesting and tasty! Often found in Latin restaurants, yuca fries have become a family favorite for their unique fluffy inside texture and crisp outer crunch. Pair them with our Peruvian Chicken (page 342) and Fried Sweet Plantains (page 268), and you will be a believer, too!

YUCA FRIES

PREHEAT OVEN: 350°F · SERVES: 4 TO 6

Ingredients

1 yuca, peeled and cut into 1-x-1-x-3-inch fries (see Note)

2 cups lard, avocado oil, or coconut oil

Kosher or sea salt to taste

For serving:

1 batch Garlic and Herb Aioli (page 122), or other dipping sauce of choice

SPECIAL TOOLS:

Deep-fryer or deep, heavy-bottomed pot

fryer

1. Bring a pot of water to a boil over high heat.

2. Boil the yuca for 10 minutes until softened.

3. Heat the fat in an electric deep-fryer or deep, heavy-bottomed pot to 350°F over medium heat. When the fat comes to temperature, reduce the heat and watch the temperature so that it stays as close to 350°F as possible.

4. Fry the yuca spears in batches, only 6 or so at a time, for about 6 minutes or until golden brown.

5. Remove from the oil and set on a paper towel–lined cooling rack to drain the excess oil. Sprinkle each batch with salt while still hot.

6. Serve warm with the aioli or the dipping sauce of your choice.

Note: Yuca is very long and very knotty, making peeling and slicing a bit challenging. To make this task easier, chop your yuca into 3-inch sections first and handle each section individually.

✓ Egg-Free
✓ Nut-Free
✓ Nightshade-Free

UNDER 30 MIN

under 5 INGREDIENTS

ONE POT

In an iceberg lettuce world, we're always looking for unique salads to toss together for more color and nutrients. After we began making our delicious Pickled Onions (page 128), it seemed natural to use them to enhance our favorite lettuce—arugula! This salad goes wonderfully with leftover Slow-Roasted Pork Shoulder (page 332) or Pork Belly Bites (page 224).

PICKLED ONION AND ARUGULA SALAD

SERVES: 4 TO 6

Ingredients

2½ cups arugula

1 cup Pickled Onions (page 128)

1 tablespoon freshly squeezed lemon juice

1 tablespoon olive oil or avocado oil

Salt and pepper to taste

1. In a medium mixing bowl, toss together all of the ingredients.

2. Serve immediately, as the dressed salad will wilt over time.

Note: This salad comes together so quickly that we recommend having pickled onions on hand for last-minute dinners. It will wow guests and is simple enough for everyday.

DRINKS

For the most part, we drink water. But that doesn't mean we don't enjoy a tasty beverage on occasion. This section will teach you how to make drinks special—even the humble glass of water.

	PHASE	PAGE #	UNDER 30 MIN	under 5 INGREDIENTS	ONE POT	HOLIDAY	ON the GO
Almond Milk	2	290		YES			YES
Coconut Milk	2	290	YES	YES			YES
Chai Thai Iced Tea	1	292				YES	YES
Eggnog	1	294			YES	YES	YES
Salted Caramel Frappé	1	296	YES		YES		YES
Iced Mocha	1	298	YES		YES		YES
Peppermint Hot Chocolate	1	300	YES	YES	YES	YES	
Flavored Water	3	302	YES	YES	YES		YES

Over the years, people have become conditioned to drinking something other than water when they are thirsty, forgetting that, until about 6,000 years ago, when the Egyptians invented beer, water was about the only thing humans drank. While we do not drink dairy, we often use coconut milk or almond milk in our recipes and recommend that you make your own using this method. Of course, as you transition or when you want something creamy, these milks are wonderful to drink, too.

COCONUT MILK AND ALMOND MILK

MAKES: ABOUT 1 QUART

Ingredients

Almond Milk

☑ Egg-Free
◼ Nut-Free
☑ Nightshade-Free

2 cups raw almonds
4 cups boiling water

Coconut Milk   `UNDER 30 MIN`

☑ Egg-Free
☑ Nut-Free
☑ Nightshade-Free

3 cups unsweetened shredded coconut
4 cups boiling water

SPECIAL TOOLS:

blender

1. If making Almond Milk, place the almonds in a bowl and cover the almonds with cold water. Place in the fridge overnight or up to 24 hours, until the brown skins can easily be rubbed off. Drain the water and rinse the nuts. Remove the skins by rubbing the almonds between your thumb and forefinger, until the entire batch consists of smooth skinless almonds. Rinse again if needed. Alternatively, you can purchase blanched almonds.

2. Place the skinned almonds or coconut in a high-speed blender and pour the boiling water over the top. (A food processor will also work but will not grind the almonds or coconut nearly as finely, resulting in a thinner milk.)

3. Blend on high for about 5 minutes, or until the almonds or coconut are well puréed.

4. Allow to cool for about 10 minutes.

5. Strain the milk through a cheesecloth-lined strainer into a 1-quart jar with a sealable lid; a wide-mouth mason jar is best. Press all the liquid out of the pulp until completely dry.

6. Store the milk in the refrigerator for up to a week. The pulp will last in the fridge for 3 days or so and can be used in other recipes (see Note).

Notes: You can save the almond pulp for Almond Meal Crackers (page 182). Or use the coconut pulp in Coconut Butter (page 114) by simply dehydrating the pulp on low heat until the shreds are dry again. Looking for a sweeter version? Try adding soft Medjool dates and pure vanilla extract in Step 5 for a sweetened vanilla milk that is much healthier than store-bought.

If you want to impress your party guests, you can't go wrong with this layered beverage. The trick is to prepare the ingredients ahead of time, which makes serving this elegant drink super quick and easy. We love it because the coconut milk makes it slightly sweet, yet it has only 2 tablespoons of honey for 12 servings. This pairs wonderfully with our "Want to Try Some Thai?" menu (page 85).

CHAI THAI ICED TEA

MAKES: 10 TO 12 (8-OUNCE) SERVINGS

Ingredients

10 chai teabags (see Note)

2 quarts boiling water

Ice

2 (13½-ounce) cans full-fat coconut milk or 3½ cups homemade (page 290)

1 tablespoon pure vanilla extract

½ teaspoon ground cloves

Grated zest of 1 orange

2 tablespoons raw or creamed honey

For serving:

Ground allspice, for garnish

1. Place the teabags in a 1-gallon pitcher and pour the boiling water over the teabags. Steep for 10 minutes.

2. Remove the teabags and fill the rest of the pitcher with cold water and ice. Refrigerate while you make the coconut milk syrup.

3. In a medium saucepan over medium heat, whisk together the coconut milk, vanilla, cloves, and orange zest.

4. Once the milk comes to a boil, reduce the heat to medium-low and simmer for 40 minutes, until thickened, stirring every few minutes.

5. When the milk coats the whisk, remove from the heat and allow to cool for 2 minutes.

6. Stir in the honey, and then pour into a sealable container and chill for 2 hours.

7. To serve, fill a 16-ounce glass with ice, and then fill it two-thirds full with the iced tea. Fill the remainder of the glass with the chilled coconut milk mixture and sprinkle with a pinch of allspice.

Note: You can find chai at any regular grocery store. Usually it is made by flavoring black tea. But some versions use Rooibos tea as the base, which is caffeine-free, making it a good option if you want to make this drink kid-friendly.

☐ Egg-Free
☐ Nut-Free
☑ Nightshade-Free

ONE POT
HOLIDAY
ON the GO

SPECIAL TOOLS:

food processor   blender

Ingredients

2 cups coconut milk (full-fat, canned or homemade, page 290)

2 cups Almond Milk (page 290)

½ cup maple syrup

1 teaspoon pure vanilla extract

1 teaspoon ground cinnamon

1 teaspoon freshly grated nutmeg, plus more for garnish

⅛ teaspoon ground allspice

4 large pastured egg yolks

Note: This nog can be used to replace full-fat coconut milk in many of our sweet recipes that call for it. It makes excellent ice cream and is a great replacement for cream in coffee, too!

To call us eggnog devotees would be an understatement. We used to mark the holiday season not by a calendar, but by when supermarkets would start to receive their eggnog shipments. Then we would purchase it by the gallon. With that gluttonous, unhealthy behavior now relatively under control, we still love this traditional holiday beverage and make our own special coconut milk version.

We offer two versions of this recipe: cooked and uncooked. For those using eggs of unknown quality or who are very concerned about food-borne pathogens in raw egg yolks, it's probably better to make the cooked version for safety's sake. But for those who want to experience the thickest, most delicious version of this drink, it's worth finding a reputable pastured egg purveyor and skipping the stove.

EGGNOG

MAKES: 4 (8-OUNCE) SERVINGS

To make raw nog (recommended):

1. In a blender or food processor, process all of the ingredients on high speed for 2 minutes, until the egg yolks are fully incorporated.

2. Serve chilled with freshly grated nutmeg on top.

To make cooked nog:

1. In a large saucepan, combine all of the ingredients except the egg yolks. Warm over medium heat for about 5 minutes, but stop before it starts to simmer.

2. Meanwhile, in a medium mixing bowl, whisk the egg yolks by hand until they are an even light yellow.

3. While whisking constantly, temper the egg yolks by slowly pouring 1 cup of the warmed milk mixture into the yolks. Repeat until about half of the milk has been whisked into the yolks.

4. Pour the tempered egg yolks back into the saucepan and whisk to combine.

5. Continue to heat for another 5 minutes, but do not boil. Use a candy thermometer to ensure that the temperature does not go above 160°F.

6. Chill in the fridge for at least an hour. Serve cold with freshly grated nutmeg on top.

✓ Egg-Free

☐ Nut-Free

✓ Nightshade-Free

UNDER 30 MIN

ONE POT

ON the GO

One of the most unhealthy things to start your day with is that famous coffee milkshake that features tons of sugar and chemicals and very little coffee. Inspired by our coffee-fiend friends, we tried to capture the essence of that thick frozen drink with this healthier version of a salted caramel–flavored smoothie. Of course, it's still a treat and not an everyday food.

SALTED CARAMEL FRAPPÉ

MAKES: 2 (10-OUNCE) SERVINGS

1. In a high-speed blender, purée all of the ingredients until smooth. If you do not have a high-speed blender, we recommend that you first purée the dates in a food processor and then transfer the puree to a standard blender. With the machine running, slowly add the liquids until combined, and then add the remaining ingredients and blend until smooth.

2. Divide the frappé between 2 large glasses. We love using mason jars to make this feel extra special.

Note: As you transition to a Paleo lifestyle, your palate will likely change. If this drink becomes too sweet for you, omit the maple syrup and try it with fewer dates for a less sweet treat.

Ingredients

5 soft Medjool dates, pitted

1 tablespoon maple syrup

1 cup brewed coffee, chilled

½ cup Almond Milk (page 290)

1½ cups ice

1 teaspoon kosher or sea salt

SPECIAL TOOLS:

blender

✓ Egg-Free
☐ Nut-Free
✓ Nightshade-Free

UNDER 30 MIN

ONE POT

ON the GO

If you were one of the people who happily stood in line to overpay for the simple delight of sweet coffee and milk with chocolate added, you are probably nervous about giving up that habit. The good news is, not only will you save money by making mocha yourself, but you'll find that it is so easy to assemble in your own kitchen that it saves you time as well. And you can rest assured that there is no added junk!

ICED MOCHA

MAKES: 2 (12-OUNCE) SERVINGS

Ingredients

1½ cups brewed coffee, chilled

1 cup coconut milk (full-fat, canned or homemade, page 290) or Almond Milk (page 290)

2 tablespoons cacao powder

2 tablespoons maple syrup

1 teaspoon pure vanilla extract

Ice, for serving

1. In a blender or food processor, process all of the ingredients until thoroughly combined.

2. Fill 2 large glasses with ice. Pour the mocha over the ice and serve.

Note: If you prefer a frozen smoothie version of this drink, simply include the ice in the blending process. Adding a frozen banana instead of the maple syrup is another great alternative.

SPECIAL TOOLS:

food processor   OR   blender

✓ Egg-Free
◼ Nut-Free
✓ Nightshade-Free

UNDER 30 MIN

under 5
INGREDIENTS

ONE POT

HOLIDAY

Winter evenings curled up by a fire wouldn't be complete without a cup of hot chocolate, would they? Try this rich, delicious beverage by itself, or perhaps top it with one or two of our Marshmallows (page 372) for an extra treat.

PEPPERMINT HOT CHOCOLATE

SERVES: 2

Ingredients

2 cups Almond Milk (page 290) or coconut milk (full-fat, canned or homemade, page 290)

¼ cup cacao powder

2 tablespoons maple syrup

¾ teaspoon peppermint extract

2 to 4 Marshmallows (page 372; optional)

1. Pour the almond milk into a small saucepan. Place over medium heat and whisk in the cacao powder and maple syrup.

2. Bring to a simmer, and then reduce the heat to medium-low. Simmer, uncovered, for 5 to 10 minutes, until the cacao lumps have dissolved.

3. Remove from the heat and stir in the peppermint extract.

4. Pour into 2 mugs. Top each mug with one or two 1-inch marshmallows, if desired, and serve.

Note: Not a fan of peppermint? Replace the peppermint extract with a flavor you enjoy, such as vanilla or almond.

☑ Egg-Free
☑ Nut-Free
☑ Nightshade-Free

While universally acknowledged for the qualities of being "life-giving" and "thirst-quenching," water is equally considered to be boring, hence the billion-dollar soda, beer, and juice industries. If you are not quite ready to give up flavors in your beverages, with a few simple additions you can turn regular water into something you look forward to drinking.

FLAVORED WATER

MAKES: 4 (8-OUNCE) SERVINGS

1. Fill a 1-quart pitcher with cold water.

2. Stir in the flavoring ingredients. Place in the refrigerator to chill for at least 30 minutes before serving.

Note: We highly recommend using carbonated water in these recipes. It's available at all major stores, or you can even make it yourself with an in-home carbonator such as a SodaStream.

Ingredients

Mint Lime

1 lime, sliced
12 fresh mint leaves

Cherry Vanilla

¼ cup pitted cherries
1 teaspoon pure vanilla
  extract

Orange Almond

1 orange, sliced
1 teaspoon almond extract

MAINS

To encourage you on your Paleo journey, this section gives you ideas of the vast array of foods you can serve for dinner or at any time of the day. Try any of these recipes and you're sure to enjoy a healthy, delicious meal!

	PHASE	PAGE #	UNDER 30 MIN	under 5 INGREDIENTS	ONE POT	HOLIDAY	ON THE GO
Sage and Citrus Roast Chicken	2	306			YES		
Juicy Pot Roast	3	308			YES		
Nona's Paprikosh (Chicken and Dumplings)	2	310					
Stacy's Soup	3	312	YES		YES		
Leftover Casserole	2	314			YES		
Macadamia-Crusted Tilapia	3	316	YES	YES			
Crab Balls	3	318				YES	YES
Mongolian Beef	2	320	YES				
Kung Pao Chicken	2	322	YES		YES		
Drunken Carrot Noodles	2	324					
Turkey Thai Basil	2	326	YES		YES		
Panang Beef Curry	3	328			YES		
Cider-Braised Brats	1	330			YES		
Slow-Roasted Pork Shoulder	2	332			YES	YES	
Lamb Stew	3	334			YES		
Apple Short Ribs	2	336		YES	YES		
Epic Bacon Meatloaf	3	338					
Linguine with Baby Clams	3	340	YES				
Peruvian Chicken	2	342					
Turkey Breasts Stuffed with "Cheese" and Cranberries	2	344				YES	
Restaurant Steaks	2	346	YES	YES	YES	YES	
Brisket with Onion Jam	3	348			YES		
Beef Tongue Carnitas	3	350					
Eastern Market Shrimp Salad	3	352	YES				
Garden Tuna Salad	3	354	YES		YES		YES
Chicken Waldorf Salad	2	356	YES		YES		YES
Grilled Kabobs with Pineapple	2	358			YES		
Grilled Spareribs	2	360			YES		
Butternut Squash Lasagna	2	362		YES			

We find that leg quarters are the most economical of all chicken parts. We often pick up pastured, organic chicken leg quarters for less than the price of conventionally raised breasts. This is a steal, because the thighs and legs are the most flavorful and juiciest parts of a chicken. Although we usually love roasting leg quarters with just salt and pepper, this dish is super simple to put together, and the flavor combination can't be beat. One of our favorite meals using this recipe can be found on page 81.

SAGE AND CITRUS ROAST CHICKEN

PREHEAT OVEN: 400°F · SERVES: 6 TO 8

Ingredients

6 chicken leg quarters

3 tablespoons lard or fat of choice

1 teaspoon kosher or sea salt

⅛ teaspoon ground black pepper

1 orange, washed and sliced into rounds

12 to 15 fresh sage leaves

1. Preheat the oven to 400°F.

2. Dry the skin of each leg quarter completely with a paper towel. Rub the lard over the skin. Place in a large baking dish and sprinkle with the salt and pepper.

3. Place the orange rounds and sage leaves on top of the chicken.

4. Place the chicken in the oven and roast for 1 hour, or until the juices run clear and the internal temperature reaches 160°F.

✓ Egg-Free
✓ Nut-Free
✓ Nightshade-Free

Most people think of pot roast as that dried-out hunk of meat you had to pretend to enjoy for the sake of your mom's feelings. But it doesn't have to be that way! As long as you prepare it with enough braising liquid, you will enjoy a fantastic one-pot meal. Though amazing on its own, we recommend serving it with Cauli-Mash (page 244) and Biscuits (page 250).

JUICY POT ROAST

SERVES: 6 TO 8

Ingredients

1 (3- to 4-pound) chuck beef roast or similar (not lean) cut

2 tablespoons lard or fat of choice

5 carrots, peeled and cut into 3-inch chunks

½ medium butternut squash (about ¾ pound), peeled, seeded, and cut into 3-inch chunks

4 turnips, peeled and cut into 3-inch chunks

1 large yellow onion, sliced

1 tablespoon tapioca flour

¼ cup red wine

2 cups Stock, beef recommended (page 132)

2 bay leaves

1 teaspoon kosher or sea salt

⅛ teaspoon ground black pepper

For serving (optional):

1 batch Cauli-Mash (page 244)

1. Dry the roast with a paper towel, and then season each side with salt and pepper.

2. In a large Dutch oven, melt the lard over medium-high heat.

3. Sear the roast on each side, about 3 minutes per side. Remove from the pot and set aside.

4. Add the carrots, squash, turnips, and onion to the pot. Sauté until the onion is translucent, about 10 minutes.

5. Add the tapioca flour and stir constantly for 1 minute. Add the wine and stir, scraping the bottom of the pot to deglaze.

6. Return the roast to the pot and add the stock, bay leaves, salt, and pepper. Increase the heat to high and bring to a boil.

7. Reduce the heat to medium-low and cover. Simmer for 2 hours or until the meat pulls apart easily. Discard the bay leaves. Serve atop Cauli-Mash, if desired.

Note: Braised foods are easy to chew and digest. Young children with weak jaw muscles will love this dish! Made with broth and grass-fed beef high in omega-3s, it's also wonderfully healing. We make ours without tomato paste since Stacy avoids nightshades due to her autoimmune disease, yet it still delivers on flavor— we promise! Because this one-pot meal is so nourishing, we make it at least once a week in the fall and winter.

Stacy's grandmother, Nona, often hosted large Sunday get-togethers for her family, and when she did, chicken and dumplings was frequently on the menu. An Italian woman married to a Hungarian man, she perfected this dish with warm broth, chewy dumplings, and slightly spicy paprika. We have tried to do her memory justice with this recipe, leaving out the traditional sour cream and wheat dumplings.

NONA'S PAPRIKOSH (CHICKEN AND DUMPLINGS)

SERVES: 4 TO 6

Ingredients

2 tablespoons lard or fat of choice

6 chicken thighs

½ cup tapioca flour

1 onion, sliced

⅓ cup white wine

4 cups Stock, chicken recommended (page 132)

2 tablespoons paprika

2 teaspoons kosher or sea salt

¼ teaspoon ground black pepper

Cauli-Gnocchi dough (page 260)

½ cup plain coconut milk yogurt

½ cup coconut milk (full-fat, canned or homemade, page 290)

For serving (optional):

1 batch Biscuits (page 250)

1. In a large Dutch oven, melt the lard over medium-high heat.

2. Dredge each chicken thigh in the tapioca flour and then brown on both sides, about 3 minutes per side. Remove to a plate.

3. Reduce the heat to medium. Sauté the onion until translucent, about 5 minutes.

4. Pour in the wine and whisk to deglaze the pan. Pour in the stock and return the chicken to the pan. Season with the paprika, salt, and pepper and bring to a boil over high heat.

5. Reduce the heat to low, cover, and simmer for 30 minutes.

6. Remove the lid and increase the heat to medium. Drop in the dough by the tablespoon.

7. When all the dumplings firm up and float to the top, add the yogurt and milk and stir to combine. When the coconut milk and yogurt have dissolved and are fully incorporated, remove from the heat and serve with biscuits, if desired.

Note: If you are unable to find or make coconut milk yogurt, use ½ cup of coconut cream mixed with 1 tablespoon of apple cider vinegar instead.

Every morning Matt, the homemaker in our family, wakes early and makes Stacy soup to eat for breakfast. That may seem impossible, but we have it down to a serious science. Matt can now make a rich and flavorful soup, provided that we already have broth on hand, in under 30 minutes. If you don't have time each morning, a big pot made once a week will last a long time and freezes well.

STACY'S SOUP

SERVES: 1

Ingredients

2 tablespoons lard or fat of choice

1 cup diced vegetables, cooked or raw (leftovers work great)

½ cup diced meat, cooked or raw (leftovers preferred)

3 cups Stock (page 132), preferably paired with your chosen meat

Herbs and spices of choice (see pages 48 and 49 for suggestions)

Salt and pepper to taste

1. In a medium saucepan, melt the lard over medium heat.

2. Add the vegetables and sauté until softened if raw, or until heated through if precooked.

3. Add the meat and brown if raw, or heat through if precooked.

4. Pour in the stock and increase the heat to high. Bring to a boil.

5. Reduce the heat to medium-low and add the herbs and spices. Cover and simmer for 15 minutes. Season with salt and pepper and serve.

Note: Adding Cashew Cheese Sauce (page 126) to this soup makes it an incredibly rich and creamy delight. Our favorite combo uses Leftover Casserole (page 314), which brings this soup together in mere minutes.

✓ Egg-Free
☐ Nut-Free
✓ Nightshade-Free

ONE POT

When you've reached that last day before you go grocery shopping and you've run out of ideas for what to cook for dinner, free up some fridge space by throwing together a Leftover Casserole. Our Cashew Cheese Sauce (page 126) is the perfect creamy complement to your fridge remainders.

LEFTOVER CASSEROLE

PREHEAT OVEN: 350°F · SERVES: 6 TO 8

1. Preheat the oven to 350°F.

2. In a food processor, combine the cheese sauce, garlic, and tarragon and process until the garlic is thoroughly minced.

3. In a medium bowl, mix together by hand the chicken, broccoli, and sauce from the food processor.

4. Press this mixture into a 13-by-9-inch baking dish and bake for 25 minutes, or until the top just begins to brown.

5. Serve warm, or freeze for the next time you're running short on time for making dinner.

Note: We use leftover chicken and broccoli for this dish, but any cooked meat and vegetables will work just as well. Use the leftovers of this casserole the next day by transforming them into a creamy version of Stacy's Soup (page 312). Heat your portion of casserole in a small pot, breaking it up as you cook. Then add your stock and bring to a boil. Finally, simmer on low for 20 minutes and serve.

Ingredients

2 cups Cashew Cheese Sauce (page 126)

2 cloves garlic

2 teaspoons fresh tarragon leaves (or herb of choice)

4 cups shredded cooked chicken (or meat of choice)

3 cups broccoli florets, steamed (or vegetable of choice)

SPECIAL TOOLS:

food processor

✓ Egg-Free
☐ Nut-Free
✓ Nightshade-Free

The omega-3 fats in fish are extremely important to our health, especially for their anti-inflammatory properties. But if you haven't acquired a taste for fish, you may be avoiding seafood dishes altogether and missing out. Try this recipe, which uses one of the mildest flavored fishes and packs in some extra delicious flavors with our favorite nut—macadamias.

MACADAMIA-CRUSTED TILAPIA

PREHEAT OVEN: 400°F · SERVES: 4 TO 6

Ingredients

6 (6-ounce) tilapia fillets

Salt and pepper to taste

1 cup raw macadamia nuts

½ cup blanched almond flour

¼ cup lard or fat of choice, melted

2 tablespoons tapioca flour

SPECIAL TOOLS:

food processor

1. Preheat the oven to 400°F. Line a rimmed baking sheet with aluminum foil.

2. Lay out the tilapia fillets on the prepared baking sheet. Sprinkle with salt and pepper.

3. In a food processor, chop the macadamia nuts into a coarse meal.

4. In a separate bowl, stir together the macadamia meal, almond flour, lard, and tapioca flour into a thick paste.

5. Press a thin layer of this paste onto the fillets. Place in the oven and bake for 12 minutes, or until the fish is white all the way through and no longer translucent.

6. Serve warm. We recommend pairing with a flavorful mash (page 278).

Note: We also enjoy replacing the tilapia with mahi mahi or even trout, so when you're ready to step up your adventure with fish, use this recipe as a starting point.

Egg-Free
Nut-Free
Nightshade-Free

In the Chesapeake Bay area, crab cakes are on everyone's menu in the summer. Even our local butcher shops prepare and sell their own. Unfortunately, all of them are made with breadcrumbs. These crab balls, which replicate an appetizer at our favorite waterfront restaurant, will satisfy your crab cake craving, and they're simple to make. When we serve them to friends, they're sometimes gone before we get one!

CRAB BALLS

PREHEAT OVEN: 425°F · SERVES: 4 TO 6

Ingredients

Coconut oil, for greasing the pan

16 ounces backfin crabmeat

½ cup blanched almond flour

3 tablespoons Mayonnaise (page 122)

2 large eggs, lightly beaten

2 teaspoons Old Bay seasoning

1 teaspoon grated lemon zest

½ teaspoon garlic powder

½ teaspoon kosher or sea salt

¼ teaspoon ground black pepper

For serving:

1 recipe Tartar Sauce (page 122)

1. Preheat the oven to 425°F. Line a rimmed baking sheet or other shallow pan with parchment paper or lightly grease it with coconut oil.

2. In a medium mixing bowl, combine the crabmeat, almond flour, mayonnaise, and eggs and mix together with your hands.

3. Add the rest of the ingredients and mix together until evenly incorporated.

4. Using a rounded tablespoon for consistency, roll the crab mixture into 1-inch balls and place on the prepared pan.

5. Place in the oven and bake for 25 to 30 minutes, until browned on the outside.

6. Serve with the tartar sauce.

Note: We recommend using backfin or even claw meat for crab cakes. Since you're oven-baking them, the larger jumbo lump meat is not necessary and would be much more expensive.

We were very pleased to learn that a large Chinese restaurant chain was implementing a gluten-free menu featuring wheat-free tamari in place of regular soy sauce for many of their dishes. On that menu was a dish called Mongolian Beef consisting of fried beef in a sticky, sweet sauce, which became a favorite of ours. That's why we created our own rendition at home. It's still a sweet treat but is much healthier than the restaurant version. For a special night, we recommend serving this as a part of the Chinese Take-Out Dinner (page 67), but it's easy enough for any weeknight!

MONGOLIAN BEEF

SERVES: 2 TO 4

Ingredients

¼ cup tapioca flour

Pinch of salt and pepper

1½ pounds sirloin, cut into ½-by-1-inch pieces

Lard or fat of choice for frying

2 teaspoons minced garlic

1 teaspoon minced fresh ginger

½ cup coconut aminos or tamari

¼ cup water

¼ cup blackstrap molasses

¼ cup unrefined granulated palm, date, or maple sugar

6 green onions, cut into 1-inch lengths, plus more for garnish

For serving:

1 batch Plain Cauli-Rice (page 246)

1. In a wide-bottomed bowl, combine the tapioca flour with a pinch of salt and pepper. Dredge each piece of beef in the flour mixture, shaking off the excess. Set aside.

2. In a large skillet over medium-high heat, melt enough lard to reach halfway up the meat pieces. Preheat for about 8 minutes until it reaches 350°F.

3. Fry the beef in batches until browned on both sides, about 3 minutes per side. Transfer to a paper towel–lined plate.

4. In a separate skillet, heat 3 tablespoons of lard over medium heat until melted and hot. Add the garlic and ginger and sauté for 90 seconds. Any longer than that and you will burn the garlic.

5. Pour in the coconut aminos and water and simmer for 3 minutes.

6. Stir in the molasses and palm sugar until dissolved. Continue to simmer for 5 minutes, until the sauce is thickened.

7. Add the cooked beef and onions to the skillet and stir to coat. Continue to cook for 6 minutes, stirring frequently.

8. While still warm, garnish with green onions, if desired, and serve with Plain Cauli-Rice.

Note: If your family likes green onions, like we do, we suggest doubling or tripling the amount called for in the recipe so that you aren't fighting over who gets the greens.

✓ Egg-Free
☐ Nut-Free
☐ Nightshade-Free

Spicy chicken with peppers and peanuts is a classic on most Chinese take-out menus, and it's one of our favorites. Although it's difficult to visualize how the dish is assembled or made Paleo-friendly, the trick is spicy chili paste. It can be found in your grocer's international foods aisle. And the walnuts provide a crunch that is far superior to peanuts in flavor and texture. Serve over our Plain Cauli-Rice (page 246).

KUNG PAO CHICKEN

SERVES: 2 TO 4

1. In a small bowl, whisk together the ingredients for the marinade.

2. In an airtight container, toss the chicken in the marinade until coated. Place the chicken in the fridge and allow to marinate for at least 1 hour.

3. In a small bowl, combine the ingredients for the sauce and set aside.

4. Remove the chicken from the marinade and discard the remaining marinade.

5. In a wok or large skillet, heat the lard over medium-high heat. Add the chicken and brown until the juices run clear.

6. Pour in the sauce and stir constantly until the sauce is fragrant and the chicken is coated.

7. Add the celery, walnuts, water chestnuts, and green onions and continue to stir until well incorporated.

8. When the onions and celery are softened, remove from the heat and serve.

Ingredients

For the marinade:

1 tablespoon coconut aminos or tamari

1 tablespoon rice wine or white wine

1 tablespoon untoasted, cold-pressed sesame oil

1 tablespoon tapioca flour

1 cup diced raw chicken breast or thigh meat

For the sauce:

1 tablespoon coconut aminos or tamari

1 tablespoon rice wine or white wine

1 tablespoon untoasted, cold-pressed sesame oil

1 tablespoon tapioca flour

1 tablespoon chili paste

1 teaspoon grated fresh ginger

2 cloves garlic, minced

1 tablespoon lard or fat of choice

½ cup diced celery

¼ cup raw walnuts, coarsely chopped

1 (6-ounce) can water chestnuts, drained and sliced

3 green onions, sliced

Drunken noodles is a Thai dish that pairs a sweet, sticky sauce with hot peppers and unique, wide rice noodles. It is a favorite in our family, and re-creating it took many attempts. This unique dish uses a very interesting noodle replacement that is naturally sweet, so there is no need to add much sweetener. It pairs well with any dish from the "Want to Try Some Thai?" menu (page 85) or works great any day of the week to add vegetables to your table in the most fun and delicious way we know!

DRUNKEN CARROT NOODLES

SERVES: 2 TO 4

Ingredients

3 thick carrots, peeled

2 tablespoons lard

1 pound cubed chicken, beef, or pork or whole medium shrimp, peeled and deveined

½ onion, cut into 8 wedges

2 cloves garlic, minced

1 cup broccoli florets

1 Thai bird chile pepper or jalapeño pepper, sliced (optional)

1 tablespoon fish sauce

2 tablespoons coconut aminos or tamari

1 tablespoon blackstrap molasses

1 cup fresh Thai basil leaves

1. Using a mandoline or julienne peeler, slice the carrots lengthwise into long, wide "noodles." Set aside.

2. Melt the lard in a large skillet or wok over medium-high heat.

3. Sauté the meat or shrimp, onion wedges, and garlic in the lard, stirring frequently, until the meat is browned and cooked through or the shrimp turns pink. Remove from the heat and set aside.

4. Add the carrot noodles and broccoli to the skillet and cook until softened, stirring frequently. After about 8 minutes, when the carrots are soft enough to pierce, add the Thai bird chile pepper (if using), fish sauce, coconut aminos, and molasses. Stir to combine.

5. Return the meat or shrimp, onion, and garlic to the skillet and stir to combine. When everything is coated in the sauce, stir in the Thai basil leaves. As soon as the leaves have wilted, remove from the heat and serve.

Note: Our recommendations and info on unique products can be found on pages 32–38.

✓ Egg-Free
✓ Nut-Free
☐ Nightshade-Free

UNDER 30 MIN

ONE POT

After Thanksgiving one year, we were at a loss for what to do with our leftover turkey, which was a first for us. Just when we were about to give up and reach for the take-out menu, family friends gave us the following inspiration. Thanks to a brilliant eight-year-old girl, we made the unlikely pairing of turkey and Thai ingredients. When you're tired of Thanksgiving leftovers, this recipe will transform your leftover turkey into something your palate will find new and refreshing.

TURKEY THAI BASIL

SERVES: 2 TO 4

Ingredients

4 cups shredded cooked turkey (about 1 pound)

2 tablespoons fish sauce

3 tablespoons coconut aminos or tamari

1 tablespoon water

1 teaspoon kosher or sea salt

½ teaspoon ground white pepper

2 tablespoons lard or fat of choice

4 baby bok choy, leaves pulled apart and hearts halved

1 red bell pepper, sliced

1 yellow bell pepper, sliced

1 large onion, sliced

3 cloves garlic, minced

1½ cups fresh Thai basil leaves

For serving (optional):

1 batch Thai Fried Cauli-Rice (page 247)

1. In a medium bowl, combine the turkey, fish sauce, coconut aminos, water, salt, and pepper and stir until the turkey is thoroughly coated. Set aside.

2. Melt the lard in a large skillet or wok over medium-high heat.

3. Add the baby bok choy, bell peppers, onion, and garlic and sauté until softened, stirring frequently, about 8 minutes.

4. Add the seasoned turkey to the skillet and stir for about 3 minutes, until the turkey is fully incorporated and heated through.

5. Remove from the heat and add the Thai basil leaves, stirring until the basil has wilted. Serve warm with Thai Fried Cauli-Rice, if desired.

Note: This recipe is fantastic with any leftover meat, including chicken and lean beef. It's a wonderful way to transform yesterday's dinner. Wondering about some of these ingredients? See pages 32–38.

☑ Egg-Free

■ Nut-Free

■ Nightshade-Free

In the Paleo scene, Thai food is very popular. Unlike its distant Chinese cousin, Thai food is often naturally gluten-free and uses Paleo favorites like coconut milk and fish sauce. Because our family loves Thai food so much, Matt actually took cooking lessons from a local chef who won a Throwdown TV competition against Bobby Flay. Matt loved learning how to bring those authentic flavors home to our kitchen. This spicy Thai curry is not only quick to make, but intensely flavorful as well.

PANANG BEEF CURRY

SERVES: 2 TO 4

Ingredients

2 tablespoons lard or fat of choice

2 pounds skirt steak, cut into ½-by-2-inch strips

1 onion, sliced

3 medium carrots, peeled and cut into 1-inch pieces

2 tablespoons Thai red curry paste or Panang curry paste (or more for spice lovers)

1 (13½-ounce) can full-fat coconut milk or 1¾ cups homemade (page 290)

1 tablespoon coconut aminos or tamari

1½ tablespoons fish sauce

1 tablespoon freshly squeezed lemon juice

20 fresh Thai basil leaves, plus extra for garnish (optional)

For serving:

1 batch Plain Cauli-Rice (page 246)

Unsalted roasted cashews, for garnish (optional)

1. In a large skillet or wok, melt the lard over medium-high heat.

2. Add the beef and stir constantly until browned on all sides, about 7 minutes.

3. Transfer the meat to a plate and set aside. Add the onion and carrots to the skillet and cook until soft, stirring constantly, about 8 minutes.

4. Return the meat and accumulated juices to the skillet. Add the curry paste, stirring to coat.

5. Pour in the coconut milk and stir until uniformly red. Add the coconut aminos, stir, and reduce the heat to medium-low. Simmer for 15 minutes.

6. Before serving, add the fish sauce, lemon juice, and Thai basil leaves and stir until the leaves have wilted. Serve over Plain Cauli-Rice and garnish with the cashews or however else you'd like.

Note: Though this dish is spicy, the coconut milk has a cooling effect. If you've never braved curry before, this is one to try!

✓ Egg-Free
✓ Nut-Free
✓ Nightshade-Free

ONE POT

Bratwursts, which we made and stuffed ourselves in our previous cookbook, *Beyond Bacon,* are delicious, mild sausages that are perfect for grilling during the hot summer months. You can easily find them at the store, but a local butcher shop will likely have freshly prepared ones in the natural casings perfect for this dish.

Ingredients

12 Bratwurst

1 (12-ounce) bottle hard apple cider or apple juice

1 cup Stock, beef or pork recommended (page 132)

2 cloves garlic

2 teaspoons black peppercorns

2 teaspoons kosher or sea salt

SPECIAL TOOLS:

grill
(optional)

CIDER-BRAISED BRATS

PREHEAT GRILL: MEDIUM OR PREHEAT OVEN: 350°F · SERVES: 6 TO 8

1. Preheat the grill to medium, or preheat the oven to 350°F.

2. Place the Bratwursts in a shallow roasting pan or Dutch oven.

3. Pour the cider and stock over the top of the brats. Add the garlic, peppercorns, and salt.

4. If grilling, place the pan on the grill and braise for 20 minutes or until the brats are cooked through. When ready, the liquid will have reduced, allowing the outer skin of the brats to start to caramelize and brown. Alternatively, place the pan in the oven and roast the brats for 20 minutes.

5. When cooked through, the meat will not be soft to the touch, and the center will reach 160°F. Remove the brats from the liquid. Sear the outside of each brat on the grill or on the stovetop in a skillet over medium-high heat, about 3 minutes per side.

✓ Egg-Free
✓ Nut-Free
✓ Nightshade-Free

You've probably been underestimating the wonderful pork shoulder in favor of more popular cuts like chops, bacon, and sausages. But that's a mistake! Pork shoulder is not at all difficult to prepare and is always a crowd-pleaser. In fact, we almost always make one when we have company because everyone loves the leftovers—especially for breakfast.

We perfected the art of cooking pork shoulder in our previous cookbook, *Beyond Bacon.* This method is similar to the recipe in that book, only this version is nightshade-free so that those avoiding spicy foods can enjoy it, too. Pulled pork can be paired with just about any side, but our favorites are Roasted Rainbow Carrots (page 266) and Pickled Onion and Arugula Salad (page 286).

SLOW-ROASTED PORK SHOULDER

PREHEAT OVEN: 325°F · SERVES: 6 TO 8

Ingredients

- 1 tablespoon kosher or sea salt
- 1 tablespoon unrefined granulated palm, date, or maple sugar
- 1 teaspoon ginger powder
- 1 teaspoon garlic powder
- 1 teaspoon dried thyme leaves
- ½ teaspoon ground black pepper
- ⅛ teaspoon ground cloves
- 1 (5-pound) bone-in pork shoulder (aka picnic roast or Boston butt)
- ½ cup lard or fat of choice, melted
- ½ cup apple cider vinegar

For serving:

- 1 batch Apple Butter BBQ Sauce (page 112) or Carolina-Style Sauce (page 234)

1. Preheat the oven to 325°F.

2. In a small bowl, mix together the seasonings with a fork.

3. Pat the pork dry with a paper towel, and then coat the outside with the seasoning mix. Place in an 11-by-7-inch baking dish, fat side up.

4. In a separate bowl, whisk together the lard and vinegar.

5. Place the baking dish in the oven and roast the pork for about 4 hours. Baste with the vinegar mixture every 30 to 45 minutes, whisking before each use. To avoid overcooking the meat, begin checking it after about 3 hours to make sure that it is still soft to the touch. Continue checking every 30 minutes. As soon as the meat begins to firm up and pull apart easily, remove it from the heat. The internal temperature should reach 185°F.

6. Serve as a roast or pulled with the barbecue sauce and the sides of your choice. To make pulled pork, shred the roasted pork with 2 forks; it should pull apart with a gentle nudge. If the pork is too dry, reincorporate some of the liquid left in the baking dish as you shred it.

Note: Most picnic roasts have one bone in them that runs half the length of the roast. There is no need to remove this bone, but as you pull the meat apart, be aware that it's there. Bone-in or boneless, this recipe works for both. Don't get confused when purchasing pork. Ask your butcher or farmer for the shoulder. Either the picnic or the Boston butt (which isn't the rear end, the ham, but rather the butt end of the front leg bone) works well.

Of all the readily available land-based meat animals out there, grass-fed lamb is the best source of inflammation-reducing omega-3 fatty acids. Even conventionally raised lamb will provide you with a good omega-3 punch, as most lamb tends to be pasture-raised at least to some extent. On the next cold night when you want to make a rich stew, try using lamb instead of beef or chicken.

LAMB STEW

SERVES: 4 TO 6

Ingredients

- 1 cup coconut flour
- 1 tablespoon paprika
- 1 tablespoon plus 2 teaspoons kosher or sea salt, divided
- 2 teaspoons ground black pepper, divided
- 2 pounds cubed lamb stew meat
- 2 tablespoons lard or fat of choice
- 1 large onion, sliced
- 3 cloves garlic, smashed with the side of a knife
- 8 medium carrots, peeled and cut into 2-inch pieces
- 4 cups Stock, beef recommended (page 132)
- 1 cup red wine (or more stock)
- 1 bay leaf
- 2 sprigs fresh rosemary
- 2 sprigs fresh thyme
- 2 teaspoons kosher or sea salt
- 1 teaspoon ground black pepper

For serving:

- 1 batch Cauli-Mash (page 244)
- Chopped fresh parsley, for garnish

1. In a large bowl, combine the flour, paprika, 1 tablespoon of the salt, and 1 teaspoon of the pepper. Dredge the lamb in the flour mixture, shaking off the excess flour.

2. In a large Dutch oven, melt the lard over medium-high heat. Brown the lamb, about 4 minutes per side. Transfer the browned meat to a plate and set aside.

3. Add the onion, garlic, and carrots to the pot. Sauté for about 8 minutes, until the onion is soft.

4. Add the stock and wine and return the meat to the pot over high heat. Stir to combine and bring to a boil.

5. If you have a mesh or cheesecloth sachet for herbs, put the bay leaf and sprigs of herbs inside, or, for a more rustic look, place the bay leaf and herbs directly in the pot. Stir in the remaining 2 teaspoons of salt and 1 teaspoon of pepper.

6. Reduce the heat to low and cover. Simmer for 90 minutes, until the meat is very tender and the carrots are easily pierced.

7. Remove the bay leaf and herb sprigs.

8. Serve warm over Cauli-Mash with a sprinkle of chopped parsley. Store in an airtight container for up to several days—it makes wonderful leftovers.

✓ Egg-Free
✓ Nut-Free
☐ Nightshade-Free

When you first get beef short ribs, you'll be tempted to grill them. But do not give in to that temptation! Short ribs are best slow-roasted. This recipe enhances their flavor while transforming the chewiness that is inherent to the cut into a soft, buttery, and fall-apart-tender piece of meat.

APPLE SHORT RIBS

PREHEAT OVEN: 325°F · SERVES: 4 TO 6

Ingredients

1 large yellow onion, sliced

2 medium apples, peeled and sliced thin

4 pounds beef short ribs

Salt and pepper to taste

1 cup Apple Butter BBQ Sauce (page 112)

For serving:

1 batch Cauli-Mash (page 244)

1. Preheat the oven to 325°F.

2. Spread the onion and apple slices in a single layer across the bottom of a 13-by-9-inch baking dish. Place the ribs on top, meat side up.

3. Sprinkle the ribs generously with salt and pepper and pour the barbecue sauce over the top.

4. Cover the baking dish and place in the oven. Cook for 2 hours, or until the meat is falling-apart-tender.

5. This dish is best served warm over Cauli-Mash.

Note: This method also works with pork spareribs. Simply make a foil packet in which to place your spareribs and other ingredient, seal, and roast directly on the oven rack for 90 minutes.

When most people make meatloaf, we wonder where their imagination went. We always add vegetables to our meatloaf for extra flavor and nutrition. Then, instead of topping it with ketchup, we top ours with bacon, making it a moist, flavorful, and epic meal indeed! Dried-out, boring meatloaf is a thing of the past.

EPIC BACON MEATLOAF

PREHEAT OVEN: 350°F · SERVES: 4 TO 6

Ingredients

2 tablespoons lard or fat of choice

½ cup diced onion

½ cup diced celery

½ cup diced carrots

2 cups baby spinach

1 tablespoon minced garlic

2 pounds ground beef

2 large eggs

¾ cup blanched almond flour

2 tablespoons fresh parsley, chopped

½ teaspoon kosher or sea salt

⅛ teaspoon ground black pepper

3 strips bacon

1. Preheat the oven to 350°F.

2. Melt the lard in a large skillet over medium heat.

3. Add the onion, celery, and carrots and sauté until softened, about 7 minutes.

4. Add the spinach and garlic and cook, stirring constantly, until wilted into the rest of the vegetables.

5. With a slotted spoon, transfer the vegetables to a large mixing bowl. Add the beef, eggs, almond flour, parsley, salt, and pepper to the bowl and mix by hand to incorporate.

6. Press the meat into a 9-by-5-inch loaf pan and top with the bacon strips.

7. Place in the oven and bake for about 60 minutes. When the meatloaf is done, there will likely be a lot of liquid that has drained, both fat from the meat and water from the spinach. To ensure that it holds together firmly, let the meatloaf rest in the pan for at least 10 to 20 minutes before removing it.

Note: Meatloaf is one of the best ways to "sneak" nutrient-rich organ meat into your food. To add it, simply grind up liver, heart, or kidney and incorporate it into the ground meat mixture.

✓ Egg-Free
✓ Nut-Free
☐ Nightshade-Free

UNDER 30 MIN

If you're looking to eat a little more healthy seafood during the week, keeping a can of baby clams on hand makes throwing this meal together a snap. Matt grew up fighting his brothers for leftovers of this dish, and he is thrilled to be able to share such a healthy version without the traditional pasta with his boys, who argue over the leftovers as well.

LINGUINE WITH BABY CLAMS

SERVES: 4 TO 6

Ingredients

4 large zucchini or yellow squash, cut into long strands using a julienne peeler or into noodles using a spiral slicer

2 tablespoons lard or unsalted butter

⅓ cup olive oil or fat of choice

1 medium Vidalia or other sweet onion, diced

3 cloves garlic, minced

¼ teaspoon cayenne pepper (optional)

¼ cup white wine or apple juice

2 (10-ounce) cans whole baby clams, juice reserved

1 tablespoon chopped fresh parsley

SPECIAL TOOLS:
Spiral slicer (optional)

1. Bring a large pot of water to boil over high heat. When boiling, submerge the zucchini "noodles" in the water and cook for 90 seconds.

2. Pour the noodles into a colander to drain and rinse with cold water to stop the cooking. Drain well.

3. Transfer the noodles to a serving bowl and toss with the lard.

4. In a medium saucepan, heat the olive oil over medium heat.

5. Sauté the onion and garlic in the oil until soft, about 6 minutes. Add the cayenne, if using, and stir to incorporate.

6. Pour in the wine and juice from the clams and increase the heat to high. Boil for about 10 minutes to reduce the liquid, stirring frequently.

7. Reduce the heat to medium and add the clams. Stir and simmer for 5 minutes until the clams are heated through.

8. Pour the sauce on top of the zucchini noodles, and then sprinkle on the parsley. Toss to combine, and serve.

Note: This dish can also be made with spaghetti squash noodles. See page 144 for our how-to on making squash.

Washington, D.C., has a sizable Peruvian community; it seems like every shopping center is selling *pollo a la brasa,* or rotisserie chicken grilled over hot coals. A common take-out item in our home, it is honestly the most flavorful chicken you could ever eat. While this version is not exactly the same, considering that your home likely doesn't have a rotisserie grill, this method will get you close. For the full experience, we recommend serving it with Yuca Fries (page 284) and Fried Sweet Plantains (page 268).

PERUVIAN CHICKEN

PREHEAT OVEN: 400°F · SERVES: 4 TO 6

Ingredients

1 whole (4-pound) chicken

1 tablespoon tapioca flour

1 teaspoon kosher or sea salt

1 teaspoon ground cumin

1 teaspoon paprika

½ teaspoon garlic powder

⅛ teaspoon ground black pepper

1 cup hard apple cider, white wine, or apple juice

SPECIAL TOOLS:

Vertical roaster or empty aluminum can

1. Place an oven rack in the bottom position. Preheat the oven to 400°F.

2. Pat the chicken dry, inside and out, with a paper towel.

3. In a small bowl, combine the tapioca flour, salt, and spices with a fork.

4. Apply this rub over the skin of the chicken and on the inside of the cavity. Be sure to apply on both the breast side and the spine side.

5. Pour the cider into the cup of a vertical roaster or into a clean aluminum can. Insert the cup or can into the cavity of the chicken as far as possible, and adjust so that chicken balances. If using a can, place the chicken on a rimmed baking sheet to catch the juices.

6. Roast for 75 minutes or until the skin is crispy and the chicken is cooked through. When done, the juices will run clear and the internal temperature will reach 160°F.

Note: Using a different size chicken? Just cook it until it reaches the correct internal temperature; the time will vary depending on the size of the bird.

☑ Egg-Free
◼ Nut-Free
☑ Nightshade-Free

Having a small Thanksgiving with only a couple of friends? This is what you should serve: turkey and stuffing made in a fraction of the cook time, with minimal leftovers. The flavors of the dish are so incredible, however, that we highly recommend that you try it year-round.

TURKEY BREASTS STUFFED WITH "CHEESE" AND CRANBERRIES

PREHEAT OVEN: 325°F · SERVES: 4 TO 6

Ingredients

2 boneless turkey breasts (about 3 pounds total)

Salt and pepper to taste

2 tablespoons lard or fat of choice

½ cup diced onion

½ cup diced cooked chestnuts (see Note)

½ cup diced mushrooms

1 cup Cashew Cheese Sauce (page 126)

½ cup dried cranberries

1. Preheat the oven to 325°F.

2. Using a sharp knife, slice into the side of each turkey breast to create a pocket running the length of the breast. Sprinkle salt and pepper on the skin side.

3. Melt the lard in a medium skillet over medium heat. Add the onion, chestnuts, and mushrooms and sauté until the onion is translucent, about 8 minutes.

4. Transfer the cooked onion, chestnuts, and mushrooms to a medium mixing bowl. Add the cheese sauce and cranberries and stir to combine.

5. Stuff each turkey breast with this mixture. Place the breasts in an 11-by-7-inch or larger Pyrex baking dish.

6. Place in the oven and bake for 1 hour or until the juices run clear, the skin is crisped, and the internal temperature reaches 165°F.

Note: During the holiday season especially, preroasted fresh chestnuts are sold in many produce sections.

✓ Egg-Free
✓ Nut-Free
✓ Nightshade-Free

UNDER 30 MIN

under 5 INGREDIENTS

ONE POT

HOLIDAY

Ever wonder how restaurants seem to be able to cook steaks perfectly, and no matter how hard you try, you can't replicate the flavor and texture? Or perhaps you struggle to get your steaks perfectly medium-rare without having to slice into the meat to check? This is our foolproof method for cooking steaks. Once you do it this way, you'll never find yourself with blue meat or overcooked hockey pucks again. We recommend serving these steaks with any of the other dishes highlighted in the incredibly nutrient-filled Restaurant Dinner (page 99).

RESTAURANT STEAKS

PREHEAT OVEN: 350°F · SERVES: 2

Ingredients

2 (2½-inch-thick) rib-eye steaks

2 tablespoons lard or butter

Salt and pepper to taste

1. Preheat the oven to 350°F, and preheat a large cast-iron skillet over medium-high heat.

2. Melt the lard in the skillet.

3. Pat the steaks dry and liberally sprinkle each side with salt and pepper.

4. Sear the steaks for about 3 minutes on each side, until a brown crust forms and it easily releases to flip.

5. Once both sides are browned, transfer the skillet to the oven and cook until medium-rare (135°F), about 9 minutes.

6. Allow the steaks to rest for at least 5 minutes before serving.

Note: To check the doneness of steak (or any meat) without cutting it open, you can either 1) use a meat thermometer or 2) touch the meat. If using a meat thermometer, use the general guidelines for the type of meat being cooked on page 412. If using the touch method, with the pad of your finger, try to bounce the center of the steak. If it has a lot of give (like uncooked meat would), it's still too rare; if it is very sturdy and doesn't move when pressed, it is well-done. A medium-cooked steak will have a slight give and bounce when pressed, similar to the way the meaty part of your palm feels. The more often you do this and see what the meat looks like inside, the more you'll know what the different cooking temperatures feel like.

✓ Egg-Free
✓ Nut-Free
✓ Nightshade-Free

Braising tougher cuts of meat really pays dividends at the dinner table (not to mention in your wallet, since tougher cuts are often the most affordable). This dish may take a long time to cook, but you'll love the flavor. Additionally, by braising the meat in broth, you're adding tons of healthful micronutrients.

BRISKET WITH ONION JAM

PREHEAT OVEN: 350°F · SERVES: 4 TO 6

Ingredients

2 yellow onions, sliced ½-inch thick

3 pounds beef brisket

¾ teaspoon dried basil

¾ teaspoon dried oregano leaves

¾ teaspoon dried parsley

Salt and pepper to taste

2 to 3 cups Stock, beef recommended (page 132)

1. Preheat the oven to 350°F.

2. Place the onions on the bottom of shallow roasting pan. (We recommend enameled cast iron.)

3. Rub both sides of the brisket with the herbs and generously sprinkle both sides with salt and pepper. Place the brisket on top of the onions.

4. Place the brisket in the oven and roast for 90 minutes to cook the onions.

5. Add 2 cups of stock, cover, and reduce the heat to 325°F; cook for an additional 4 hours. Baste the meat with the stock every 30 to 60 minutes, if you're able, until it's no longer liquid-y and an onion jam forms. If the jam forms before the brisket is tender, add another cup of stock and continue to baste and cook until the meat is juicy and tender and the liquid is cooked off.

Note: To make a flavorful dish while you're out of the house, place the onions in the bottom of a slow cooker and then place the remaining ingredients on top of the onions. Cook on low for 8 hours. It won't be quite as good, but it will be easier for you!

Tongue may not seem appetizing at first, but once you see how juicy and tender you can make it, you'll be a believer. Unlike most organ meats (aka offal), tongue is a muscle and tastes very similar to traditional carnitas. Using a slow cooker to braise tongue is the perfect way to ensure that it is perfectly tender.

BEEF TONGUE CARNITAS

SERVES: 4 TO 6

Ingredients

2 beef tongues (about 3 pounds)

1 cup beef Stock (page 132)

4 cloves garlic, smashed with the side of a knife

1 teaspoon kosher or sea salt

2 teaspoons chili powder

1 teaspoon ground cumin

⅛ teaspoon ground black pepper

Suggested toppings:

Chopped fresh cilantro

Squeeze of fresh lime juice

Avocado slices or guacamole

Salsa

Enchilada Sauce from our Breakfast Burritos (page 160)

½ batch Tostadas (page 262)

1 batch Fiesta Cauli-Rice (page 247)

SPECIAL TOOLS:

Slow cooker

1. Place the whole tongues in the bottom of a slow cooker. Pour the stock over the top and add the garlic.

2. Cover and cook on low for 8 hours.

3. Remove the tongues from the braising liquid. Using a knife, gently cut away the skin of the tongue and discard.

4. Using 2 forks or your fingers, gently shred the meat, leaving no large chunks. If you are having a difficult time pulling the meat apart, it needs more time to braise and soften; return it to the broth and cook for a bit longer, and then try again.

5. Place the shredded meat in a bowl and sprinkle on the salt and spices. Stir until the salt and spices are evenly incorporated into the meat.

6. In a large dry skillet over medium-high heat, fry the seasoned meat in batches until seared.

7. Serve in our tostadas with fiesta cauli-rice and any combination of the suggested toppings.

Note: If the skin of the tongue is too much for you, ask your butcher to trim your tongues. The skin helps to seal in moisture and peels away easily when cooked, but taking baby steps to organ meat is better than none at all!

Egg-Free
✓ Nut-Free
✓ Nightshade-Free

UNDER 30 MIN

One of the traditions Stacy has with the boys is to go to the Eastern Market in downtown Washington, D.C., and visit one particular stand that sells a mayonnaise-based shrimp salad for lunch. The boys love it so much that they insisted we learn to make it at home, since the store-bought is considered a treat. Once made, it never lasts long!

EASTERN MARKET SHRIMP SALAD

SERVES: 2 TO 4

Ingredients

2 tablespoons lard or fat of choice

1 pound medium shrimp, peeled and deveined

¼ cup Garlic and Herb Aioli (page 122)

1 tablespoon honey

Grated zest of ½ lemon

Juice of ½ lemon

½ teaspoon kosher or sea salt

¼ teaspoon ground black pepper

1. Melt the lard in a large skillet over medium heat. Cook the shrimp in the lard for 2 to 3 minutes per side, just until they've turned a vibrant pink color all the way through. Be careful not to overcook them; you want them tender on the inside. Remove from the heat and set aside.

2. In a medium mixing bowl, combine the rest of the ingredients.

3. Add the shrimp and toss to combine. Let rest for a few hours to allow the flavors to meld, if you can wait that long. Serve cold.

Note: This versatile salad is great over greens or even paired with crudités. We love it best fresh with a fork.

Egg-Free
☑ Nut-Free
☑ Nightshade-Free

At a certain point, our son Cole decided that the garden tuna salad from our local grocery store was the best lunch he had ever had, and he insisted that he needed it daily. We would place a pound of it in the fridge and be shocked to find it gone by the next afternoon. With his help, we re-created this tuna salad at home, using him as our taste-tester. It's much more affordable to make at home, and we love all the healthy fats in this version!

GARDEN TUNA SALAD

SERVES: 2 TO 4

Ingredients

2 cups chunk light tuna, drained, about 2 (5-ounce) cans

⅓ cup diced yellow onion

⅓ cup diced celery

⅓ cup shredded carrots

¼ cup diced dill pickle or dill relish (Bubbies brand preferred)

2 teaspoons Dijon mustard

¾ cup Mayonnaise (page 122)

Salt and pepper to taste

1. In a medium mixing bowl, stir together all of the ingredients until thoroughly mixed. Chill for at least 15 minutes before serving.

Note: Try this salad inside our collard green wraps (page 356) or alongside your favorite veggie. Organic carrot chips have become a favorite in our house.

- Egg-Free
- Nut-Free
- ✓ Nightshade-Free

UNDER 30 MIN

ONE POT

ON the GO

Whether you serve it on a bed of lettuce, by itself, or stuffed in a hollowed-out apple half, this classic chicken salad will delight your taste buds. No matter what you may have been told, not everything needs to be radically altered to make it Paleo.

CHICKEN WALDORF SALAD

SERVES: 2 TO 4

Ingredients

- 2 cups diced cooked chicken
- ⅓ cup diced celery
- ⅓ cup diced apple
- ⅓ cup raw walnuts, chopped
- ⅓ cup quartered red seedless grapes
- ½ cup Mayonnaise (page 122)
- 1 tablespoon freshly squeezed lemon juice
- Salt and pepper to taste

1. In a medium mixing bowl, stir together all of the ingredients until thoroughly mixed. Chill for at least 15 minutes before serving.

Note: This salad is perfect when you need to use leftover chicken from dinner. Feel free to add carrots or your favorite fruits and veggies. For added micronutrients, use young, tender collard greens as wraps: Simply wash the greens, remove the thick stems, and roll!

✓ Egg-Free
✓ Nut-Free
✓ Nightshade-Free

ONE POT

Kabobs are a favorite for parties at our house. Simply lay out all the meat and veggie options in separate bowls and allow your guests to choose what they want to make their very own kabobs. These kabobs are wonderful served atop Cauli-Rice (page 246) or Carrot Mash (page 278). Add a salad and you've got a quick, flavorful dinner.

GRILLED KABOBS WITH PINEAPPLE

PREHEAT GRILL: MEDIUM-HIGH · SERVES: 4 TO 6

Ingredients

½ cup coconut aminos or tamari

1 tablespoon fish sauce

1 tablespoon freshly squeezed lime juice

3 cloves garlic, minced

1 teaspoon onion powder

½ teaspoon five-spice powder

2 pounds cubed beef, such as top sirloin

Any combination of veggies:

Onion, chopped into eighths

Green bell pepper, sliced into eighths

Pineapple cubes

White button mushrooms, stems removed

Zucchini and/or yellow squash, sliced into rounds or chunks

1. In a sealable container, whisk together the coconut aminos, fish sauce, lime juice, garlic, onion powder, and five-spice powder. Place the meat in the container and toss in the marinade to coat. Seal and refrigerate for 4 hours or overnight.

2. Prior to grilling, soak wooden skewers in water for 20 minutes. Preheat the grill to medium-high.

3. Skewer the veggies and meat on the soaked skewers, leaving 2 ends empty. Since we like our beef cooked medium-rare, we thread the veggies with the meat, which allows the flavors to infuse. If you like more well-done beef, we recommend skewering the veggies and meat separately so that the veggies do not overcook while the beef stays on longer.

4. Grill the kabobs on all 4 sides for 4 minutes per side until the meat is medium-rare, or longer for well-done. (See our tip on page 346 for touch-testing the doneness of beef.)

5. Allow the kabobs to rest for a few minutes before serving.

SPECIAL TOOLS:

grill

✓ Egg-Free
✓ Nut-Free
☐ Nightshade-Free

ONE POT

After cooking up whole pigs for our last book, *Beyond Bacon,* we feel like we've become barbecue experts, or at least avid fans. As a result of grilling racks of ribs many times during the summer months, this is our favorite "quick" way to prepare them. Our family friend Sam loved them so much that she wanted to be part of the photograph for them!

GRILLED SPARERIBS

PREHEAT GRILL: MEDIUM · SERVES: 2 TO 4

1. Preheat the grill to medium.

2. In a small bowl, mix together the ingredients for the rub with a fork.

3. Evenly coat each side of the ribs with the rub.

4. Place the ribs in the center of a long sheet of aluminum foil. Fold over and seal the edges to create a securely closed packet.

5. Place the foil packet on the top rack of the grill and roast for 90 minutes with the lid closed, flipping halfway through. If your grill has no top rack, turn off the gas burners on one side and place ribs on that side. If using a charcoal grill, push the coals to one side and place the ribs on the opposite side.

6. Once cooked through, remove the ribs from the foil and place on the main surface of the grill, directly over the heat source, and grill on high heat just long enough to sear each side of the ribs.

7. Serve warm with the barbecue sauce.

Ingredients

For the rub:

1 tablespoon kosher or sea salt

1 tablespoon unrefined granulated palm, date, or maple sugar

1 teaspoon paprika

1 teaspoon ground cumin

½ teaspoon dry mustard

½ teaspoon ground black pepper

⅛ teaspoon cayenne pepper

3 pounds pork spareribs

For serving:

Carolina-Style Sauce (page 234), Apple Butter BBQ Sauce (page 112), or barbecue sauce of choice

SPECIAL TOOLS:

grill

When life says no noodles, we make lasagna anyway. Butternut squash lends a unique flavor to this classic Italian casserole. Unlike our Veggie Lasagna side dish (page 240), this version is a complete meal that goes great with a simple salad and Garlic Breadsticks (page 282). We recommend doubling the recipe and freezing one for later; it is a perfect dish to give to a new mom or sick friend or for when the babysitter is watching the kids.

BUTTERNUT SQUASH LASAGNA

PREHEAT OVEN: 350°F · SERVES: 4 TO 6

Ingredients

- 1 medium butternut squash (about 1½ pounds)
- 2 pounds uncooked Traditional Beef Breakfast Sausage (page 164)
- 2 cups tomato sauce, divided
- 1 cup Cashew Cheese Sauce (page 126), divided
- 1 tablespoon chopped fresh parsley, plus more for garnish

Note: If you've made this lasagna ahead of time and chilled or frozen it before baking, you will need to increase the cooking time by 10 minutes if chilled or 30 minutes if frozen.

1. Preheat the oven to 350°F. Bring a large pot of water to boil over high heat.

2. Cut the squash in half lengthwise, and then remove the seeds and peel it. Cut the 2 squash pieces in half crosswise, right above the bulbous section, at the base of the slender "neck" portion, creating a total of 4 pieces. Using a mandoline or other slicer, slice the squash quarters lengthwise into thin slices. Alternatively, this can be done carefully with a sharp knife.

3. Add the squash slices to the boiling water and blanch for 90 seconds. Drain and rinse with cool water to stop the cooking.

4. In a medium skillet over medium heat, brown the sausage, breaking it up into small pieces. Drain off the excess fat and set the sausage aside.

5. Pour ½ cup of the tomato sauce into an 8-by-8-inch baking dish and spread evenly over the bottom.

6. Add a layer of the butternut squash "noodles," using about one-quarter of the noodles.

7. Sprinkle one-third of the sausage over the top of the squash.

8. Dollop ⅓ cup of the cheese sauce over the sausage and spread evenly.

9. Add more tomato sauce, about ⅓ cup.

10. Repeat Steps 5 to 8 to create a total of 3 layers. Place the remaining squash noodles on top and spoon the remaining tomato sauce over the squash. (This prevents the squash from drying out, so make sure to cover all the edges.) Sprinkle the parsley on top.

11. Place in the oven and bake for 30 minutes. The lasagna is done when the top is browned and a knife can easily pierce the center pieces of butternut squash. Serve warm with an extra sprinkle of fresh parsley.

SWEETS AND TREATS

At our house, treats aren't a daily indulgence (nor should they be), but it's nice to partake in something sweet every once in a while, especially as you start your transition. Not only that, but what's more fun than making cookies or cakes for a special occasion? We hope that these recipes will cover all your dessert desires and make for interesting and palate-pleasing experiences, without the most offending junk.

	PHASE	PAGE #	UNDER 10 MIN	under 5 INGREDIENTS	ONE POT	HOLIDAY	ON the GO
Chocolate Layer Cake with Fresh Fruit	1	366				YES	
Frosting	1	368	YES	YES	YES	YES	
Snickerdoodle Whoopie Pies	1	370				YES	YES
Marshmallows	1	372		YES		YES	YES
Rocky Road Blondies	1	374			YES		
Samoa Brownies	1	376					
Chocolate Chip and Walnut Cookies	1	378		YES		YES	YES
Creamy Dreamy Frozen Custard	2	380		YES			
Peach Cobbler	1	382					
Healthiest Ice Cream Ever	3	384					
Jack-O'-Lantern Cookies	1	386				YES	YES
Pecan Pralines	1	388				YES	
Pumpkin Parfait	1	390				YES	
Key Lime Pie	1	392					
Lemon Drop Thumbprint Cookies	1	394					YES
Lemon Blueberry Bundt Cake	1	396					
Chia Seed Pudding	1	398		YES	YES		
Monster Cookie Dough Dip	1	400	YES		YES	YES	
Creamy Coconut Chocolate Chip Macaroons	1	402		YES	YES		YES
Salted Dark Chocolate Truffle Cookies	1	404	YES				YES
Chocolate Custard	2	406					

You might think it's impossible to still have a luscious real chocolate layer cake, but even our non-Paleo family and friends love this one. When we first made this cake, we topped it with our Strawberry Frosting (page 368) and fresh berries. We had a houseful of guests, and eventually everyone ended up at the kitchen counter, standing over this cake eating multiple slices with a fork and insisting we share the recipe with them immediately. We feel confident this will be a treat worthy of your next birthday party.

CHOCOLATE LAYER CAKE WITH FRESH FRUIT

PREHEAT OVEN: 350°F · MAKES: ONE 1-LAYER, 9-INCH CAKE (12 SERVINGS)

1. Preheat the oven to 350°F. Grease a 9-inch cake pan with lard and then dust it with cacao powder.

2. In a large mixing bowl, cream the lard and sugar with the coconut milk until smooth, starting slowly to avoid splattering.

3. Add the eggs and vanilla and beat to incorporate.

4. In a separate bowl, sift together the flours.

5. Slowly stir the flours into the wet ingredients until the batter is smooth.

6. Pour the batter into the prepared pan and smack it against the counter to release any air bubbles.

7. Place in the oven and bake for 30 to 40 minutes, until a toothpick inserted in the center comes out clean.

8. Remove from the oven and let cool in the pan for 30 minutes.

9. Run a knife around the outer edge of the cake to help loosen it. Turn the cake out onto a serving platter. Using a spatula, frost the cake evenly. Arrange the berries on top of the frosting.

Ingredients

Per layer:

- ½ cup lard, plus more for greasing the pan
- ½ cup cacao powder, plus more for dusting the pan
- ½ cup unrefined granulated cane sugar (see Notes)
- 1 cup coconut milk (full-fat, canned or homemade, page 290)
- 3 large eggs
- 2 teaspoons pure vanilla extract
- ½ cup tapioca flour
- 3 cups blanched almond flour
- 1 cup Strawberry Frosting (page 368)
- 1 cup fresh berries of choice, sliced or quartered (optional)

Notes: This recipe makes a 9-inch-round single-layer cake. Double the recipe for a double-layer cake as pictured, or slice the single layer in half for the same effect. If you cut one layer in half, prepare to need more frosting to frost the sides as well.

Typically, we would not recommend using granulated cane sugar, but we find that it contributes to the texture in an important way, creating the classic cakelike texture you would expect. Obviously this is a special treat and ought to be treated as such, but if you need an alternative, granulated palm or maple sugar can be substituted.

✓ Egg-Free
✓ Nut-Free
✓ Nightshade-Free

UNDER 30 MIN

under 5 INGREDIENTS

ONE POT

HOLIDAY

SPECIAL TOOLS:

High-speed blender, coffee grinder, or spice grinder

blender

The modern world has come to think that frosting comes from a can. But, filled with artificial food color and chemicals, it couldn't be further from food. Real buttercream frosting is traditionally made simply with butter and powdered cane sugar. Our versions of the classic use homemade powdered palm sugar and bring back the simplicity of traditional buttercream with a punch of flavor perfect for cakes, cupcakes, cookies, and whoopie pies. We've even heard people say that they love to use them as dips for fruit.

FROSTING

MAKES: ABOUT 2 CUPS EACH

Ingredients

Vanilla Bean

¾ cup unrefined granulated palm sugar

1 cup palm shortening or unsalted butter, softened

2 tablespoons pure vanilla extract

Seeds of 2 vanilla pods

Up to 2 tablespoons coconut milk (full-fat, canned or homemade, page 290) or Almond Milk (page 290)

Cinnamon Ginger

3 tablespoons unrefined granulated palm sugar

1 cup palm shortening or unsalted butter, softened

3 tablespoons maple syrup

3 tablespoons honey

1 teaspoon ground cinnamon

½ teaspoon ginger powder

¼ teaspoon ground nutmeg

Up to 2 tablespoons coconut milk (full-fat, canned or homemade, page 290) or Almond Milk (page 290)

Strawberry

½ cup unrefined granulated palm sugar

1 cup freeze-dried strawberries

1 cup palm shortening or unsalted butter, softened

2 teaspoons almond extract

1 teaspoon pure vanilla extract

Up to 2 tablespoons coconut milk (full-fat, canned or homemade, page 290) or Almond Milk (page 290)

1. To make with a high-speed blender, grind the sugar and freeze-dried strawberries, if making the strawberry frosting, to a powder. Add the rest of the ingredients except the coconut or almond milk to the blender and blend until smooth. Then slowly add the coconut or almond milk, a little at a time, until the desired consistency is reached. (Depending on the humidity and altitude, the frosting may need a touch more or less liquid, which is why it's important to work slowly.)

2. To make with a coffee grinder or spice grinder, grind the sugar and freeze-dried strawberries, if making the strawberry frosting, to a powder, working in batches as needed. Transfer the powder to a mixing bowl. Add the rest of the ingredients except the coconut or almond milk to the bowl and whip with a hand-held electric mixer until smooth. Then, while whipping, slowly add the coconut or almond milk, a little at a time, until the desired consistency is reached. (Depending on the humidity and

altitude, the frosting may need a touch more or less liquid, which is why it's important to work slowly.)

3. Store leftover frosting in the refrigerator. Because the frosting will stiffen when cooled, we recommend making it when the cake or other treat is cool and ready to be iced. Frosted treats should be removed from the refrigerator 20 minutes before serving to let the frosting soften at room temperature.

Note: If you tolerate dairy, then organic grass-fed butter is a good substitute for palm shortening. It adds some nutrients and lots of flavor. In our home, we use sustainably sourced palm shortening (see page 26 for trusted sources). If you do not have a coffee grinder or high-speed blender, most health food stores sell organic powdered cane sugar (aka confectioners' sugar). Look for a brand that uses tapioca flour as the anticlumping agent (instead of cornstarch).

Egg-Free

Nut-Free

☑ Nightshade-Free

HOLIDAY ON the GO

Soft cinnamon sandwich cookies with a terrific ginger bite to the frosting make for a great nostalgia trip. Of course, these snickerdoodle cookies are also delicious on their own.

SNICKERDOODLE WHOOPIE PIES

PREHEAT OVEN: 350°F · MAKES: 1 DOZEN WHOOPIE PIES

Ingredients

½ cup palm shortening, ghee, or unsalted butter, plus more for greasing the pan (if not using parchment)

½ cup Almond Butter (page 186)

½ cup maple syrup

2 large eggs

1 tablespoon pure vanilla extract

2 cups blanched almond flour

1 teaspoon baking soda

2 teaspoons ground cinnamon

For the topping:

Unrefined granulated palm, date, or maple sugar

1 tablespoon ground cinnamon

For the filling:

1 batch Cinnamon Ginger Frosting (page 368)

1. Preheat the oven to 350°F. Line 3 baking sheets with parchment paper or grease them with palm shortening.

2. In a large bowl, beat together the palm shortening, almond butter, maple syrup, eggs, and vanilla until smooth.

3. In a separate bowl, whisk together the flour, baking soda, and cinnamon.

4. While beating the wet mixture, slowly add the dry mixture until combined. The dough will be wet and sticky.

5. Drop tablespoons of the dough several inches apart onto the prepared baking sheets, 8 per sheet. Using the back of a spoon or a spatula and a circular motion, spread the cookies into flat disks, about ½ inch thick.

6. In a small bowl, combine the ingredients for the topping. Sprinkle the topping over the cookies, about ⅛ teaspoon per cookie.

7. Bake the cookies for 8 to 10 minutes, until the edges are golden brown and the centers are still slightly wet-looking and spongy and bounce back if you press on them. (If baking 2 sheets at once, swap the sheets between the racks midway through baking.)

8. Let the cookies rest on the baking sheet for 10 minutes, and then transfer them to a cooling rack. Let cool thoroughly, at least an hour. You can store unfrosted cookies in an airtight container at room temperature for up to a week.

9. Once the cookies are cool, spread about a tablespoon of the frosting onto the flat side of one cookie and then top with a second cookie to create a whoopie pie. Repeat with the remaining cookies and frosting. Store the whoopie pies in an airtight container in the refrigerator for up to 2 weeks. Allow to come to room temperature before serving.

Note: To change the flavor, try our Vanilla Bean Frosting (page 368) for a sandwich cookie reminiscent of a Little Debbie Oatmeal Creme Pie.

☑ Egg-Free
☑ Nut-Free
☑ Nightshade-Free

Yes, marshmallows! It turns out that they're surprisingly easy to make at home and twice as delicious as store-bought versions. You'll be amazed when the syrup and gelatin suddenly form thick white marshmallow fluff. Although they're perfect on their own, we love to add them to our Rocky Road Blondies (page 374).

MARSHMALLOWS

MAKES: 2 DOZEN MARSHMALLOWS

Ingredients

½ cup honey

½ cup maple syrup

1 cup water, divided

¼ cup gelatin powder

1 teaspoon pure vanilla extract

Coconut oil, for greasing the spatula and knife

Tapioca flour, for dusting the marshmallows

SPECIAL TOOLS:

Candy thermometer (see Note)

1. Whisk together the honey, maple syrup, and ½ cup of the water in a small saucepan over medium heat. Attach a candy thermometer.

2. While the sweeteners are heating, bloom the gelatin: In the bowl of a stand mixer, combine the gelatin powder and the remaining ½ cup of water. Stir to moisten the gelatin powder. Set aside.

3. Stir frequently as the syrup mixture increases in temperature. When it reaches 240°F (referred to as the soft ball stage), remove from the heat and pour over the gelatin.

4. Immediately start whipping, using the whisk attachment, on medium speed. When the syrup begins to get frothy, increase the speed to high and add the vanilla.

5. Continue whipping until the mixture becomes fluffy, about 12 minutes. Stop whipping when the mixture is very thick, stiff, and white and coats the whisk completely.

6. Line an 11-by-7-inch baking dish with parchment paper, allowing extra length to hang outside of the dish.

7. Grease a rubber spatula with coconut oil and use it to transfer the marshmallow mixture to the dish. Smooth the top and gently press with the spatula so that the mixture expands to each corner. Dust lightly with tapioca flour to prevent sticking during storage.

8. Allow to cool completely before removing with the parchment paper "handles" to a cutting board. Grease a knife with coconut oil and use it to cut the marshmallows into 1½-inch squares. Dust lightly again with tapioca flour on all sides. Store in an airtight container at room temperature for up to a week.

Note: Candy thermometers are affordable and are easily found at almost any grocery store or even a dollar store. Using one is essential to this recipe.

After making Marshmallows (page 372), the logical next step is to travel the rocky road! Instead of cocoa powder, we give these blondies their chocolate kick with ground cacao nibs for a unique take on this classic flavor combination.

ROCKY ROAD BLONDIES

PREHEAT OVEN: 350°F · MAKES: 16 (2-INCH) SQUARES

Ingredients

- ⅓ cup lard or palm shortening, plus more for greasing the pan (if not using parchment)
- ½ cup maple syrup
- 2 large eggs
- 2½ cups blanched almond flour
- 1 teaspoon baking soda
- ½ teaspoon kosher or sea salt
- ¼ cup cacao nibs, coarsely ground (see Note)
- ½ cup chocolate chips
- ½ cup diced Marshmallows (page 372)
- ½ cup raw walnuts, chopped

1. Preheat the oven to 350°F. Line an 8-by-8-inch baking dish with parchment paper or grease it with lard.

2. In a large bowl, whisk together the lard and maple syrup until combined.

3. Add the eggs and beat to incorporate.

4. In a separate bowl, sift together the almond flour, baking soda, and salt. Stir in the cacao nibs.

5. Slowly whisk the dry ingredients into the wet ingredients until a thick batter forms.

6. Fold in the chocolate chips, marshmallows, and walnuts.

7. Pour the batter into the prepared baking dish.

8. Place in the oven and bake for 25 minutes, until the edges begin to brown and a toothpick inserted in the center comes out clean. Allow to cool in the pan for 15 minutes before slicing. Store in an airtight container at room temperature for up to a week.

Note: Cacao nibs are cocoa beans before they are processed into chocolate, cocoa, or any of the other products of the cocoa bean.

Yes, like the famous Girl Scout cookie. The coconut, caramel, and chocolate merge to make a delectable dessert. If you love Samoas, then you will love these brownies more. And since this recipe is based off of our award-winning brownie recipe featured in the *Paleo Magazine's* Best of 2013 competition, we're confident that you'll love it!

SAMOA BROWNIES

PREHEAT OVEN: 350°F · MAKES: 12 TO 15 BROWNIES

Ingredients

For the brownies:

⅓ cup coconut oil, melted, plus more for greasing the dish

½ cup maple syrup

2 large eggs

2½ cups blanched almond flour

¼ cup cacao powder

1 teaspoon baking soda

½ teaspoon kosher or sea salt

½ cup raw macadamia nuts, chopped

½ cup chocolate chips

For the caramel sauce:

½ cup maple syrup

½ cup honey

1 teaspoon baking soda

For the toasted coconut topping:

½ cup unsweetened coconut flakes

1. Preheat the oven to 350°F. Grease an 11-by-7-inch baking dish.

2. Make the brownies: In a medium bowl, whisk together the coconut oil and maple syrup. Add the eggs and beat together.

3. In a separate bowl, mix the flour, cacao powder, baking soda, and salt.

4. Add the dry ingredients to the wet ingredients and mix until a thick batter forms. Fold in the nuts and chocolate chips.

5. Pour the batter into the prepared baking dish. Place in the oven and bake for 25 minutes, or until a toothpick inserted in the center comes out clean.

6. Meanwhile, make the caramel sauce: Heat the maple syrup and honey in a small saucepan over medium heat. Once bubbles begin to form, reduce the heat to medium-low and cook until it thickens and the color darkens, about 10 minutes, stirring continuously with a whisk to prevent burning. Watch carefully; the mixture can potentially bubble up and flow over the edge of the pan. If that happens, remove the pan from the heat and stir, returning the pan to the heat once the bubbling subsides.

7. Once the sauce has thickened, remove the pan from the heat and whisk in the baking soda until thoroughly combined (it will expand and bubble as you whisk).

8. Return the pan to medium heat for 2 to 3 minutes, whisking constantly, until the mixture becomes a thick, rich, bubbly sauce that does not deflate when moved off the heat. Remove from the heat and let cool for 15 minutes, stirring occasionally to reincorporate any liquid that separates.

9. Let the caramel sauce and brownies cool for a few minutes (a tough one, we know!).

10. Make the toasted coconut topping: In a small skillet, toast the coconut flakes over medium heat, stirring frequently, until slightly browned, about 5 minutes. Remove from the pan and set aside.

11. Pour HALF of the caramel sauce over the baked brownies and top with the toasted coconut flakes. (Save the other half for other recipes, like our Chocolate Layer Cake on page 366, or use it as a topping on our Creamy Dreamy Frozen Custard on page 380.) Store the leftover caramel sauce in a sealable jar like a mason jar in the fridge for up to 2 weeks. The brownies can be stored in an airtight container at room temperature for up to a week.

Note: These brownies are intended to be a bit more cakey. If you prefer a fudgy brownie, then double the chocolate chips and bake for 20 to 22 minutes. The brownies will still be slightly soft in the center when removed from the oven.

☐ Egg-Free
☐ Nut-Free
☑ Nightshade-Free

Classic chocolate chip cookies are a favorite in our household. Nothing beats the taste of a warm cookie filled with gooey chocolate. Both of us have wonderful memories of baking this classic cookie as kids, and it's something we like to share with our children. This fruit-sweetened version allows us to do that and give them something healthy at the same time. We've tried dozens of recipes over the years, and this cookie is by far our favorite. We love to eat a couple cookies dipped in a cold glass of Coconut or Almond Milk (page 290). This dough is a wonderful base for lots of cookies. Add raisins, cinnamon, and almond slivers instead of chocolate chips for a version that will taste like an oatmeal cookie.

CHOCOLATE CHIP AND WALNUT COOKIES

PREHEAT OVEN: 350°F · MAKES: 3 DOZEN COOKIES

Ingredients

1 cup raw cashews

½ cup soft Medjool dates, pitted

¾ cup palm shortening, ghee, lard, or unsalted butter, plus more for greasing the pan (if not using parchment)

2 large eggs

1 teaspoon pure vanilla extract

2 tablespoons coconut flour

2 cups blanched almond flour

½ teaspoon baking soda

1 teaspoon kosher or sea salt

¾ cup chocolate chips

½ cup raw walnuts, chopped

SPECIAL TOOLS:

food processor

1. Place the cashews in a bowl and cover with water. Set aside to soak for 2 hours.

2. After the cashews have soaked for 2 hours, preheat the oven to 350°F. Line a baking sheet with parchment paper or grease it with palm shortening.

3. Pour the soaked cashews into a colander and rinse them; drain well. Place the cashews and dates in a food processor and pulse until very finely chopped.

4. Add the palm shortening, eggs, and vanilla to the processor and pulse until smooth and blended.

5. Add the flours, baking soda, and salt to the processor and pulse until just combined.

6. Empty out the dough into a mixing bowl and fold in the chocolate chips and chopped walnuts.

7. Roll the dough into tablespoon-sized balls and place on the prepared baking sheet. Flatten each ball with the palm of your hand.

8. Place in the oven and bake for 8 to 10 minutes, until the cookies are slightly brown but still soft in the center. Let sit on the baking sheet for about 5 minutes before transferring to a cooling rack; they will firm up as they cool. Store at room temperature for a couple of days, or refrigerate to keep longer (although we highly doubt that they'll last that long!). They freeze well, too, if you want to bake them in advance.

Note: We like a soft, chewy cookie. If you'd like a crispier version, add 2 tablespoons of arrowroot flour when you mix in the other flours.

■ Egg-Free
■ Nut-Free
✓ Nightshade-Free

When bringing home eggs fresh from the farm one hot July afternoon, we decided that they must be used to make homemade frozen custard. Custard is just like ice cream with egg yolks included. The result is a rich and flavorful ice cream that you're sure to enjoy. The dates help to keep the texture creamy while providing natural sweetness without any added sweeteners. The end result is a sweet frozen treat that has added nutrients from the egg yolks—so no need to feel guilty for enjoying a scoop or two. For an extra indulgence, sandwich this custard between Chocolate Chip and Walnut Cookies (page 378) or serve with our Peach Cobbler (page 382) or Samoa Brownies (page 376) à la mode.

CREAMY DREAMY FROZEN CUSTARD

MAKES: 2 PINTS

Ingredients

2 (13½-ounce) cans full-fat coconut milk or 3½ cups homemade (page 290)

8 soft Medjool dates, pitted (or more to your taste)

1½ teaspoons hazelnut, almond, or pure vanilla extract

1 to 2 teaspoons kosher or sea salt

4 large pastured egg yolks

SPECIAL TOOLS: Food processor or blender; ice cream maker

food processor   OR   blender

1. In a blender or food processor, purée the milk, dates, extract, and 2 teaspoons of the salt. If using vanilla extract, use only 1 teaspoon of salt. (We like this custard salty when we use hazelnut or almond extract, as it reminds us of a peanut butter–flavored ice cream.)

2. Add the egg yolks one at a time, pulsing to combine until smooth.

3. Place the mixture in an ice cream maker and churn, following the manufacturer's instructions, until thickened, about 20 minutes.

4. Freeze in an airtight container for at least 30 minutes before serving. If frozen for more than 4 hours, let rest at room temperature for about 20 minutes before serving. (Because they don't have chemical softeners, natural ice creams set hard like ice and require time to soften.)

Note: Concerned about raw egg yolks? You can certainly heat the egg yolks by warming the coconut milk over medium heat (do not bring to a simmer) and then tempering the yolks into the warm milk and simmering gently. Don't overheat, or you'll be left with scrambled eggs floating in coconut milk!

We have a good friend who is severely allergic to nuts and chocolate, so making sweet treats for him can be challenging. After some brainstorming, we perfected this dish and were thrilled when it got his thumbs-up without an ambulance called to the scene. This unique, nut-free cobbler makes a great summertime dessert. In the fall or winter, try replacing peaches with other seasonal fruit, like apples or pears.

PEACH COBBLER

PREHEAT OVEN: 350°F · SERVES: 8

Ingredients

- 2 cups unsweetened dried banana chips
- 1 cup raw sunflower seeds
- ½ cup unrefined granulated palm, date, or maple sugar
- 1½ cups unsweetened shredded coconut
- 1 cup palm shortening, ghee, or unsalted butter, softened
- 2 pounds peaches, peeled and sliced, or 32 ounces thawed frozen or canned in juice peach slices
- ¼ cup arrowroot flour

For serving (optional):
- 1 batch Creamy Dreamy Frozen Custard (page 380)

SPECIAL TOOLS:

food processor

1. Preheat the oven to 350°F.

2. In a food processor, pulse the banana chips, sunflower seeds, sugar, and coconut 10 times for 1 second each time.

3. Add the palm shortening and continue to pulse until a crumbly meal forms.

4. Spread the fruit in the bottom of an 8-inch-square baking dish and stir in the arrowroot flour.

5. Sprinkle the dough on top of the fruit and coat evenly and completely.

6. Place in the oven and bake for 35 minutes, until the dough turns golden brown. We recommend putting the baking dish on a rimmed baking sheet in case the juice bubbles and spills over.

7. Serve warm with the Creamy Dreamy Frozen Custard, if desired.

Note: Although you can make your own banana chips, it's not hard to find high-quality store-bought ones. We always keep them in the house as a versatile snack or ingredient.

We originally made this recipe at the height of peach season after our family went to a pick-your-own farm and came back with tons of very ripe peaches. We blanched them and then peeled, pitted, sliced, and froze them to have that organic, farm-fresh taste available all year long.

Do we dare to call ice cream healthy? We created this unique ice cream with zero sweeteners and roasted squash as its centerpiece. The result is a barely sweet and refreshing dessert that allows you to enjoy a frozen treat without guilt.

HEALTHIEST ICE CREAM EVER

PREHEAT OVEN: 350°F · MAKES: 2 PINTS

Ingredients

- 1 medium butternut squash (about 1½ pounds)
- 1½ teaspoons kosher or sea salt
- 1 (13½-ounce) can full-fat coconut milk or 1¾ cups homemade (page 290)
- 2 large pastured egg yolks
- 2 tablespoons coconut oil
- 1 teaspoon pure vanilla extract
- 1 teaspoon almond extract
- 1 teaspoon ground cinnamon
- Slightly Sweet & Salty Snack Mix (page 184), for garnish

1. Preheat the oven to 350°F.

2. Remove the ends of the squash, slice it in half lengthwise, and remove the seeds. Then peel and cube the squash. Spread out the squash cubes in a rimmed baking sheet and roast in the oven for 30 minutes or until easily pierced with a fork. Let cool completely.

3. Place 2 packed cups of the cooled squash and the remaining ingredients in a food processor or high-speed blender and purée until smooth.

4. Put the mixture in an ice cream maker and churn, following the manufacturer's directions, until stiffened, about 10 minutes.

5. Freeze in an airtight container for at least 30 minutes before serving. If frozen for more than 4 hours, let rest at room temperature for about 20 minutes before serving. (Natural ice creams don't contain chemical softeners, so they set hard like ice and require time to soften.)

6. Scoop into bowls and top with the Slightly Sweet & Salty Snack Mix.

Note: If you can't find butternut squash, any winter squash will do. Most grocery stores sell prepackaged peeled and cubed butternut squash to make this recipe even easier, but we've heard that pumpkin is a fan favorite.

Don't have an ice cream maker? Never fear! After cooking and cooling the squash, place it in the freezer to harden for a few hours. Then, once partially frozen, add the squash and remaining ingredients to a high-speed blender and purée—you'll have instant soft-serve.

SPECIAL TOOLS:
Food processor or high-speed blender; ice cream maker

 OR

food processor   blender

Growing up, Stacy loved the prepackaged snacks she could find at convenience stores for a quarter. Of course, you get what you pay for, and those treats didn't do great things for her health. Missing those flavors one afternoon, Stacy and the kids came up with this fun and flavorful recipe perfect for seasonal celebrations. These cookies will certainly satisfy your own craving for a Little Debbie Pumpkin Delight! Using our Pumpkin or Apple Butter (page 110) as a filling makes these smiling pumpkin faces worth the effort for a terrific Halloween party treat.

JACK-O'-LANTERN COOKIES

PREHEAT OVEN: 350°F · MAKES: 8 COOKIE SANDWICHES

Ingredients

½ cup raw pumpkin seeds (preferred) or 1¼ cups raw sunflower seeds

1¼ cups blanched almond flour

½ cup coconut flour

½ cup tapioca flour, plus extra for flouring the rolling surface

1½ teaspoons ground cinnamon

½ teaspoon ground nutmeg

¼ teaspoon ginger powder

⅛ teaspoon ground cloves

½ teaspoon baking soda

¼ teaspoon kosher or sea salt

½ cup pumpkin puree

¼ cup coconut oil, softened, plus more for greasing the pan (if not using parchment)

¼ cup honey

2 large eggs

½ cup Pumpkin Butter or Apple Butter (page 110)

SPECIAL TOOLS:
High-speed blender, coffee grinder, or spice grinder; pumpkin-shaped cookie cutter

1. In a high-speed blender, coffee grinder, or spice grinder, grind the pumpkin seeds or sunflower seeds on high until they are a fine powder.

2. In a medium mixing bowl, sift together the flours, ground seeds, spices, baking soda, and salt.

3. In a large bowl, beat together the pumpkin puree, oil, honey, and eggs until well blended. Pour in the dry ingredients slowly while mixing. Continue to mix until a thick dough forms.

4. Divide the dough in half and flatten each half into a disk. Wrap each disk in plastic wrap and chill for at least 20 minutes.

5. When you're ready to make the cookies, preheat the oven to 350°F. Line a baking sheet with parchment paper or grease it with coconut oil.

6. Remove a dough disk and roll it out on a tapioca-floured surface to ¼ inch thick.

7. Using a 3-inch-wide, pumpkin-shaped cookie cutter, cut out the cookies and place them on the prepared baking sheet. If the dough becomes warm, it will become sticky and difficult to work with. If that happens, return it to the fridge to cool.

8. Spoon about 1 tablespoon of the pumpkin or apple butter on top of each cookie and spread it out, leaving a ⅛-inch edge all the way around.

9. Remove the second dough disk from the refrigerator and roll it out to the same ¼-inch thickness. Cut out more pumpkins.

10. With a knife, cut out fun faces on this second set of pumpkins, and then place them on top of the buttered cookies. Lightly press the edges together to seal.

11. Place in the oven and bake for about 15 minutes, until the cookies just begin to brown. Store at room temperature for only a day or two; otherwise, keep chilled and bring to room temperature before serving.

Candied nuts are a favorite treat in our house. They're fun to make, and these pralines have just the right amount of sweetness and crunch to satisfy your sweet tooth after only a few bites. We add these to our Pumpkin Parfait (page 390), but they go quick at parties when set out in a candy bowl.

PECAN PRALINES

SERVES: 8

Ingredients

½ cup coconut milk (full-fat, canned or homemade, page 290)

1 cup unrefined granulated palm sugar

¼ cup maple syrup

¼ cup palm shortening or unsalted butter

1 teaspoon pure vanilla extract

½ teaspoon kosher or sea salt

2 cups raw pecans

SPECIAL TOOLS:

Candy thermometer

1. Line a rimmed baking sheet with parchment paper.

2. In a small saucepan over medium heat, whisk together the coconut milk, palm sugar, and maple syrup. Attach a candy thermometer and allow to come to a simmer.

3. When the mixture reaches 240°F, remove the pan from the heat and stir in the palm shortening, vanilla, and salt.

4. Add the pecans and stir to coat. Pour the pecans onto the prepared baking sheet in a single layer and allow to cool completely.

5. When the pecans are cool, break apart and store in an airtight container for up to 2 weeks.

Note: Whole pecans are prettier, but pieces are much more affordable; feel free to use whichever you prefer.

After making our Pumpkin Pudding (page 154), we wanted to see what we could do to enhance it for our pumpkin-loving photographer, Aimee. We realized that our Cinnamon Bread (page 156) and Pecan Pralines (page 388) would be the perfect complements to the rich pudding. Although it takes quite a bit of effort, this special treat is certainly worth it for the pumpkin lover in your life. And once each component is made, it's simple and fun to assemble this deluxe parfait for any special occasion.

PUMPKIN PARFAIT

SERVES: 10 TO 12 (OR SERVES 8 IN 8-OUNCE GLASSES)

Ingredients

For the Whipped Coconut Cream:

1 (13½-ounce) can full-fat coconut milk or 1 cup organic grass-fed heavy whipping cream

1 batch Pumpkin Pudding (page 154)

1 loaf Cinnamon Bread (page 156), cooled and cut into 1-inch cubes

1 batch Pecan Pralines (page 388)

SPECIAL TOOLS:
Stand mixer or hand-held electric mixer

1. Make the Whipped Coconut Cream: Chill the coconut milk in the can in the fridge overnight. Chill a metal bowl in the freezer for at least 15 minutes before starting. (If using a stand mixer, chill the metal bowl that comes with the mixer.)

2. Open the can of coconut milk, scoop off the thick, creamy portion that has risen to the surface, and place it in the chilled bowl.

3. In a stand mixer or using a hand-held electric mixer, whip the coconut cream on high speed until soft peaks form, about 5 minutes. Alternatively, if you tolerate dairy, unsweetened grass-fed heavy whipping cream will whip more easily following this step.

4. Assemble the parfait: In the bottom of a clear glass serving bowl with high sides and about a 2-quart capacity, layer 1 cup of the pumpkin pudding, then one-third of the cinnamon bread cubes, then one-third of the Whipped Coconut Cream, and finally one-third of the pralines. Repeat this layering 3 times.

5. Alternatively, make individual servings using clear glass bowls or parfait glasses. This recipe will make eight 8-ounce servings.

Egg-Free
Nut-Free
☑ Nightshade-Free

Since going Paleo four years ago, we've regularly made Key Lime Pie because it's a favorite of Stacy's dad, who raves about the homemade versions he finds when visiting the Florida Keys. Although Stacy's dad still eats grains and has had the very best pies made with fresh Key limes from Florida, he asks for our Key Lime Pie. The secret is to use real lime juice; never compromise with a bottled lime juice.

KEY LIME PIE

PREHEAT OVEN: 350°F · MAKES: 1 (9-INCH) PIE OR 16 (2-INCH) SQUARES

1. Preheat the oven to 350°F.

2. In a food processor, chop the almonds, walnuts, and dates into a thick paste.

3. Press the crust into the bottom of a 9-inch pie pan. Place in the oven and bake for 8 minutes. Remove from the oven and allow to cool as you make the filling. Leave the oven on.

4. In a medium mixing bowl, whisk together the lime juice, eggs, egg yolk, coconut milk, honey, and coconut flour. Fold in the lime zest.

5. Pour the filling on top of the cooled crust and bake for 30 minutes or until the middle is set and the edges are browned.

6. Allow to cool in the pan for 15 minutes. Top with the whipped coconut cream, if desired. Leftover pie can be stored in the fridge for up to a week.

Variation: Key Lime Bars
This recipe can be made as bars instead. Press the crust into an 8-by-8-inch baking dish and skip the coconut cream topping. The bars are perfect for a party!

Ingredients

For the crust:

1 cup raw almonds

½ cup raw walnuts

½ cup soft Medjool dates, pitted

For the filling:

½ cup freshly squeezed Key lime or regular lime juice

3 large eggs

1 large egg yolk

1 cup coconut milk (full-fat, canned or homemade, page 290)

¼ cup honey

2 tablespoons coconut flour

1 tablespoon grated lime zest

For serving (optional):

1 batch Whipped Coconut Cream (page 390)

SPECIAL TOOLS:

food processor

The best part of these cookies is the sweet lemon curd bite in the center of each one. You can make your own curd or, to save time, use a prepared version. You'll find fairly Paleo-friendly products on store shelves because curd is traditionally made with just juice, eggs, sugar, and butter.

LEMON DROP THUMBPRINT COOKIES

PREHEAT OVEN: 350°F · MAKES: 3 DOZEN COOKIES

Ingredients

For the lemon curd:

3 large eggs

½ cup maple syrup

2 teaspoons grated lemon zest

⅓ cup freshly squeezed lemon juice

¼ cup lard or unsalted butter, softened

For the cookies:

¼ cup coconut oil, melted

½ cup honey

2 large eggs

1 teaspoon grated lemon zest

2 tablespoons freshly squeezed lemon juice

1 teaspoon pure vanilla extract

4 cups blanched almond flour, sifted

1 cup tapioca flour, sifted

SPECIAL TOOLS:
Double boiler assembly

1. To make the curd: Whisk the eggs, maple syrup, lemon zest, and lemon juice in a double boiler over medium heat. If you don't have a double boiler, simply place a heatproof glass bowl over a simmering pot of water, ensuring that only the steam touches the bottom of the bowl.

2. Simmer the curd, stirring constantly, for 8 minutes until thickened and well mixed.

3. Fold in the lard until melted and incorporated. Transfer to the refrigerator and allow to thicken for at least 2 hours. The curd is now ready to be used, or it can be stored in an airtight container, like a mason jar, for 2 weeks or more in the refrigerator.

4. When you're ready to make the cookies, preheat the oven to 350°F.

5. To make the cookies: In a large mixing bowl, beat together the oil, honey, and eggs until well combined.

6. Stir in the lemon zest, lemon juice, and vanilla.

7. Slowly add the sifted flours while whisking until a dough forms.

8. Using your hands, form the dough into 1½-inch-wide cookies and place them on a baking sheet, ½ inch apart. Then use your thumb or the back of rounded tablespoon to create a divot in the center of each cookie. Spoon the cooled lemon curd into the divot.

9. Place in the oven and bake for 18 minutes or until lightly browned on the edges. Let cool on the baking sheet for 10 minutes before transferring to a cooling rack and allowing to cool completely. Store the cookies in an airtight container in the refrigerator for up to 2 weeks.

Note: Our children love making these cookies because they get to stick their thumbs in the center and fill the holes with curd. They say it's like a volcano of deliciousness!

Egg-Free
Nut-Free
☑ Nightshade-Free

This cake manages to be elegant, simple, *and* delicious. Combining lemon and blueberries is a fantastic way to make a cake with minimal sweeteners memorable to your guests. We've even served this cake as a birthday treat instead of a traditional layer cake.

LEMON BLUEBERRY BUNDT CAKE

PREHEAT OVEN: 325°F · SERVES: UP TO 12

Ingredients

½ cup lard, ghee, or palm shortening, softened, plus more for greasing the pan

4 cups blanched almond flour

1 tablespoon ground cinnamon

1 teaspoon baking soda

1 teaspoon kosher or sea salt

¼ cup maple syrup

¼ cup honey

4 large eggs

1 tablespoon pure vanilla extract

2 teaspoons grated lemon zest

2 tablespoons freshly squeezed lemon juice

2 cups blueberries

1 cup raw walnuts, chopped (optional)

SPECIAL TOOLS:
Bundt pan

1. Preheat the oven to 325°F. Grease a 12-cup Bundt pan with lard. Be sure to get the fat into all of the creases, where the cake is most likely to stick.

2. In a medium mixing bowl, sift together the almond flour, cinnamon, baking soda, and salt.

3. In a large mixing bowl, beat together the maple syrup, honey, eggs, vanilla, lemon zest, lemon juice, and lard until well combined.

4. Stir the dry ingredients slowly into the wet ingredients until fully incorporated.

5. With a spatula, fold in the blueberries and walnuts, if using.

6. Pour the batter into the greased Bundt pan, smoothing the top. Tap the pan on the countertop a couple times to release any trapped air bubbles.

7. Place in the oven and bake for 1 hour, or until a knife inserted in the center of the cake comes out clean.

8. Let cool in the pan for 20 to 30 minutes, and then turn out onto a plate. The cooling-in-the-pan step cannot be skipped! Letting the cake cool allows it to retract from the edges of the Bundt pan, which will make for a beautiful release (instead of a crumbly mess).

Note: Yes, you could use thawed-from-frozen blueberries, but they would change texture of the resulting cake due to much more juice.

☑ Egg-Free
☐ Nut-Free
☑ Nightshade-Free

One of our favorite desserts is this easy chia seed pudding. These little seeds are rumored to pack a nutritional punch, but what we love is that they absorb fluid and become jellylike bubbles in the pudding, reminiscent of tapioca or rice pudding. All you need is some liquid and chia seeds and the pudding will form itself, although we recommend adding some more flavor.

CHIA SEED PUDDING

Ingredients

SERVES: 8

Cinnamon Raisin

- ⅔ cup coconut milk (full-fat, canned or homemade, page 290)
- ⅔ cup Almond Milk (page 290)
- 1 tablespoon honey
- 2 tablespoons chia seeds
- ½ teaspoon pure vanilla extract
- 1 teaspoon ground cinnamon
- 2 tablespoons raw walnuts, finely chopped
- ½ cup raisins

Mango Sticky (Not) Rice

- 1 (13½-ounce) can full-fat coconut milk or 1¾ cups homemade (page 290)
- 1 cup water
- ⅓ cup unrefined granulated palm, date, or maple sugar
- ½ cup chia seeds
- 2 cups diced ripe juicy mango (or thawed from frozen)

Chocolate

- 1 (13½-ounce) can full-fat coconut milk or 1¾ cups homemade (page 290)
- 2 cups Almond Milk (page 290)
- ¼ cup honey
- 2 tablespoons cacao powder
- ½ cup chia seeds
- 1 teaspoon pure vanilla extract
- ¼ teaspoon ground cinnamon
- ½ cup chocolate chips (optional)

1. Pour the milk(s), water (if needed), honey or sugar, and cacao powder (if needed) into a small saucepan and warm over medium heat. Stir frequently until the sweetener is thoroughly dissolved.

2. Place the chia seeds along with the vanilla and cinnamon (if needed) in a medium mixing bowl. Pour the warm milk into the bowl and whisk thoroughly to moisten the seeds.

3. Stir in any remaining add-ins. Chill the pudding in the refrigerator until completely cooled, about 1 hour, before serving in 4-ounce portions.

☑ Egg-Free
◼ Nut-Free
☑ Nightshade-Free

UNDER 30 MIN

ONE POT

HOLIDAY

You know how the best part of making cookies is eating the cookie dough? Well, what if you made cookie dough with the intention of eating it by itself? When you serve this at your next party, even non-Paleo people will be clamoring for more!

MONSTER COOKIE DOUGH DIP

SERVES: 10 TO 12

Ingredients

2 cups blanched almond flour

½ cup palm shortening or unsalted butter, softened

¼ cup honey

¼ cup maple syrup

1 tablespoon pure vanilla extract

½ teaspoon kosher or sea salt

Optional add-ins:

½ cup soft Medjool dates, pitted and chopped

½ cup raw walnuts, chopped

½ cup chocolate chips

For dipping:

Tart apples

Carrots

Banana chips

1. Mix together the flour, palm shortening, sweeteners, vanilla, and salt until a thick dough forms. This can easily be done in a stand mixer or food processor.

2. Fold in the add-ins, if using, by hand.

3. Transfer to a serving bowl and serve alongside your favorite dipping foods at room temperature. An excellent make-ahead food, this dip stores well chilled.

Note: We recommend sustainably harvested non-hydrogenated palm shortening for this recipe because it's a flavorless, shelf-stable fat. That means you can transport this dip at room temperature without worrying about it going bad.

Variation: Frozen Cookie Dough Pops

After completing Step 1, form the dough into rounded tablespoon-sized balls and place on a rimmed baking sheet lined with parchment paper. Poke the balls with skewers or popsicle sticks and freeze until hardened. Once frozen, dip in melted chocolate to make incredibly decadent cookie dough pops, perfect for a child's birthday party.

SPECIAL TOOLS:

food processor

✓ Egg-Free
✓ Nut-Free
✓ Nightshade-Free

Many people who have tried this cookie tell us that it quickly becomes their favorite. Even people who don't like coconut love them. This recipe comes together incredibly fast, and because there are no eggs in the batter, it's delicious just as dough. In fact, we use this dough base in our Cranberry-Orange No-Bake Coconut Bars (page 172). These macaroons are one of those rare nut- and egg-free treats that are still delicious—try them and you'll see that they are indeed creamy!

CREAMY COCONUT CHOCOLATE CHIP MACAROONS

PREHEAT OVEN: 300°F · MAKES: 2 DOZEN COOKIES

Ingredients

1 cup coconut cream concentrate, or 1 cup Coconut Butter (page 114) blended with 1 tablespoon coconut oil until loose and almost liquid

⅔ cup maple syrup

1 teaspoon kosher or sea salt

2 cups unsweetened shredded coconut

½ cup chocolate chips (optional)

1. Preheat the oven to 300°F.

2. In a medium mixing bowl, stir together the coconut cream concentrate, maple syrup, and salt with a spatula until well combined.

3. Fold in the coconut and then the chocolate chips.

4. Use a rounded tablespoon to form the dough into 1-inch balls. Place the balls 1 inch apart on a baking sheet and press flat.

5. Place in the oven and bake for 25 minutes, until the edges are slightly brown. Let cool on the baking sheet for 10 minutes before removing to a cooling rack. Store in an airtight container at room temperature for up to a week.

Note: When first combining the ingredients, you may think that this is going to be a salty cookie, but trust us— the salt makes these macaroons taste great! For those who do not eat chocolate, these are delicious even without the chocolate chips.

These fudgy cookies are a true delight for the chocolate lovers among us. And who doesn't love melting chocolate in a double boiler? We packed all the chocolate flavor we could into each delicious bite and accented it with a sprinkle of coarse sea salt on top.

SALTED DARK CHOCOLATE TRUFFLE COOKIES

PREHEAT OVEN: 350°F · MAKES: 2 DOZEN COOKIES

Ingredients

⅓ cup lard, unsalted butter, or palm shortening, softened, plus more for greasing the baking sheet (if not using parchment)

6 ounces unsweetened baking chocolate

1¼ cups chocolate chips

1 cup blanched almond flour

¼ cup cacao powder

¼ teaspoon kosher or sea salt

¼ teaspoon baking powder

3 large eggs

¾ cup unrefined granulated palm, date, or maple sugar

1 tablespoon pure vanilla extract

Coarse kosher or sea salt to sprinkle on top

SPECIAL TOOLS:
Double boiler assembly

1. Preheat the oven to 350°F. Line a baking sheet with parchment paper or grease it with lard, unsalted butter, or palm shortening.

2. Melt the baking chocolate and chocolate chips in a double boiler over medium heat, stirring constantly. Once the chocolate has melted completely, remove from the heat so that the chocolate doesn't overcook and seize. If the oil has begun to separate from the solid part of the chocolate, it has seized and will ruin the cookies if you use it.

3. In a medium bowl, sift together the almond flour, cacao powder, salt, and baking powder. Set aside.

4. In a large bowl, whisk together the eggs, lard, sugar, and vanilla until combined.

5. Temper the egg mixture with the melted chocolate by adding about ¼ cup of the warm chocolate to the bowl with the wet ingredients and whisking until combined. Then add another ¼ cup of the warm chocolate and whisk again. Then add the remaining melted chocolate to the wet batter.

6. Gradually add the dry ingredients to the wet batter, stirring constantly until just incorporated. The final dough will be smooth and pliable.

7. Form tablespoon-sized balls of the dough and place 1½ inches apart on the prepared baking sheet. Sprinkle with coarse salt and press semiflat.

8. Place in the oven and bake for 9 to 10 minutes, or until the centers of the cookies begin to firm up—they will harden further as they cool. Remove to a cooling rack and let cool for 10 minutes. Store in an airtight container at room temperature for up to a week.

Notes: If you'd like these to be more like dense, undercooked brownies than thick, cakelike cookies, use ¼ cup less almond flour. Our recommendations for chocolate and chocolate chip brands can be found on page 38.

An easy chocolate custard made with true superfoods: egg yolks and gelatin! It is rich and thick like the original homemade custards, not the boxed stuff people eat these days. And it's a great make-ahead dish. We love topping ours with fresh fruit or Whipped Coconut Cream (page 390).

CHOCOLATE CUSTARD

SERVES: 6

1. In a medium saucepan over medium heat, whisk together the coconut milk, almond milk, and cacao powder. Bring to a slow simmer.

2. In a small mixing bowl, whisk the egg yolks, maple syrup, and vanilla until incorporated.

3. Pour about one-third of the warm milk mixture into the egg yolk mixture and whisk to incorporate.

4. Pour the egg yolk mixture back into the saucepan and whisk to combine. Simmer gently for 2 minutes, and then remove from the heat.

5. Whisk in the gelatin powder until completely dissolved, and then whisk for another minute after you think it's dissolved to make sure that it's fully dissolved.

6. Pour into medium ramekins or bowls and chill in the refrigerator until stiffened, about 1 hour. To prevent a skin from forming on the top layer of the custard, press plastic wrap directly onto the surface before chilling and remove before serving. Store chilled for up to several days.

7. Serve cold topped with fresh berries, chopped nuts, or whipped coconut cream.

Ingredients

For the custard:

1 (13½-ounce) can full-fat coconut milk or 1¾ cups homemade (page 290)

1 cup Almond Milk (page 290)

½ cup cacao powder

3 large egg yolks

½ cup maple syrup

1½ teaspoons pure vanilla extract

1 tablespoon gelatin powder

For serving:

Fresh berries

Chopped nuts

Whipped Coconut Cream (page 390)

Note: *If you love a rich, deep chocolate flavor, try adding a teaspoon of almond or hazelnut extract or a tablespoon or two of chilled espresso or strong-brewed coffee. The chocolate flavor is enhanced by the essence of coffee and nut.*

RECIPE ALLERGEN INDEX

CONDIMENTS, SAUCES, AND DIPS	PAGE #	EGG-FREE	NUT-FREE	NIGHTSHADE-FREE
Apple and Pumpkin Butters	110	YES	YES	YES
Apple Butter BBQ Sauce	112	YES	YES	
Coconut Butter	114	YES	YES	YES
Sautéed Mushrooms and Onions	116	YES	YES	YES
Hollandaise Sauce	118		YES	YES
Ketchup	120	YES	YES	
Mayonnaise and Mayo-Based Dips	122		YES	YES
Ranch Dressing	124		YES	YES
Caesar Dressing	124		YES	YES
Berry Balsamic Dressing	124	YES	YES	YES
Cashew Cheese Sauce	126	YES		YES
Pickled Onions	128	YES	YES	YES
Roasted Garlic	130	YES	YES	YES
Stock (also known as "Bone Broth")	132	YES	YES	YES

BREAKFAST	PAGE #	EGG-FREE	NUT-FREE	NIGHTSHADE-FREE
Easy Peasy Pancakes	136			YES
Strawberry Streusel Muffins	138			YES
Blueberry Breakfast Cookies	140			YES
CC's Perfect Hash Browns	142	YES	YES	
Eggs in a Nest	144		YES	YES
Quick Banana-Chocolate Soufflé Cake	146		YES	YES
Green Salad with Poached Egg	148		YES	YES
Apple Cinnamon Crumb Cake	150	YES		YES
Eggs Stacy	152		YES	
Pumpkin Pudding	154			
Cinnamon Bread	156			YES
Sweet Potato Apple Hash	158	YES	YES	
Breakfast Burritos	160		YES	
Egg Pizza (Frittata)	162		YES	YES
Breakfast Sausage: Blueberry Sage	164	YES	YES	YES
Breakfast Sausage: Turkey Cranberry	164	YES	YES	YES
Breakfast Sausage: Traditional Beef	164	YES	YES	
Waffles	166		YES	YES

SNACKS AND ON-THE-GO

	PAGE #	EGG-FREE	NUT-FREE	NIGHTSHADE-FREE
Snack Balls: Apple Pie	170	YES	YES	YES
Snack Balls: Banana Bread	170	YES	YES	YES
Snack Balls: Coconut Cream	170	YES		YES
Snack Balls: Chocolate Chip Cookie	170	YES		YES
Cranberry-Orange No-Bake Coconut Bars	172	YES		YES
Pizza Kale Chips	174	YES		
Salt and Vinegar Kale Chips	174	YES	YES	YES
Sweet Potato Chips	176	YES	YES	YES
Roasted Pumpkin Seeds	178	YES	YES	YES
Sweet Heart Jerky	180	YES	YES	YES
Superfood Jerky	180	YES	YES	
Teriyaki Jerky	180	YES	YES	YES
Almond Meal Crackers	182	YES		YES
Slightly Sweet & Salty Snack Mix	184	YES		YES
Nut Butter	186	YES		YES
Energy Bars	188	YES		YES
Smoothies: Blueberry	190	YES	YES	YES
Smoothies: Strawberry Mango	190	YES	YES	YES
Smoothies: PB&J	190	YES	YES	YES
Smoothies: Elvis Presley	190	YES	YES	YES

CHILDHOOD FAVORITES

	PAGE #	EGG-FREE	NUT-FREE	NIGHTSHADE-FREE
Chunky Monkey Muffins	194	YES	YES	YES
Honey Nut Cereal	196	YES		YES
Pumpkin Cider Latte	198	YES	YES	YES
Not Beanie Weenies	200	YES	YES	
Chicken Fingers with Honey Mustard	202			YES
Mini Corn Dog Muffins	204			YES
Zucchini Cauliflower Tots	206			YES
Meatza: Prosciutto, Arugula, and Pear	208			YES
Meatza: Supreme	208			
Monkey Bread	210			YES
Gummy Snacks	212	YES	YES	YES

APPETIZERS	PAGE #	EGG-FREE	NUT-FREE	NIGHTSHADE-FREE
Braunschweiger Burger Sliders	216			YES
Chinese Lettuce Cups	218	YES	YES	YES
Chicken Liver Mousse	220	YES	YES	YES
Prosciutto-Wrapped Pears	222	YES	YES	YES
Pork Belly Bites with Arugula	224	YES	YES	YES
Spinach and Artichoke Dip	226	YES	YES	YES
Stuffed Mushrooms	228	YES		YES
Mint Lamb Meatballs	230		YES	YES
Meatballs in a Pig Blanket	230		YES	
Orange Sesame Meatballs	230			YES
Steamed Mussels in Tomato Broth	232	YES	YES	
Crispy Oven-Baked Chicken Wings: Lemon Garlic Sauce	234	YES	YES	YES
Crispy Oven-Baked Chicken Wings: Carolina-Style Sauce	234	YES	YES	
Crispy Oven-Baked Chicken Wings: Spicy Sauce	234	YES	YES	
Crispy Oven-Baked Chicken Wings: Sweet BBQ Sauce	234	YES	YES	

SIDES	PAGE #	EGG-FREE	NUT-FREE	NIGHTSHADE-FREE
Green Onion and Bacon Mac 'n' Cheese	238			YES
Veggie Lasagna	240	YES		
Breakfast Puree	242	YES	YES	YES
Cauli-Mash	244	YES	YES	YES
Cauli-Rice: Plain	246	YES	YES	YES
Cauli-Rice: Fiesta	246	YES	YES	
Cauli-Rice: Thai Fried	246		YES	YES
Green Bean Casserole	248	YES	YES	YES
Biscuits	250			YES
Baked Potato Soup	252	YES	YES	YES
Creamed Kale	254	YES	YES	YES
Cucumber Salad	256	YES	YES	YES
Spinach, Walnut, and Bacon Salad	258	YES		YES
Cauli-Gnocchi with Brussels Sprouts and Lemon Zest	260			YES
Tostadas	262	YES		YES
Butternut Bisque	264	YES	YES	YES
Roasted Rainbow Carrots	266	YES	YES	YES
Fried Sweet Plantains	268	YES	YES	YES
Grilled Asparagus	270	YES	YES	YES
Winter Salad	272	YES		YES
Sautéed Apples	274	YES	YES	YES
Citrus Broccoli	276	YES	YES	YES
Carrot Mash	278	YES	YES	YES
Caesar Salad	280		YES	YES
Garlic Breadsticks	282			YES
Yuca Fries	284	YES	YES	YES
Pickled Onion and Arugula Salad	286	YES	YES	YES

DRINKS	PAGE #	EGG-FREE	NUT-FREE	NIGHTSHADE-FREE
Almond Milk	290	YES		YES
Coconut Milk	290	YES	YES	YES
Chai Thai Iced Tea	292	YES	YES	YES
Eggnog	294			YES
Salted Caramel Frappé	296	YES		YES
Iced Mocha	298	YES		YES
Peppermint Hot Chocolate	300	YES		YES
Flavored Water	302	YES	YES	YES

MAINS	PAGE #	EGG-FREE	NUT-FREE	NIGHTSHADE-FREE
Sage and Citrus Roast Chicken	306	YES	YES	YES
Juicy Pot Roast	308	YES	YES	YES
Nona's Paprikosh (Chicken and Dumplings)	310			
Stacy's Soup	312	YES	YES	YES
Leftover Casserole	314	YES		YES
Macadamia-Crusted Tilapia	316	YES		YES
Crab Balls	318			
Mongolian Beef	320			YES
Kung Pao Chicken	322	YES		
Drunken Carrot Noodles	324	YES	YES	
Turkey Thai Basil	326	YES	YES	
Panang Beef Curry	328	YES		
Cider-Braised Brats	330	YES	YES	YES
Slow-Roasted Pork Shoulder	332	YES	YES	YES
Lamb Stew	334	YES	YES	
Apple Short Ribs	336	YES	YES	
Epic Bacon Meatloaf	338			YES
Linguine with Baby Clams	340	YES	YES	
Peruvian Chicken	342	YES	YES	
Turkey Breasts Stuffed with "Cheese" and Cranberries	344	YES		YES
Restaurant Steaks	346	YES	YES	YES
Brisket with Onion Jam	348	YES	YES	YES
Beef Tongue Carnitas	350	YES		
Eastern Market Shrimp Salad	352		YES	YES
Garden Tuna Salad	354		YES	YES
Chicken Waldorf Salad	356			YES
Grilled Kabobs with Pineapple	358	YES	YES	YES
Grilled Spareribs	360	YES	YES	
Butternut Squash Lasagna	362	YES		

SWEETS AND TREATS

SWEETS AND TREATS	PAGE #	EGG-FREE	NUT-FREE	NIGHTSHADE-FREE
Chocolate Layer Cake with Fresh Fruit	366			YES
Frosting: Vanilla Bean	368	YES	YES	YES
Frosting: Cinnamon Ginger	368	YES	YES	YES
Frosting: Strawberry	368	YES	YES	YES
Snickerdoodle Whoopie Pies	370			YES
Marshmallows	372	YES	YES	YES
Rocky Road Blondies	374			YES
Samoa Brownies	376			YES
Chocolate Chip and Walnut Cookies	378			YES
Creamy Dreamy Frozen Custard	380		YES	YES
Peach Cobbler	382	YES	YES	YES
Healthiest Ice Cream Ever	384		YES	YES
Jack-O'-Lantern Cookies	386			YES
Pecan Pralines	388	YES		YES
Pumpkin Parfait	390			YES
Key Lime Pie	392			YES
Lemon Drop Thumbprint Cookies	394			YES
Lemon Blueberry Bundt Cake	396			YES
Chia Seed Pudding: Cinnamon Raisin	398	YES		YES
Chia Seed Pudding: Mango Sticky (Not) Rice	398	YES	YES	YES
Chia Seed Pudding: Chocolate	398	YES		YES
Monster Cookie Dough Dip	400	YES		YES
Creamy Coconut Chocolate Chip Macaroons	402	YES	YES	YES
Salted Dark Chocolate Truffle Cookies	404			YES
Chocolate Custard	406			YES

INTERNAL COOKING TEMPERATURES

TYPE OF MEAT	TEMPERATURE TO REACH
CHICKEN & TURKEY	165°F
BEEF & LAMB	
RARE	125°F
MEDIUM-RARE	130°F TO 135°F
MEDIUM	135°F TO 140°F
MEDIUM-WELL	145°F
PORK	
MEDIUM-RARE	145°F
MEDIUM	150°F
WELL-DONE	160°F

RESOURCES

You've now read a whole book on the Paleo diet. Perhaps you're thirsty for more. Well, the Paleo community has many, many participants with their own unique takes on the diet and how to do it. Here is just a small portion of them:

- **Sarah Ballantyne** of ThePaleoMom.com, cohost of *The Paleo View Podcast,* and author of *The Paleo Approach* and *The Paleo Approach Cookbook:* A scientific mind who specializes in helping people with autoimmune diseases and family adaptations and shares many of her recipes.

- **Robb Wolf** of RobbWolf.com, host of *The Paleo Solution Podcast,* and author of *The Paleo Solution:* A Paleo pioneer who shares his commentary on the science of Paleo.

- **Mark Sisson** of MarksDailyApple.com and author of *The Primal Blueprint:* Mark is the founder of the very similar primal movement. He has been answering questions on his site and forum for years, so he likely has the answer you are seeking.

- **Chris Kresser** of ChrisKresser.com: A practitioner of functional medicine, Chris breaks down what the medical science says about Paleo and health.

- **Danielle Walker** of AgainstAllGrain.com and author of *Against All Grain* and *Meals Made Simple:* Danielle is a truly remarkable cook and baker whose recipes never fail to impress.

- **Diane Sanfilippo** of BalacedBites.com, cohost of *The Balanced Bites Podcast,* and author of *Practical Paleo:* Diane's book *Practical Paleo* is the definitive guide to the hows and whys of the Paleo diet and is certainly a must-read.

- **George Bryant** of CivilizedCavemanCooking.com and coauthor of *The Paleo Kitchen:* A renowned cook who specializes in improving bacon.

- **Juli Bauer** of PaleOMG.com and coauthor of *The Paleo Kitchen:* Talented, funny, and awesome, Juli is a joy to read and writes delicious recipes.

- **Bill and Hayley Staley** of PrimalPalate.com and authors of *Make it Paleo:* Great food and beautiful photographs fill every post Bill and Hayley write.

- **Michelle Tam** of NomNomPaleo.com and author of *Food for Humans:* Michelle, often affectionately known only as Nom Nom, is Paleo's greatest comedian and shows us how to cook in her own entertaining style.

- **Liz Wolfe** of RealFoodLiz.com, cohost of *The Balanced Bites Podcast,* and author of *Eat the Yolks:* Liz is a nutritionist and homesteader who educates people on eating for health.

- **Jill Ciciarelli** of FirstComesHealth.com and author of *Fermented:* Jill is an expert on fermentation and teaches people how to bring the gut-healing power of fermented foods into the home.

- **Stephanie Gaudreau** of StupidEasyPaleo.com and author of *The Paleo Athlete* and *The Performance Paleo Cookbook:* Stephanie not only shares her recipes on her blog, but she's also an accomplished athlete and nutritionist.

- **Diana Rodgers** of SustainableDish.com and author of *Paleo Lunches and Breakfasts On the Go:* Diana is both a nutritionist and a farmer who writes on both topics in an informative way.

- **Russ Crandall** of TheDomesticMan.com and author of *The Ancestral Table:* Russ's traditional and ethnic recipes are amazing.

- **Elana Amsterdam** of ElanasPantry.com: Elana's was one of the first popular grain-free bloggers and helped us when we were first starting.

- **Melissa Joulwan** of TheClothesMaketheGirl.com and author of *Well Fed:* Melissa's recipes combine the often incompatible qualities of simple and flavorful.

- **Kelly Brozyna** of TheSpunkyCoconut.com and author of *The Paleo Chocolate Lovers' Cookbook* and *Dairy-Free Ice Cream:* Kelly makes desserts on a restricted diet simple with tons of great recipes and is especially talented with ice cream and chocolate.

ACKNOWLEDGMENTS

You never realize how many hands work on a project like this until you look back and actually count them! Thanks first to Erich, Michele, and the entire Victory Belt Publishing juggernaut. You plucked us out of obscurity and have let us pursue every crazy idea we've pitched.

Both this book and our last book are really defined by their unique visual style. We would never have been able to achieve anything close to it without the immensely talented Aimee Buxton, who was not just a hired gun, but a true partner on those photo shoots who worked tirelessly to capture the goods.

In addition to Aimee, the cover of this book was an incredibly collaborative group project. Who knew it would take eight people to take one picture? Thanks to Russ Crandall, who provided the technical equipment and expertise to capture that one perfect shot, as well as Janey Crandall, Brent Schraeder, and especially Heather Gerum, who has the superpower of holding still for over an hour. You should definitely check out new Floridian Russ at TheDomesticMan.com and the mud-running couple Brent and Heather at VaHunterGatherers.com. Additionally, a huge thanks to our intern Sam, who ran to the store several times and helped us remake the food for the cover several times in the span of eight hours.

Samantha Scott, our "intern" whom we sincerely hope was able to learn something during her time helping us, was absolutely indispensible as we not only wrote a book while three kids ran underfoot, but also prepared up to twenty dishes for each photo shoot. She has an amazing knack with food, children, animals, and frazzled dads who are simultaneously cooking and typing up 175 recipes. You can read more about Sam's exploits at PaleoSitter.com and find her photos throughout the book, as she was always a willing hand (pun intended).

We'd be remiss if we did not acknowledge that the rolling snowball that PaleoParents.com has become would have hit a stone wall if it wasn't for the team that Stacy has assembled in the past eighteen months. Courtney McGregor came with us to several photo shoots to help us cook, keep us company, and step in as the occasional model, a role she's been training for all her life. Courtney is responsible for helping us mature the three-phase idea as well. Katy Galvin (freerangekaty.com) spent the past year running and organizing Paleo Parents while we made this book happen. And thanks to Monica Kenney, the once and future queen bee of Paleo Parents operations, who helped keep us all organized while pregnant, no less.

We're very grateful to everyone who tested our recipes for us just to make sure that we were intelligible and knowledgeable and could actually make the food we say we could. Your feedback was invaluable!

To our family and friends who have patiently participated in our lives as we come in and out of availability, thank you. Many of you we have known since before our lives turned around with Paleo, some of you even inspired to change your own lives as a result. The remainder of you have come into our lives like a firehouse of love and support, your encouragement and inspiration helps us lead the lives we do. We are beyond lucky to have our lives filled with such joy, for which you are all responsible.

And finally, we thank our patient boys, Cole, Finian, and Wesley, who made sacrifices themselves these past three years so that Mommy and Daddy could become cookbook authors. We hope that this legacy gives us enough cool points that you can look back on these years fondly; we know the boredom of "cookbook weekends" almost certainly wasn't the fun we promised. We have committed to you, and ourselves, that this book be our last (for at least a long while), and we look forward to weekends filled with board games, farm visits, and cooking together without a camera present.

INDEX

GROCERY LIST *Guide*

SUPERMARKETS

Organic veggies*

Grass-fed, pastured, organic meat

Pastured poultry

Rotisserie chicken

Lunch meat

Free-range, pastured, organic eggs

Kerrygold butter

High-quality cheeses

Grass-fed, organic heavy cream

Yogurt

Coconut aminos or wheat-free tamari

Palm shortening

Fermented foods (e.g., Bubbies pickles, sauerkraut)

Kombucha

LaraBars

Buying produce that is already cleaned, chopped, or prepped will save you time in the kitchen.

TRADER JOE'S *or* NATURAL GROCERS

Applegate Farms deli meat

Canned salmon

Canned tuna

Frozen fish

Salami (we like the stick kind)

Smoked salmon

Boxed almond and coconut milk for drinking

Cold-brew coffee

Coconut milk yogurt

Ketchup

Mustard

Olive oil

Canned black olives

Pre-bagged trail mix, nuts, and dried fruit

Applesauce and squeezers (no sugar added)

Organic bananas

Canned fruit in 100% juice

Frozen fruit

Fruit juice (100% juice)

Low-sugar juice boxes

Butternut squash

Beets

Mirepoix

Sliced and cleaned mushrooms

Seasonal produce*

Bagged salad

COSTCO *or other* BULK STORES

Coconut oil

Fresh dates

Honeyville almond flour

MaraNatha almond butter

Raw bagged nuts (almonds, pecans, walnuts)

Bulk nuts

Organic frozen wild berries

Organic canned diced tomatoes

Produce (organic salad mix, baby spinach, carrots, asparagus, Brussels sprouts, romaine lettuce, and more)

Lunch meat

Frozen natural sausage patties

Frozen seafood

Canned and deboned wild salmon and tuna

Smoked salmon

FOOD SWAPS

NOW	→ BETTER	→ BEST
Fruit cup in syrup	Organic fruit cup in juice	Organic fruit
Pancake syrup	100% maple syrup	Apple and Pumpkin Butters *(page 110)*
Deli meat	Minimally processed deli meat (MSG- and gluten-free)	Beef Tongue Carnitas *(page 350)*, Chicken Waldorf Salad *(page 356)*, or Garden Tuna Salad *(page 354)*
Breakfast cereal	Gluten-free rice or corn cereal	Honey Nut Cereal *(page 196)*
Jelly	Organic jams	Homemade compotes and fruit preserves, Apple and Pumpkin Butters *(page 110)*
Fruit snacks	Organic fruit snacks	Dried fruit
Slim Jim/jerky	Gluten-free, nitrate-free jerky	Jerky *(page 180)*
Standard salad dressing	Organic dressings and dips	Ranch Dressing, Caesar Dressing, or Berry Balsamic Dressing *(page 124)*
Tortillas and wraps	Gluten-free tortillas	Lettuce or collard green wraps *(page 356)* or Tostadas *(page 262)*
Bread	Tapioca- or rice-based gluten-free bread	More vegetables, Cinnamon Bread *(page 156)*, or Biscuits *(page 250)*
Skim milk	Organic and/or raw whole milk	Coconut or Almond Milk *(page 290)*
Ice cream	Store-bought grass-fed or coconut milk ice cream	Healthiest Ice Cream Ever *(page 384)* or Creamy Dreamy Frozen Custard *(page 380)*
Chips	Store-bought sweet potato chips or avocado oil potato chips	Kale Chips *(page 174)* or Sweet Potato Chips *(page 176)*
Vegetable oil	Olive oil, avocado oil, or butter	Lard, duck fat, or coconut oil
Pasta	Rice-based, gluten-free pasta	Spaghetti squash or zucchini noodles
Conventional eggs	Organic, cage-free eggs	Pastured eggs
Conventional meat	Organic or pasture-raised meat from the grocery store	Local pasture-raised meat direct from a farm
Conventional produce	Use the Dirty Dozen and Clean 15 lists to strategically buy organic produce	All organic and/or local and seasonal produce

TRUSTED SOURCES

TROPICAL TRADITIONS:	U.S. WELLNESS MEATS:	TESSEMAE'S:	STEVE'S PALEO GOODS:	CAPPELLO'S:
Coconut oil, palm shortening, maple syrup, raw honey	Pasture-raised meats and lard	Salad dressings, marinades, and sauces	Jerky, dried fruit, grain-free granola	Almond flour–based pasta

GOING OUT *Guide*

EVERYONE NEEDS A BREAK *from* COOKING SOMETIMES, EVEN THE MOST SEASONED PALEO PRACTITIONER. WITH THAT IN MIND, HERE ARE SOME SUGGESTIONS *for* PLACES TO GO *and* WHAT TO LOOK FOR WHEN YOU'RE EATING OUTSIDE YOUR HOME.

GENERAL TIPS

▶ When you arrive, ask if the restaurant has a gluten-free menu. Many restaurants have one available; if not, your server may be able to tell you which menu items are gluten-free.

▶ While you are being seated, be sure to ask for no bread basket or they'll bring one for you automatically.

▶ Ask questions about ingredients! "What is in this side dish?" "Is it coated in flour, or is flour used as a thickener?" "Can I replace the rice with vegetables?" "Do you have an alternative to the bread?" Everyone who works at the restaurant has a vested interest in satisfying you. We always joke, "We're high maintenance, but we tip well!"

▶ When in doubt, a steak, broiled fish, or bunless burger is usually available and generally within the Paleo bounds.

TAKE-OUT OPTIONS

▶ You may be able to find gluten-free pizza made with a non-gluten-grain crust, but be careful! Chains often take zero precautions against cross-contamination and may actually dust their gluten-free crusts with wheat flour on purpose. A truly gluten-free pizza will be cooked in a separate pan and prepared on a separate surface.

▶ Chinese food may be off-limits unless the restaurant in question offers gluten-free options, which is rare. Also ask about MSG.

▶ Thai food, if prepared in the traditional way, is often naturally gluten-free. Just confirm that items are made with rice and without soy sauce.

▶ Our favorite take-out is Peruvian chicken, which we replicate on page 342. If you do not have this option where you live, most supermarkets offer rotisserie chicken.

FAST-CASUAL AND FAST-FOOD OPTIONS

▶ Avoid McDonald's and Burger King, whose patties contain a lot of soy, and Burger King coats its fries in flour. Wendy's has soy-free patties and flour-free fries.

▶ Burger joints are almost always safe, offering lettuce wraps or gluten-free bread.

▶ More upscale, build-your-own fast-casual restaurants, such as Chipotle, are much more likely to cater to your needs than other fast-food restaurants. They will likely be able to tell you the ingredients of any of their components and steer you toward building a safe meal.

▶ Casual American restaurants such as Jason's Deli and Ruby Tuesday often offer gluten-free bread and an excellent salad bar.

▶ If coffee is what you're after, you may be able to find independent coffee shops that offer almond milk. The major chains do not offer it, so you may be stuck with black coffee. Starbucks will blend their Kerrygold butter into your coffee if you are brave enough to ask!

RESTAURANTS *for* FINER DINING

▶ Sushi restaurants are safe if you avoid dishes that contain soy sauce and imitation crab. Be sure to inquire about the crab, as many menus will say "crab" even when it's imitation. Bring your own coconut aminos or tamari for dipping sashimi. Salad rounds out the meal nicely.

▶ Brazilian steakhouses are an all-you-can-eat meat experience and offer many safe options.

▶ Often, the fancier the restaurant, the less likely it uses unhealthy ingredients and the more likely it can accommodate your needs. Ask questions and make requests!

🍎 SIMPLE SAFE FOODS

STARCHES

Acorn squash
Beets
Butternut squash
Parsnips
Plantains
Pumpkin
Rutabagas
Spaghetti squash
Sweet potatoes
Yams
Yuca

SWEETENERS

Date sugar
Honey
Maple syrup
Molasses
Palm sugar

NUTS *and* SEEDS

Almonds
Brazil nuts
Cacao nibs
Cashews
Chia seeds
Macadamia nuts
Pecans
Pine nuts
Pumpkin seeds
Sunflower seeds
Walnuts

VEGETABLES

Asparagus
Artichokes
Arugula
Avocados
Bell peppers
Broccoli
Brussels sprouts
Cabbage
Carrots
Cauliflower
Celery
Chile peppers
Collard greens
Cucumbers
Garlic
Kale
Leeks
Lettuce
Mushrooms
Onions
Radishes
Rhubarb
Romaine lettuce
Seaweed
Spinach
Tomatillos
Tomatoes
Turnips
Zucchini

FRUITS

Apples
Apricots
Bananas
Blackberries
Blueberries
Cantaloupes
Cherries
Coconut
Cranberries
Dates
Figs
Grapefruit
Grapes
Lemons
Limes
Mangos
Oranges
Papaya
Passion fruit
Peaches
Pears
Pineapples
Plums
Pomegranates
Prunes
Tangerines
Raspberries
Strawberries
Watermelons

MEAT/PROTEIN

Anchovies
Bacon
Chicken
Crab
Duck
Eggs
Elk
Gelatin
Lamb
Lobster
Pork
Prosciutto
Salmon
Sardines
Shellfish
Shrimp
Tuna
Turkey
Salami
Steak
Veal

OTHER

Cocoa powder
Coconut aminos
Coconut oil
Coffee
Ghee (clarified butter)
Tea

PALEO STAPLES

For THE PANTRY

Fats and Oils

Coconut oil (we recommend Nutiva and Tropical Traditions brands)

Avocado oil (we recommend Chosen Foods brand)

Macadamia nut oil

Olive oil

Chocolate

Dark chocolate chips (we recommend Equal Exchange and Enjoy Life brands)

Unsweetened chocolate squares

Cocoa powder (we recommend Navitas, Rapunzel, and Equal Exchange brands)

Coconut Products

Full-fat canned coconut milk (we recommend Natural Value brand)

Coconut cream concentrate/ coconut butter (we recommend Tropical Traditions and Nikki's Coconut Butter brands)

Flours

Blanched almond flour (we recommend Honeyville brand)

Arrowroot flour (we recommend Bob's Red Mill brand)

Coconut flour (we recommend Tropical Traditions brand)

Tapioca flour (we recommend Bob's Red Mill brand)

Sweeteners

Unrefined granulated palm sugar (we recommend Sweet Tree and Navitas brands)

Unrefined granulated date sugar

Unrefined granulated maple sugar

Grade B maple syrup

Raw honey

Additional Items

Canned anchovies

Canned salmon

Canned sardines

Canned tuna

Canned black olives

Canned tomatoes

Apple cider vinegar

Balsamic vinegar

Dried fruit and nuts

Honey Nut Cereal (page 196)

Gelatin

Nut Butters

Almond butter (page 186, or we recommend MaraNatha and Traders Joe's brands)

Sunflower seed butter (we recommend SunButter, MaraNatha, and Trader Joe's brands)

Umami Flavors

Coconut aminos (we recommend Coconut Secrets and Naked Coconuts brands)

Wheat-free tamari

Fish sauce (we recommend Red Boat brand)

For THE FRIDGE

Ketchup (page 120)

Mayonnaise (page 122)

Mustard

Pickles

Sauerkraut

Salad Dressing (page 124)

Almond Milk (page 290)

Coconut Milk (page 290)

Organic deli meats

Premade salads (page 50)

Stock (page 132)

Fresh produce

Organic deli meats

Thawed meat

Kombucha

For YOUR PURSE or GLOVE BOX

Jerky (page 180; we also recommend Steve's PaleoGoods brand)

Dried fruit

Snack Balls (page 170)

FAMILY FUN *Guide*

PURSUING A HEALTHIER LIFESTYLE *as a* FAMILY ISN'T JUST ABOUT CHANGING WHAT YOU EAT, IT'S ALSO ABOUT MAKING A CHANGE TOGETHER. FAMILY ACTIVITIES ARE A GREAT WAY *to* ENCOURAGE EVERYONE TO GROW HEALTHIER TOGETHER. HERE ARE SOME *of* OUR FAVORITE WAYS TO PURSUE BETTER HEALTH *with* OUR FAMILY.

VISIT LOCAL FARMS Many farms, orchards, and other agricultural centers encourage visitors, and these trips are a great way to learn more about where your food comes from. The more natural and sustainable the farm's practices, the more likely they'll let you wander the fields and explore. For kids, this might mean getting to see and touch farm animals! EatWild.com is an excellent resource for finding sustainable farms in your area.

PICK YOUR OWN PRODUCE In many areas, farms let you onto their fields to pick in-season produce. Check out PickYourOwn.org to find one near you. Each farm tells you by phone or on its website what is available to pick, but you can expect to find a variety through the seasons, depending on your location.

HIKE, BIKE, *and* CAMP When we made our switch to Paleo, we suddenly had a huge jump in energy and wanted to go exploring. Going to local parks and wilderness areas is a great way to experience the natural world and get in touch with nature. We highly recommend geocaching as a reason to go exploring!

EXERCISE Whatever your preferred method— from swimming to CrossFit, from soccer to flashlight tag—playing and exercising together can be great fun. Getting active as a family sets a good example for the kids and creates healthy habits for years to come. Plus, it's fun! Our family has had dedicated months where we all practice something together, like handstands.

PLANT A GARDEN, RAISE CHICKENS Nothing is more organic than the vegetables you grow yourself! If you have the space, plant your own food and learn how much work it takes to put food on a plate. If your local laws allow it, you may even be able to raise chickens for eggs. We find inspiration in the truly adventurous homesteaders Liz Wolfe at RealFoodLiz.com and Diana Rogers at SustainableDish.com.

COOK *and* EAT TOGETHER We know, that probably seems boring, but you would be surprised how often families don't participate in the most obvious communal activity in the home: eating together. If you are able, make cooking and eating a family affair. And this goes for not just kids but adults as well. Many couples have found that working together in the kitchen translates into a more lasting bond. Just look at the websites PrimalPalate.com and VaHunterGatherers.com for inspiration. For date night, we love to grocery shop and then cook an extravagant meal that costs a fraction of what a restaurant would charge but is twice as healthy.

THE TRUE SUPERFOODS

AFTER YOU'VE ELIMINATED THE BAD STUFF, IT'S TIME TO REPLACE IT *with* HEALTHY *and* HEALING FOODS. HERE'S WHAT YOU SHOULD BE THINKING ABOUT *in* PHASE 3.

ORGAN MEATS Consuming organ meats, also known as offal, can be a big hurdle because of their unusual appearance, taste, and texture. But they're certainly the healthiest of all meats, rich in vitamins and minerals found in few other sources. To make them more palatable, we recommend grinding them up and adding them to ground meat dishes, such as Epic Bacon Meatloaf (page 338), or making them into a mousse or pâté, such as Chicken Liver Mousse (page 220).

STOCK *and* GELATIN The unique amino acid profile of stock and gelatin is ideal for supporting joint and bone health as well as building collagen and keratin. Ever admire a Paleo adherent's great skin, hair, and nails? This might be the secret!

PASTURED PROTEIN Studies have shown that one of the keys to good health, especially heart health, is eating more omega-3 fats and fewer omega-6 fats. One of the quickest ways to tilt the balance toward omega-3 is to switch from grain-finished meats to pastured or grass-fed, grass-finished meats. All pastured proteins have a better ratio of omega-3 to omega-6 than their grain-fed counterparts, as well as more nutrients.

VEGETABLES This may seem obvious, but it's worth emphasizing: Paleo is not a meat-only diet. Vegetables are very important sources of antioxidants, vitamins, and minerals and should make up a significant portion of your meals.

FERMENTED FOODS Healthy gut bacteria is very important to overall health. Sauerkraut, pickles, kefir, and kombucha all support healthy bacteria in your gut.

SEAFOOD Not only are fish and shellfish rich in vitamins and minerals, they're also the best source of omega-3 fats. Replacing chicken with salmon once a week is an excellent way to tilt your ratio of omega-3 to omega-6 in the right direction.

SUPPLEMENTS We use fermented cod liver oil for its boost of omega-3, vitamin A, and vitamin K, but you may want to consult with a health professional to see what you're deficient in and take steps to make up the difference.

MAKING HEALTHY LIFESTYLE CHOICES

FOOD ALONE CAN'T FIX EVERYTHING THAT AILS YOU. TO OPTIMIZE YOUR HEALTH, YOU ALSO NEED *to* CHANGE OTHER PARTS *of* YOUR LIFE.

GET PROPER SLEEP With a full night's sleep, you not only feel rested and have improved brain function, but also reduce your stress hormones, have a stronger immune system, and improve thyroid and insulin function—key factors for losing fat.

REDUCE STRESS Our stress hormones aren't only activated when death or injury is imminent. They also surge when we're stuck in traffic, working hard to meet a deadline, or facing a long to-do list. Learning to manage stress is beneficial to your heart health and any autoimmune conditions you may have, and it allows your hormones to regulate properly.

EXERCISE Exercise, particularly resistance and strength training, has been shown to increase overall health, including bone strength and cardiovascular health. It also increases your feel-good hormones. Incorporating some movement into your life, however small the commitment, will definitely pay off.

ABSORB SUNLIGHT It's easy to stay inside, where the temperature is regulated and comfortable and we don't have to expend much energy moving around. The human body, though, needs to be outside in the sun every day. Not only does sunlight activate mood-enhancing hormones, but your body also needs it to make vitamin D, a nutrient in which most people are now deficient.